C-4112

THIS IS YOUR **PASSBOOK**® FOR ...

# POSTAL ELECTRONIC/ MAINTENANCE/ MECHANIC EXAM (955)

NATIONAL LEARNING CORPORATION®
passbooks.com

# PASSBOOK® SERIES

THE *PASSBOOK® SERIES* has been created to prepare applicants and candidates for the ultimate academic battlefield – the examination room.

At some time in our lives, each and every one of us may be required to take an examination – for validation, matriculation, admission, qualification, registration, certification, or licensure.

Based on the assumption that every applicant or candidate has met the basic formal educational standards, has taken the required number of courses, and read the necessary texts, the *PASSBOOK® SERIES* furnishes the one special preparation which may assure passing with confidence, instead of failing with insecurity. Examination questions – together with answers – are furnished as the basic vehicle for study so that the mysteries of the examination and its compounding difficulties may be eliminated or diminished by a sure method.

This book is meant to help you pass your examination provided that you qualify and are serious in your objective.

The entire field is reviewed through the huge store of content information which is succinctly presented through a provocative and challenging approach – the question-and-answer method.

A climate of success is established by furnishing the correct answers at the end of each test.

You soon learn to recognize types of questions, forms of questions, and patterns of questioning. You may even begin to anticipate expected outcomes.

You perceive that many questions are repeated or adapted so that you can gain acute insights, which may enable you to score many sure points.

You learn how to confront new questions, or types of questions, and to attack them confidently and work out the correct answers.

You note objectives and emphases, and recognize pitfalls and dangers, so that you may make positive educational adjustments.

Moreover, you are kept fully informed in relation to new concepts, methods, practices, and directions in the field.

You discover that you arre actually taking the examination all the time: you are preparing for the examination by "taking" an examination, not by reading extraneous and/or supererogatory textbooks.

In short, this PASSBOOK®, used directedly, should be an important factor in helping you to pass your test.

# POSTAL ELECTRONIC / MAINTENANCE / MECHANIC EXAM

## Sample Questions

### Examination 955 – Postal Electronic / Maintenance / Mechanic

The purpose of this booklet is to illustrate the types of questions that will be used in Test 955. The samples will also show how the questions in the test are to be answered.

Test 955 measures knowledge, skills, and abilities (KSAs) used by a variety of maintenance positions. Exhibit A lists the actual KSAs that are measured. However, not all KSAs that are measured in this test are scored for every position. The qualification standard for each position lists the KSAs required for the position. Only those questions that measure KSAs required for the position(s) for which you are applying will be scored for the position(s).

The suggested answers to each question are lettered A, B, C, etc. Select the BEST answer and make a heavy pencil mark in the corresponding space on the Sample Answer Sheet. Each mark must be dense black. Each mark must cover more than half the space and must not extend into neighboring spaces. If the answer to Sample 1 is B, you would mark the Sample Answer Sheet like this:

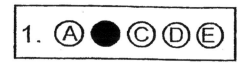

Test consists of Personal Inventory, General Aptitude and Spatial Relations sections. Subject areas to be tested are listed on the following page.

**STUDY CAREFULLY BEFORE YOU GO THE EXAMINATION ROOM**

(1) **Knowledge of basic mechanics** refers to the theory of operation, terminology, usage, and characteristics of basic mechanical principles as they apply to such things as gears, pulleys, cams, pawls, power transmissions, linkages, fasteners, chains, sprockets, and belts; and including hoisting, rigging, roping, pneumatics, and hydraulic devices.

(2) **Knowledge of basic electricity** refer to the theory, terminology, usage, and characteristics of basic electrical principles such as Ohm's Law, Kirchoff's Law, and magnetism, as they apply to such things as AC-DC circuitry and hardware, relays, switches, and circuit breakers.

(3) **Knowledge of basic electronics** refers to the theory, terminology, usage, and characteristics of basic electronic principles concerning such things as solid state devices, vacuum tubes, coils, capacitors, resistors, and basic logic circuitry.

(4) **Knowledge of digital electronics** refers to the terminology, characteristics, symbology, and operation of digital components as used in such things as logic gates, registers, adders, counters, memories, encoders and decoders.

(5) **Knowledge of safety procedures and equipment** refers to the knowledge of industrial hazards (e.g., mechanical, chemical, electrical, electronic) and procedures and techniques established to avoid injuries to self and others such as lock-out devices, protective clothing, and waste disposal techniques.

(6) **Knowledge of basic computer concepts** refers to the terminology, usage, and characteristics of digital memory storage/processing devices such as internal memory, input-output peripherals, and familiarity with programming concepts.

(19) **Ability to perform basic mathematical computations** refers to the ability to perform basic calculations such as addition, subtraction, multiplication and division with whole numbers, fractions and decimals.

(20) **Ability to perform more complex mathematics** refers to the ability to perform calculations such as basic algebra, geometry, scientific notation, and number conversions, as applied to mechanical, electrical and electronic applications.

(21) **Ability to apply theoretical knowledge to practical applications** refers to mechanical, electrical and electronic maintenance applications such as inspection, troubleshooting equipment repair and modification, preventive maintenance, and installation of electrical equipment.

(22) **Ability to detect patterns** refers to the ability to observe and analyze qualitative factors such as number progressions, spatial relationships, and auditory and visual patterns. This includes combining information and determining how a given set of numbers, objects, or sounds are related to each other.

(23) **Ability to use written reference materials** refers to the ability to locate, read, and comprehend text material such as handbooks, manuals, bulletins, directives, checklists and route sheets.

(26) **Ability to follow instructions** refers to the ability comprehend and execute written and oral instructions such as work orders, checklists, route sheets, and verbal directions and instructions.

(31) **Ability to use hand tools** refers to knowledge of, and proficiency with, various hand tools. This ability involves the safe and efficient use and maintenance of such tools as screwdrivers, wrenches, hammers, pliers, chisels, punches, taps, dies, rules, gauges, and alignment tools.

(35) **Ability to use technical drawings** refers to the ability to read and comprehend technical materials such as diagrams, schematics, flow charts, and blueprints.

(36) **Ability to use test equipment** refers to the knowledge of, and proficiency with, various types of mechanical, electrical and electronic test equipment such as VOMS, oscilloscopes, circuit tracers, amprobes, and tachometers.

(37) **Ability to solder** refers to the knowledge of, and ability to safely and effectively apply, the appropriate soldering techniques.

## Job Description

Maintenance positions require highly skilled and experienced individuals. All applicants must meet the knowledge, skills, and abilities requirements listed.
Maintenance duties require prolonged standing, walking, climbing, bending, reaching, and stooping. Employees must lift and carry heavy objects on level surfaces, on ladders, and/or on stairways. For positions requiring driving, applicants must have a valid state driver's license, a safe driving record, and at least two years of documented driving experience.

**Electronic Technician** -- Performs the full range of diagnostic, preventive maintenance, alignment and calibration, and overhaul tasks, on both hardware and software on a variety of mail processing, customer service, and building equipment and systems, applying advanced technical knowledge to solve complex problems.

1. The primary function of a take-up pulley in a belt conveyor is to

    A)  carry the belt on the return trip.
    B)  track the belt.
    C)  maintain proper belt tension.
    D)  change the direction of the belt.

2. Which device is used to transfer power and rotary mechanical motion from one shaft to another?

    A)  Bearing
    B)  Lever
    C)  Idler roller
    D)  Gear
    E)  Bushing

3. Which of the following circuits is shown in Figure III-A-22?

    A)  Series circuit
    B)  Parallel circuit
    C)  Series, parallel circuit
    D)  Solid state circuit
    E)  None of the above

Figure III-A-22

4. A circuit has two resistors of equal value in series. The voltage and current in the circuit are 20 volts and 2 amps respectively. What is the value of EACH resistor?

    A)  5 ohms
    B)  10 ohms
    C)  20 ohms
    D)  Not enough information given

5. What is the total net capacitance of two 60-farad capacitors connected in series?

    A)  30 farads
    B)  60 farads
    C)  90 farads
    D)  120 farads
    E)  360 farads

6. Select the Boolean equation that matches the circuit diagram in Figure 79-4-17B.

    A)  Z = AB+CD+EF
    B)  Z = (A+B) (C+D) (E+F)
    C)  Z = A+B+C+D+EF
    D)  Z = ABCD (E+F)

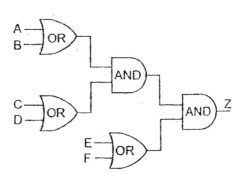

FIGURE 79-4-17B

7. If two 30-mH inductors are connected in series, what is the total net inductance of the combination?

   A)   15 mH
   B)   20 mH
   C)   30 mH
   D)   45 mH
   E)   60 mH

8. In pure binary the decimal number 6 would be expressed as

   A)   001
   B)   011
   C)   110
   D)   111

9. In Figure 75-8-11, which of the following scores will be printed?

   A)   All scores > 90 and < 60

   B)   All scores < 90

   C)   All scores ≤ 90 and ≥ 60

   D)   All scores < 60

10. Crowbars, light bulbs and vacuum bags are to be stored in the cabinet shown in Figure 75-25-1. Considering the balance of weight, what would be the safest arrangement?

   A)   Top Drawer – Crowbars
        Middle Drawer - Light Bulbs
        Bottom Drawer - Vacuum bags
   B)   Top Drawer – Crowbars
        Middle Drawer - Vacuum bags
        Bottom Drawer - Light Bulbs
   C)   Top Drawer - Vacuum Bags
        Middle Drawer – Crowbars
        Bottom Drawer - Light Bulbs
   D)   Top Drawer - Vacuum Bags
        Middle Drawer - Light Bulbs
        Bottom Drawer - Crowbars
   E)   Top Drawer - Light Bulbs
        Middle Drawer - Vacuum Bags
        Bottom Drawer - Crowbars

11. Which is most appropriate for pulling a heavy load?

   A)   Electric lift
   B)   Fork lift
   C)   Tow Conveyor
   D)   Dolly
   E)   Pallet truck

Figure 75-8-11

Figure 75-25-1

12. The electrical circuit term "open circuit" refers to a closed loop being opened. When an ohmmeter is connected into this type of circuit, one can expect the meter to

A) read infinity.
B) read infinity and slowly return to ZERO.
C) read ZERO.
D) read ZERO and slowly return to infinity.
E) None of the above

13. Contaminants have caused bearings to fail prematurely. Which pair of the items listed below should be kept away from bearings?

A) Dirt and oil
B) Grease and water
C) Oil and grease
D) Dirt and moisture
E) Water and oil

14. In order to operate a breast drill, which direction should you turn it?

A) Clockwise
B) Counterclockwise
C) Up and down
D) Back and forth
E) Right, then left

15. Which is the correct tool for tightening or loosening a water pipe?

A) Slip joint pliers
B) Household pliers
C) Monkey wrench
D) Water pump pliers
E) Pipe wrench

16. What is one purpose of a chuck key?

A) Open doors
B) Remove drill bits
C) Remove screws
D) Remove set screws
E) Unlock chucks

17. When smoke is generated as a result of using a portable electric drill for cutting holes into a piece of angle iron, one should

A) use a fire watch.
B) cease the drilling operation.
C) use an exhaust fan to remove smoke.
D) use a prescribed coolant solution to reduce friction.
E) call the Fire Department.

18. The primary purpose of soldering is to

A) melt solder to a molten state.
B) heat metal parts to the right temperature to be joined.
C) join metal parts by melting the parts.
D) harden metal.
E) join metal parts.

19. Which of the following statements is correct of a soldering gun?

A) Tip is not replaceable
B) Cannot be used in cramped places
C) Heats only when trigger is pressed
D) Not rated by the number of watts they use
E) Has no light

20. What unit of measurement is read on a dial torque wrench?

A) Pounds
B) Inches
C) Centimeters
D) Foot-pounds
E) Degrees

21. Which instrument is used to test insulation breakdown of a conductor?

A) Ohmmeter
B) Ammeter
C) Megger
D) Wheatstone bridge
E) Voltmeter

22. 1/2 of 1/4 =

A) 1/12
B) 1/8
C) 1/4
D) 1/2
E) 8

23. 2.6 - .5 =

A) 2.0
B) 2.1
C) 3.1
D) 3.3
E) None of the above

24. Simplify the following expression in terms of amps:

$563 \times 10^{-6}$

A) 563,000,000 amps
B) 563,000 amps
C) .563 amps
D) .000563 amps
E) .000000563 amps

25. Solve the power equation

$P = I^2 R$ for R

A) $R = EI$

B) $R = I^2 P$

C) $R = PI$

D) $R = P/I^2$

E) $R = E/I$

26. The product of 3 kilo ohms times 3 micro ohms is

A) $6 \times 10^{-9}$ ohms

B) $6 \times 10^{-3}$ ohms

C) $9 \times 10^3$ ohms

D) $9 \times 10^{-6}$ ohms

E) $9 \times 10^{-3}$ ohms

In sample question 27 below, select the statement which is most nearly correct according to the paragraph.

"Prior to 1870, a conveyor that made use of rollers was developed for transporting clay. This construction substituted rolling friction at the idler bearing points for the sliding friction of the slider bed. A primitive type of troughing belt conveyor was developed about the same time for the handling of grain. This design was improved during the latter part of the century when the troughing idler was developed."

27. According to the above paragraph, which of the following statements is most nearly correct?

A) The troughing belt conveyor was developed about 1870 to handle clay and grain.

B) Rolling friction construction was replaced by sliding friction construction prior to 1870.

C) In the late nineteenth century, conveyors were improved with the development of the troughing idler.

D) The troughing idler, a significant design improvement for conveyors, was developed in the early nineteenth century.

E) Conveyor belts were invented and developed in the 1800's.

For sample question 28 below, select from the drawings of objects on the right labeled A, B, C, and D, the one that would have the TOP, FRONT, and RIGHT views shown in the drawing at the left

**28.**

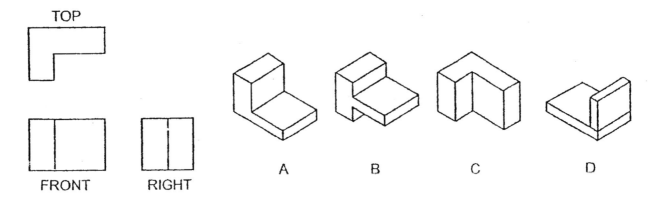

TOP

FRONT      RIGHT

A      B      C      D

In sample question 29 below, there is, on the left, a drawing of a flat piece of paper and, on the right, four figures labeled A, B, C, and D. When the paper is bent on the dotted lines it will form one of the figures on the right. Decide which alternative can be formed from the flat piece.

**29.**

A      B      C      D

In each of the sample questions below, look at the symbols in the first two boxes. Something about the three symbols in the first box makes them alike; something about the two symbols in the other box with the question mark makes them alike. Look for some characteristic that is common to all symbols in the same box, yet makes them different from the symbols in the other box. Among the five answer choices, find the symbol that can best be substituted for the question mark, because it is like the symbols in the second box, and, for the same reason different from those in the first box.

**30.**

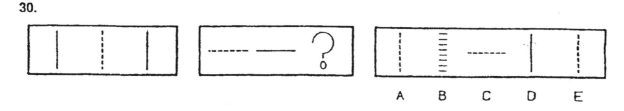

In sample question 30 above, all the symbols in the first box are vertical lines. The second box has two lines, one broken and one solid. Their likeness to each other consists in their being horizontal; and their being horizontal makes them different from the vertical lines in the other box. The answer must be the only one of the five lettered choices that is a horizontal line, either broken or solid. NOTE: There is not supposed to be a series or progression in these symbol questions. If you look for a progression in the first box and the second box, you will be wasting time. Remember, look for a likeness within each box and a difference between the two boxes.

Now do sample questions 31 and 32.

**31.**

**32.**

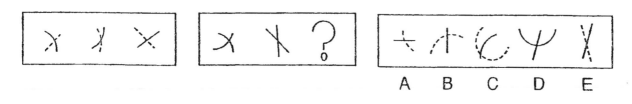

33. In Figure 3-8-6, what is the measurement of Dimension F? Drawing is not actual size.

A) 1 3/4 inches
B) 2 1/4 inches
C) 2 1/2 inches
D) 3 3/4 inches
E) None of the above

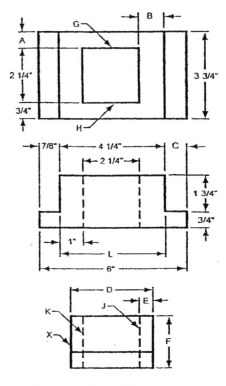

Figure 3-8-6

34. In Figure 160-57, what is the current flow through $R_3$ when:

V = 50 volts

$R_1$ = 25 ohms

$R_2$ = 25 ohms

R3 = 50 ohms

$R_4$ = 50 ohms

$R_5$ = 50 ohms

and the current through the entire circuit totals one amp?

A) 0.5 amp
B) 5.0 amps
C) 5.0 milliamps
D) 50.0 milliamps
E) None of the above

Figure 160-57

# Correct Answers to Sample Questions – Part II

1 Ⓐ Ⓑ ● Ⓓ Ⓔ      18 Ⓐ Ⓑ Ⓒ Ⓓ ●

2 Ⓐ Ⓑ Ⓒ ● Ⓔ      19 Ⓐ Ⓑ ● Ⓓ Ⓔ

3 ● Ⓑ Ⓒ Ⓓ Ⓔ      20 Ⓐ Ⓑ Ⓒ ● Ⓔ

4 ● Ⓑ Ⓒ Ⓓ Ⓔ      21 Ⓐ Ⓑ ● Ⓓ Ⓔ

5 ● Ⓑ Ⓒ Ⓓ Ⓔ      22 Ⓐ ● Ⓒ Ⓓ Ⓔ

6 Ⓐ ● Ⓒ Ⓓ Ⓔ      23 Ⓐ ● Ⓒ Ⓓ Ⓔ

7 Ⓐ Ⓑ Ⓒ Ⓓ ●      24 Ⓐ Ⓑ Ⓒ ● Ⓔ

8 Ⓐ Ⓑ ● Ⓓ Ⓔ      25 Ⓐ Ⓑ Ⓒ ● Ⓔ

9 Ⓐ Ⓑ ● Ⓓ Ⓔ      26 Ⓐ Ⓑ Ⓒ Ⓓ ●

10 Ⓐ Ⓑ Ⓒ Ⓓ ●      27 Ⓐ Ⓑ ● Ⓓ Ⓔ

11 Ⓐ Ⓑ Ⓒ Ⓓ ●      28 Ⓐ Ⓑ ● Ⓓ Ⓔ

12 ● Ⓑ Ⓒ Ⓓ Ⓔ      29 Ⓐ Ⓑ ● Ⓓ Ⓔ

13 Ⓐ Ⓑ Ⓒ ● Ⓔ      30 Ⓐ Ⓑ ● Ⓓ Ⓔ

14 ● Ⓑ Ⓒ Ⓓ Ⓔ      31 Ⓐ Ⓑ Ⓒ Ⓓ ●

15 Ⓐ Ⓑ Ⓒ Ⓓ ●      32 Ⓐ Ⓑ Ⓒ ● Ⓔ

16 Ⓐ ● Ⓒ Ⓓ Ⓔ      33 Ⓐ Ⓑ ● Ⓓ Ⓔ

17 Ⓐ Ⓑ Ⓒ ● Ⓔ      34 ● Ⓑ Ⓒ Ⓓ Ⓔ

# HOW TO TAKE A TEST

## I. YOU MUST PASS AN EXAMINATION

### A. *WHAT EVERY CANDIDATE SHOULD KNOW*

Examination applicants often ask us for help in preparing for the written test. What can I study in advance? What kinds of questions will be asked? How will the test be given? How will the papers be graded?

As an applicant for a civil service examination, you may be wondering about some of these things. Our purpose here is to suggest effective methods of advance study and to describe civil service examinations.

Your chances for success on this examination can be increased if you know how to prepare. Those "pre-examination jitters" can be reduced if you know what to expect. You can even experience an adventure in good citizenship if you know why civil service exams are given.

### B. *WHY ARE CIVIL SERVICE EXAMINATIONS GIVEN?*

Civil service examinations are important to you in two ways. As a citizen, you want public jobs filled by employees who know how to do their work. As a job seeker, you want a fair chance to compete for that job on an equal footing with other candidates. The best-known means of accomplishing this two-fold goal is the competitive examination.

Exams are widely publicized throughout the nation. They may be administered for jobs in federal, state, city, municipal, town or village governments or agencies.

Any citizen may apply, with some limitations, such as the age or residence of applicants. Your experience and education may be reviewed to see whether you meet the requirements for the particular examination. When these requirements exist, they are reasonable and applied consistently to all applicants. Thus, a competitive examination may cause you some uneasiness now, but it is your privilege and safeguard.

### C. *HOW ARE CIVIL SERVICE EXAMS DEVELOPED?*

Examinations are carefully written by trained technicians who are specialists in the field known as "psychological measurement," in consultation with recognized authorities in the field of work that the test will cover. These experts recommend the subject matter areas or skills to be tested; only those knowledges or skills important to your success on the job are included. The most reliable books and source materials available are used as references. Together, the experts and technicians judge the difficulty level of the questions.

Test technicians know how to phrase questions so that the problem is clearly stated. Their ethics do not permit "trick" or "catch" questions. Questions may have been tried out on sample groups, or subjected to statistical analysis, to determine their usefulness.

Written tests are often used in combination with performance tests, ratings of training and experience, and oral interviews. All of these measures combine to form the best-known means of finding the right person for the right job.

## II. HOW TO PASS THE WRITTEN TEST

### A. NATURE OF THE EXAMINATION

To prepare intelligently for civil service examinations, you should know how they differ from school examinations you have taken. In school you were assigned certain definite pages to read or subjects to cover. The examination questions were quite detailed and usually emphasized memory. Civil service exams, on the other hand, try to discover your present ability to perform the duties of a position, plus your potentiality to learn these duties. In other words, a civil service exam attempts to predict how successful you will be. Questions cover such a broad area that they cannot be as minute and detailed as school exam questions.

In the public service similar kinds of work, or positions, are grouped together in one "class." This process is known as *position-classification*. All the positions in a class are paid according to the salary range for that class. One class title covers all of these positions, and they are all tested by the same examination.

### B. FOUR BASIC STEPS

#### 1) Study the announcement

How, then, can you know what subjects to study? Our best answer is: "Learn as much as possible about the class of positions for which you've applied." The exam will test the knowledge, skills and abilities needed to do the work.

Your most valuable source of information about the position you want is the official exam announcement. This announcement lists the training and experience qualifications. Check these standards and apply only if you come reasonably close to meeting them.

The brief description of the position in the examination announcement offers some clues to the subjects which will be tested. Think about the job itself. Review the duties in your mind. Can you perform them, or are there some in which you are rusty? Fill in the blank spots in your preparation.

Many jurisdictions preview the written test in the exam announcement by including a section called "Knowledge and Abilities Required," "Scope of the Examination," or some similar heading. Here you will find out specifically what fields will be tested.

#### 2) Review your own background

Once you learn in general what the position is all about, and what you need to know to do the work, ask yourself which subjects you already know fairly well and which need improvement. You may wonder whether to concentrate on improving your strong areas or on building some background in your fields of weakness. When the announcement has specified "some knowledge" or "considerable knowledge," or has used adjectives like "beginning principles of…" or "advanced … methods," you can get a clue as to the number and difficulty of questions to be asked in any given field. More questions, and hence broader coverage, would be included for those subjects which are more important in the work. Now weigh your strengths and weaknesses against the job requirements and prepare accordingly.

## 3) Determine the level of the position

Another way to tell how intensively you should prepare is to understand the level of the job for which you are applying. Is it the entering level? In other words, is this the position in which beginners in a field of work are hired? Or is it an intermediate or advanced level? Sometimes this is indicated by such words as "Junior" or "Senior" in the class title. Other jurisdictions use Roman numerals to designate the level – Clerk I, Clerk II, for example. The word "Supervisor" sometimes appears in the title. If the level is not indicated by the title, check the description of duties. Will you be working under very close supervision, or will you have responsibility for independent decisions in this work?

## 4) Choose appropriate study materials

Now that you know the subjects to be examined and the relative amount of each subject to be covered, you can choose suitable study materials. For beginning level jobs, or even advanced ones, if you have a pronounced weakness in some aspect of your training, read a modern, standard textbook in that field. Be sure it is up to date and has general coverage. Such books are normally available at your library, and the librarian will be glad to help you locate one. For entry-level positions, questions of appropriate difficulty are chosen – neither highly advanced questions, nor those too simple. Such questions require careful thought but not advanced training.

If the position for which you are applying is technical or advanced, you will read more advanced, specialized material. If you are already familiar with the basic principles of your field, elementary textbooks would waste your time. Concentrate on advanced textbooks and technical periodicals. Think through the concepts and review difficult problems in your field.

These are all general sources. You can get more ideas on your own initiative, following these leads. For example, training manuals and publications of the government agency which employs workers in your field can be useful, particularly for technical and professional positions. A letter or visit to the government department involved may result in more specific study suggestions, and certainly will provide you with a more definite idea of the exact nature of the position you are seeking.

## III. KINDS OF TESTS

Tests are used for purposes other than measuring knowledge and ability to perform specified duties. For some positions, it is equally important to test ability to make adjustments to new situations or to profit from training. In others, basic mental abilities not dependent on information are essential. Questions which test these things may not appear as pertinent to the duties of the position as those which test for knowledge and information. Yet they are often highly important parts of a fair examination. For very general questions, it is almost impossible to help you direct your study efforts. What we can do is to point out some of the more common of these general abilities needed in public service positions and describe some typical questions.

## 1) General information

Broad, general information has been found useful for predicting job success in some kinds of work. This is tested in a variety of ways, from vocabulary lists to questions about current events. Basic background in some field of work, such as sociology or economics, may be sampled in a group of questions. Often these are principles which have become familiar to most persons through exposure rather than through formal training. It is difficult to advise you how to study for these questions; being alert to the world around you is our best suggestion.

2) Verbal ability

An example of an ability needed in many positions is verbal or language ability. Verbal ability is, in brief, the ability to use and understand words. Vocabulary and grammar tests are typical measures of this ability. Reading comprehension or paragraph interpretation questions are common in many kinds of civil service tests. You are given a paragraph of written material and asked to find its central meaning.

3) Numerical ability

Number skills can be tested by the familiar arithmetic problem, by checking paired lists of numbers to see which are alike and which are different, or by interpreting charts and graphs. In the latter test, a graph may be printed in the test booklet which you are asked to use as the basis for answering questions.

4) Observation

A popular test for law-enforcement positions is the observation test. A picture is shown to you for several minutes, then taken away. Questions about the picture test your ability to observe both details and larger elements.

5) Following directions

In many positions in the public service, the employee must be able to carry out written instructions dependably and accurately. You may be given a chart with several columns, each column listing a variety of information. The questions require you to carry out directions involving the information given in the chart.

6) Skills and aptitudes

Performance tests effectively measure some manual skills and aptitudes. When the skill is one in which you are trained, such as typing or shorthand, you can practice. These tests are often very much like those given in business school or high school courses. For many of the other skills and aptitudes, however, no short-time preparation can be made. Skills and abilities natural to you or that you have developed throughout your lifetime are being tested.

Many of the general questions just described provide all the data needed to answer the questions and ask you to use your reasoning ability to find the answers. Your best preparation for these tests, as well as for tests of facts and ideas, is to be at your physical and mental best. You, no doubt, have your own methods of getting into an exam-taking mood and keeping "in shape." The next section lists some ideas on this subject.

IV. KINDS OF QUESTIONS

Only rarely is the "essay" question, which you answer in narrative form, used in civil service tests. Civil service tests are usually of the short-answer type. Full instructions for answering these questions will be given to you at the examination. But in case this is your first experience with short-answer questions and separate answer sheets, here is what you need to know:

## 1) Multiple-choice Questions

Most popular of the short-answer questions is the "multiple choice" or "best answer" question. It can be used, for example, to test for factual knowledge, ability to solve problems or judgment in meeting situations found at work.

A multiple-choice question is normally one of three types—

- It can begin with an incomplete statement followed by several possible endings. You are to find the one ending which *best* completes the statement, although some of the others may not be entirely wrong.
- It can also be a complete statement in the form of a question which is answered by choosing one of the statements listed.
- It can be in the form of a problem – again you select the best answer.

Here is an example of a multiple-choice question with a discussion which should give you some clues as to the method for choosing the right answer:

When an employee has a complaint about his assignment, the action which will *best* help him overcome his difficulty is to
- A. discuss his difficulty with his coworkers
- B. take the problem to the head of the organization
- C. take the problem to the person who gave him the assignment
- D. say nothing to anyone about his complaint

In answering this question, you should study each of the choices to find which is best. Consider choice "A" – Certainly an employee may discuss his complaint with fellow employees, but no change or improvement can result, and the complaint remains unresolved. Choice "B" is a poor choice since the head of the organization probably does not know what assignment you have been given, and taking your problem to him is known as "going over the head" of the supervisor. The supervisor, or person who made the assignment, is the person who can clarify it or correct any injustice. Choice "C" is, therefore, correct. To say nothing, as in choice "D," is unwise. Supervisors have and interest in knowing the problems employees are facing, and the employee is seeking a solution to his problem.

## 2) True/False Questions

The "true/false" or "right/wrong" form of question is sometimes used. Here a complete statement is given. Your job is to decide whether the statement is right or wrong.

SAMPLE: A roaming cell-phone call to a nearby city costs less than a non-roaming call to a distant city.

This statement is wrong, or false, since roaming calls are more expensive.
This is not a complete list of all possible question forms, although most of the others are variations of these common types. You will always get complete directions for

answering questions.  Be sure you understand *how* to mark your answers – ask questions until you do.

## V.  RECORDING YOUR ANSWERS

Computer terminals are used more and more today for many different kinds of exams.

For an examination with very few applicants, you may be told to record your answers in the test booklet itself.  Separate answer sheets are much more common.  If this separate answer sheet is to be scored by machine – and this is often the case – it is highly important that you mark your answers correctly in order to get credit.

An electronic scoring machine is often used in civil service offices because of the speed with which papers can be scored.  Machine-scored answer sheets must be marked with a pencil, which will be given to you.  This pencil has a high graphite content which responds to the electronic scoring machine.  As a matter of fact, stray dots may register as answers, so do not let your pencil rest on the answer sheet while you are pondering the correct answer.  Also, if your pencil lead breaks or is otherwise defective, ask for another.

Since the answer sheet will be dropped in a slot in the scoring machine, be careful not to bend the corners or get the paper crumpled.

The answer sheet normally has five vertical columns of numbers, with 30 numbers to a column.  These numbers correspond to the question numbers in your test booklet.  After each number, going across the page are four or five pairs of dotted lines.  These short dotted lines have small letters or numbers above them.  The first two pairs may also have a "T" or "F" above the letters.  This indicates that the first two pairs only are to be used if the questions are of the true-false type.  If the questions are multiple choice, disregard the "T" and "F" and pay attention only to the small letters or numbers.

Answer your questions in the manner of the sample that follows:

32.  The largest city in the United States is
    A.  Washington, D.C.
    B.  New York City
    C.  Chicago
    D.  Detroit
    E.  San Francisco

1)  Choose the answer you think is best.  (New York City is the largest, so "B" is correct.)
2)  Find the row of dotted lines numbered the same as the question you are answering.  (Find row number 32)
3)  Find the pair of dotted lines corresponding to the answer.  (Find the pair of lines under the mark "B.")
4)  Make a solid black mark between the dotted lines.

## VI.  BEFORE THE TEST

Common sense will help you find procedures to follow to get ready for an examination.  Too many of us, however, overlook these sensible measures.  Indeed, nervousness and fatigue have been found to be the most serious reasons why applicants fail to do their best on civil service tests.  Here is a list of reminders:

- Begin your preparation early – Don't wait until the last minute to go scurrying around for books and materials or to find out what the position is all about.
- Prepare continuously – An hour a night for a week is better than an all-night cram session.  This has been definitely established.  What is more, a night a week for a month will return better dividends than crowding your study into a shorter period of time.
- Locate the place of the exam – You have been sent a notice telling you when and where to report for the examination.  If the location is in a different town or otherwise unfamiliar to you, it would be well to inquire the best route and learn something about the building.
- Relax the night before the test – Allow your mind to rest.  Do not study at all that night.  Plan some mild recreation or diversion; then go to bed early and get a good night's sleep.
- Get up early enough to make a leisurely trip to the place for the test – This way unforeseen events, traffic snarls, unfamiliar buildings, etc. will not upset you.
- Dress comfortably – A written test is not a fashion show.  You will be known by number and not by name, so wear something comfortable.
- Leave excess paraphernalia at home – Shopping bags and odd bundles will get in your way.  You need bring only the items mentioned in the official notice you received; usually everything you need is provided.  Do not bring reference books to the exam.  They will only confuse those last minutes and be taken away from you when in the test room.
- Arrive somewhat ahead of time – If because of transportation schedules you must get there very early, bring a newspaper or magazine to take your mind off yourself while waiting.
- Locate the examination room – When you have found the proper room, you will be directed to the seat or part of the room where you will sit.  Sometimes you are given a sheet of instructions to read while you are waiting.  Do not fill out any forms until you are told to do so; just read them and be prepared.
- Relax and prepare to listen to the instructions
- If you have any physical problem that may keep you from doing your best, be sure to tell the test administrator.  If you are sick or in poor health, you really cannot do your best on the exam.  You can come back and take the test some other time.

## VII.  AT THE TEST

The day of the test is here and you have the test booklet in your hand.  The temptation to get going is very strong.  Caution!  There is more to success than knowing the right answers.  You must know how to identify your papers and understand variations in the type of short-answer question used in this particular examination. Follow these suggestions for maximum results from your efforts:

## 1) Cooperate with the monitor

The test administrator has a duty to create a situation in which you can be as much at ease as possible. He will give instructions, tell you when to begin, check to see that you are marking your answer sheet correctly, and so on. He is not there to guard you, although he will see that your competitors do not take unfair advantage. He wants to help you do your best.

## 2) Listen to all instructions

Don't jump the gun! Wait until you understand all directions. In most civil service tests you get more time than you need to answer the questions. So don't be in a hurry. Read each word of instructions until you clearly understand the meaning. Study the examples, listen to all announcements and follow directions. Ask questions if you do not understand what to do.

## 3) Identify your papers

Civil service exams are usually identified by number only. You will be assigned a number; you must not put your name on your test papers. Be sure to copy your number correctly. Since more than one exam may be given, copy your exact examination title.

## 4) Plan your time

Unless you are told that a test is a "speed" or "rate of work" test, speed itself is usually not important. Time enough to answer all the questions will be provided, but this does not mean that you have all day. An overall time limit has been set. Divide the total time (in minutes) by the number of questions to determine the approximate time you have for each question.

## 5) Do not linger over difficult questions

If you come across a difficult question, mark it with a paper clip (useful to have along) and come back to it when you have been through the booklet. One caution if you do this – be sure to skip a number on your answer sheet as well. Check often to be sure that you have not lost your place and that you are marking in the row numbered the same as the question you are answering.

## 6) Read the questions

Be sure you know what the question asks! Many capable people are unsuccessful because they failed to *read* the questions correctly.

## 7) Answer all questions

Unless you have been instructed that a penalty will be deducted for incorrect answers, it is better to guess than to omit a question.

## 8) Speed tests

It is often better NOT to guess on speed tests. It has been found that on timed tests people are tempted to spend the last few seconds before time is called in marking answers at random – without even reading them – in the hope of picking up a few extra points. To discourage this practice, the instructions may warn you that your score will be "corrected" for guessing. That is, a penalty will be applied. The incorrect answers will be deducted from the correct ones, or some other penalty formula will be used.

## 9) Review your answers

If you finish before time is called, go back to the questions you guessed or omitted to give them further thought. Review other answers if you have time.

## 10) Return your test materials

If you are ready to leave before others have finished or time is called, take ALL your materials to the monitor and leave quietly. Never take any test material with you. The monitor can discover whose papers are not complete, and taking a test booklet may be grounds for disqualification.

## VIII. EXAMINATION TECHNIQUES

1) Read the general instructions carefully. These are usually printed on the first page of the exam booklet. As a rule, these instructions refer to the timing of the examination; the fact that you should not start work until the signal and must stop work at a signal, etc. If there are any *special* instructions, such as a choice of questions to be answered, make sure that you note this instruction carefully.

2) When you are ready to start work on the examination, that is as soon as the signal has been given, read the instructions to each question booklet, underline any key words or phrases, such as *least, best, outline, describe* and the like. In this way you will tend to answer as requested rather than discover on reviewing your paper that you *listed without describing*, that you selected the *worst* choice rather than the *best* choice, etc.

3) If the examination is of the objective or multiple-choice type – that is, each question will also give a series of possible answers: A, B, C or D, and you are called upon to select the best answer and write the letter next to that answer on your answer paper – it is advisable to start answering each question in turn. There may be anywhere from 50 to 100 such questions in the three or four hours allotted and you can see how much time would be taken if you read through all the questions before beginning to answer any. Furthermore, if you come across a question or group of questions which you know would be difficult to answer, it would undoubtedly affect your handling of all the other questions.

4) If the examination is of the essay type and contains but a few questions, it is a moot point as to whether you should read all the questions before starting to answer any one. Of course, if you are given a choice – say five out of seven and the like – then it is essential to read all the questions so you can eliminate the two that are most difficult. If, however, you are asked to answer all the questions, there may be danger in trying to answer the easiest one first because you may find that you will spend too much time on it. The best technique is to answer the first question, then proceed to the second, etc.

5) Time your answers. Before the exam begins, write down the time it started, then add the time allowed for the examination and write down the time it must be completed, then divide the time available somewhat as follows:

- If 3-1/2 hours are allowed, that would be 210 minutes.  If you have 80 objective-type questions, that would be an average of 2-1/2 minutes per question.  Allow yourself no more than 2 minutes per question, or a total of 160 minutes, which will permit about 50 minutes to review.
- If for the time allotment of 210 minutes there are 7 essay questions to answer, that would average about 30 minutes a question.  Give yourself only 25 minutes per question so that you have about 35 minutes to review.

6) The most important instruction is to *read each question* and make sure you know what is wanted.  The second most important instruction is to *time yourself properly* so that you answer every question.  The third most important instruction is to *answer every question*.  Guess if you have to but include something for each question.  Remember that you will receive no credit for a blank and will probably receive some credit if you write something in answer to an essay question.  If you guess a letter – say "B" for a multiple-choice question – you may have guessed right.  If you leave a blank as an answer to a multiple-choice question, the examiners may respect your feelings but it will not add a point to your score.  Some exams may penalize you for wrong answers, so in such cases *only*, you may not want to guess unless you have some basis for your answer.

7) Suggestions
   a. Objective-type questions
      1. Examine the question booklet for proper sequence of pages and questions
      2. Read all instructions carefully
      3. Skip any question which seems too difficult; return to it after all other questions have been answered
      4. Apportion your time properly; do not spend too much time on any single question or group of questions
      5. Note and underline key words – *all, most, fewest, least, best, worst, same, opposite,* etc.
      6. Pay particular attention to negatives
      7. Note unusual option, e.g., unduly long, short, complex, different or similar in content to the body of the question
      8. Observe the use of "hedging" words – *probably, may, most likely,* etc.
      9. Make sure that your answer is put next to the same number as the question
      10. Do not second-guess unless you have good reason to believe the second answer is definitely more correct
      11. Cross out original answer if you decide another answer is more accurate; do not erase until you are ready to hand your paper in
      12. Answer all questions; guess unless instructed otherwise
      13. Leave time for review

   b. Essay questions
      1. Read each question carefully
      2. Determine exactly what is wanted.  Underline key words or phrases.
      3. Decide on outline or paragraph answer

4. Include many different points and elements unless asked to develop any one or two points or elements
5. Show impartiality by giving pros and cons unless directed to select one side only
6. Make and write down any assumptions you find necessary to answer the questions
7. Watch your English, grammar, punctuation and choice of words
8. Time your answers; don't crowd material

8) Answering the essay question

Most essay questions can be answered by framing the specific response around several key words or ideas. Here are a few such key words or ideas:

M's: manpower, materials, methods, money, management
P's: purpose, program, policy, plan, procedure, practice, problems, pitfalls, personnel, public relations

  a. Six basic steps in handling problems:
    1. Preliminary plan and background development
    2. Collect information, data and facts
    3. Analyze and interpret information, data and facts
    4. Analyze and develop solutions as well as make recommendations
    5. Prepare report and sell recommendations
    6. Install recommendations and follow up effectiveness

  b. Pitfalls to avoid
    1. *Taking things for granted* – A statement of the situation does not necessarily imply that each of the elements is necessarily true; for example, a complaint may be invalid and biased so that all that can be taken for granted is that a complaint has been registered
    2. *Considering only one side of a situation* – Wherever possible, indicate several alternatives and then point out the reasons you selected the best one
    3. *Failing to indicate follow up* – Whenever your answer indicates action on your part, make certain that you will take proper follow-up action to see how successful your recommendations, procedures or actions turn out to be
    4. *Taking too long in answering any single question* – Remember to time your answers properly

## IX.  AFTER THE TEST

Scoring procedures differ in detail among civil service jurisdictions although the general principles are the same. Whether the papers are hand-scored or graded by machine we have described, they are nearly always graded by number. That is, the person who marks the paper knows only the number – never the name – of the applicant. Not until all the papers have been graded will they be matched with names. If other tests, such as training and experience or oral interview ratings have been given, scores will be combined. Different parts of the examination usually have different weights. For example, the written test might count 60 percent of the final grade, and a rating of training and experience 40 percent. In many jurisdictions, veterans will have a certain number of points added to their grades.

After the final grade has been determined, the names are placed in grade order and an eligible list is established. There are various methods for resolving ties between those who get the same final grade – probably the most common is to place first the name of the person whose application was received first. Job offers are made from the eligible list in the order the names appear on it. You will be notified of your grade and your rank as soon as all these computations have been made. This will be done as rapidly as possible.

People who are found to meet the requirements in the announcement are called "eligibles." Their names are put on a list of eligible candidates. An eligible's chances of getting a job depend on how high he stands on this list and how fast agencies are filling jobs from the list.

When a job is to be filled from a list of eligibles, the agency asks for the names of people on the list of eligibles for that job. When the civil service commission receives this request, it sends to the agency the names of the three people highest on this list. Or, if the job to be filled has specialized requirements, the office sends the agency the names of the top three persons who meet these requirements from the general list.

The appointing officer makes a choice from among the three people whose names were sent to him. If the selected person accepts the appointment, the names of the others are put back on the list to be considered for future openings.

That is the rule in hiring from all kinds of eligible lists, whether they are for typist, carpenter, chemist, or something else. For every vacancy, the appointing officer has his choice of any one of the top three eligibles on the list. This explains why the person whose name is on top of the list sometimes does not get an appointment when some of the persons lower on the list do. If the appointing officer chooses the second or third eligible, the No. 1 eligible does not get a job at once, but stays on the list until he is appointed or the list is terminated.

## X. HOW TO PASS THE INTERVIEW TEST

The examination for which you applied requires an oral interview test. You have already taken the written test and you are now being called for the interview test – the final part of the formal examination.

You may think that it is not possible to prepare for an interview test and that there are no procedures to follow during an interview. Our purpose is to point out some things you can do in advance that will help you and some good rules to follow and pitfalls to avoid while you are being interviewed.

*What is an interview supposed to test?*

The written examination is designed to test the technical knowledge and competence of the candidate; the oral is designed to evaluate intangible qualities, not readily measured otherwise, and to establish a list showing the relative fitness of each candidate – as measured against his competitors – for the position sought. Scoring is not on the basis of "right" and "wrong," but on a sliding scale of values ranging from "not passable" to "outstanding." As a matter of fact, it is possible to achieve a relatively low score without a single "incorrect" answer because of evident weakness in the qualities being measured.

Occasionally, an examination may consist entirely of an oral test – either an individual or a group oral. In such cases, information is sought concerning the technical knowledges and abilities of the candidate, since there has been no written examination for this purpose. More commonly, however, an oral test is used to supplement a written examination.

*Who conducts interviews?*

The composition of oral boards varies among different jurisdictions. In nearly all, a representative of the personnel department serves as chairman. One of the members of the board may be a representative of the department in which the candidate would work. In some cases, "outside experts" are used, and, frequently, a businessman or some other representative of the general public is asked to serve. Labor and management or other special groups may be represented. The aim is to secure the services of experts in the appropriate field.

However the board is composed, it is a good idea (and not at all improper or unethical) to ascertain in advance of the interview who the members are and what groups they represent. When you are introduced to them, you will have some idea of their backgrounds and interests, and at least you will not stutter and stammer over their names.

*What should be done before the interview?*

While knowledge about the board members is useful and takes some of the surprise element out of the interview, there is other preparation which is more substantive. It *is* possible to prepare for an oral interview – in several ways:

**1) Keep a copy of your application and review it carefully before the interview**

This may be the only document before the oral board, and the starting point of the interview. Know what education and experience you have listed there, and the sequence and dates of all of it. Sometimes the board will ask you to review the highlights of your experience for them; you should not have to hem and haw doing it.

**2) Study the class specification and the examination announcement**

Usually, the oral board has one or both of these to guide them. The qualities, characteristics or knowledges required by the position sought are stated in these documents. They offer valuable clues as to the nature of the oral interview. For example, if the job involves supervisory responsibilities, the announcement will usually indicate that knowledge of modern supervisory methods and the qualifications of the candidate as a supervisor will be tested. If so, you can expect such questions, frequently in the form of a hypothetical situation which you are expected to solve. NEVER go into an oral without knowledge of the duties and responsibilities of the job you seek.

**3) Think through each qualification required**

Try to visualize the kind of questions you would ask if you were a board member. How well could you answer them? Try especially to appraise your own knowledge and background in each area, *measured against the job sought*, and identify any areas in which you are weak. Be critical and realistic – do not flatter yourself.

**4) Do some general reading in areas in which you feel you may be weak**

For example, if the job involves supervision and your past experience has NOT, some general reading in supervisory methods and practices, particularly in the field of human relations, might be useful. Do NOT study agency procedures or detailed manuals. The oral board will be testing your understanding and capacity, not your memory.

**5) Get a good night's sleep and watch your general health and mental attitude**

You will want a clear head at the interview. Take care of a cold or any other minor ailment, and of course, no hangovers.

*What should be done on the day of the interview?*

Now comes the day of the interview itself. Give yourself plenty of time to get there. Plan to arrive somewhat ahead of the scheduled time, particularly if your appointment is in the fore part of the day. If a previous candidate fails to appear, the board might be ready for you a bit early. By early afternoon an oral board is almost invariably behind schedule if there are many candidates, and you may have to wait. Take along a book or magazine to read, or your application to review, but leave any extraneous material in the waiting room when you go in for your interview. In any event, relax and compose yourself.

The matter of dress is important. The board is forming impressions about you – from your experience, your manners, your attitude, and your appearance. Give your personal appearance careful attention. Dress your best, but not your flashiest. Choose conservative, appropriate clothing, and be sure it is immaculate. This is a business interview, and your appearance should indicate that you regard it as such. Besides, being well groomed and properly dressed will help boost your confidence.

Sooner or later, someone will call your name and escort you into the interview room. *This is it.* From here on you are on your own. It is too late for any more preparation. But remember, you asked for this opportunity to prove your fitness, and you are here because your request was granted.

*What happens when you go in?*

The usual sequence of events will be as follows: The clerk (who is often the board stenographer) will introduce you to the chairman of the oral board, who will introduce you to the other members of the board. Acknowledge the introductions before you sit down. Do not be surprised if you find a microphone facing you or a stenotypist sitting by. Oral interviews are usually recorded in the event of an appeal or other review.

Usually the chairman of the board will open the interview by reviewing the highlights of your education and work experience from your application – primarily for the benefit of the other members of the board, as well as to get the material into the record. Do not interrupt or comment unless there is an error or significant misinterpretation; if that is the case, do not hesitate. But do not quibble about insignificant matters. Also, he will usually ask you some question about your education, experience or your present job – partly to get you to start talking and to establish the interviewing "rapport." He may start the actual questioning, or turn it over to one of the other members. Frequently, each member undertakes the questioning on a particular area, one in which he is perhaps most competent, so you can expect each member to participate in the examination. Because time is limited, you may also expect some rather abrupt switches in the direction the questioning takes, so do not be upset by it. Normally, a board member will not pursue a single line of questioning unless he discovers a particular strength or weakness.

After each member has participated, the chairman will usually ask whether any member has any further questions, then will ask you if you have anything you wish to add. Unless you are expecting this question, it may floor you. Worse, it may start you off on an extended, extemporaneous speech. The board is not usually seeking more information. The question is principally to offer you a last opportunity to present further qualifications or to indicate that you have nothing to add. So, if you feel that a significant qualification or characteristic has been overlooked, it is proper to point it out in a sentence or so. Do not compliment the board on the thoroughness of their examination – they have been sketchy, and you know it. If you wish, merely say, "No thank you, I have nothing further to add." This is a point where you can "talk yourself out" of a good impression or fail to present an important bit of information. Remember, *you close the interview yourself.*

The chairman will then say, "That is all, Mr. _____, thank you." Do not be startled; the interview is over, and quicker than you think. Thank him, gather your belongings and take your leave. Save your sigh of relief for the other side of the door.

*How to put your best foot forward*
Throughout this entire process, you may feel that the board individually and collectively is trying to pierce your defenses, seek out your hidden weaknesses and embarrass and confuse you. Actually, this is not true. They are obliged to make an appraisal of your qualifications for the job you are seeking, and they want to see you in your best light. Remember, they must interview all candidates and a non-cooperative candidate may become a failure in spite of their best efforts to bring out his qualifications. Here are 15 suggestions that will help you:

**1) Be natural – Keep your attitude confident, not cocky**
If you are not confident that you can do the job, do not expect the board to be. Do not apologize for your weaknesses, try to bring out your strong points. The board is interested in a positive, not negative, presentation. Cockiness will antagonize any board member and make him wonder if you are covering up a weakness by a false show of strength.

**2) Get comfortable, but don't lounge or sprawl**
Sit erectly but not stiffly. A careless posture may lead the board to conclude that you are careless in other things, or at least that you are not impressed by the importance of the occasion. Either conclusion is natural, even if incorrect. Do not fuss with your clothing, a pencil or an ashtray. Your hands may occasionally be useful to emphasize a point; do not let them become a point of distraction.

**3) Do not wisecrack or make small talk**
This is a serious situation, and your attitude should show that you consider it as such. Further, the time of the board is limited – they do not want to waste it, and neither should you.

**4) Do not exaggerate your experience or abilities**
In the first place, from information in the application or other interviews and sources, the board may know more about you than you think. Secondly, you probably will not get away with it. An experienced board is rather adept at spotting such a situation, so do not take the chance.

**5) If you know a board member, do not make a point of it, yet do not hide it**

Certainly you are not fooling him, and probably not the other members of the board. Do not try to take advantage of your acquaintanceship – it will probably do you little good.

**6) Do not dominate the interview**

Let the board do that. They will give you the clues – do not assume that you have to do all the talking. Realize that the board has a number of questions to ask you, and do not try to take up all the interview time by showing off your extensive knowledge of the answer to the first one.

**7) Be attentive**

You only have 20 minutes or so, and you should keep your attention at its sharpest throughout. When a member is addressing a problem or question to you, give him your undivided attention. Address your reply principally to him, but do not exclude the other board members.

**8) Do not interrupt**

A board member may be stating a problem for you to analyze. He will ask you a question when the time comes. Let him state the problem, and wait for the question.

**9) Make sure you understand the question**

Do not try to answer until you are sure what the question is. If it is not clear, restate it in your own words or ask the board member to clarify it for you. However, do not haggle about minor elements.

**10) Reply promptly but not hastily**

A common entry on oral board rating sheets is "candidate responded readily," or "candidate hesitated in replies." Respond as promptly and quickly as you can, but do not jump to a hasty, ill-considered answer.

**11) Do not be peremptory in your answers**

A brief answer is proper – but do not fire your answer back. That is a losing game from your point of view. The board member can probably ask questions much faster than you can answer them.

**12) Do not try to create the answer you think the board member wants**

He is interested in what kind of mind you have and how it works – not in playing games. Furthermore, he can usually spot this practice and will actually grade you down on it.

**13) Do not switch sides in your reply merely to agree with a board member**

Frequently, a member will take a contrary position merely to draw you out and to see if you are willing and able to defend your point of view. Do not start a debate, yet do not surrender a good position. If a position is worth taking, it is worth defending.

**14) Do not be afraid to admit an error in judgment if you are shown to be wrong**

The board knows that you are forced to reply without any opportunity for careful consideration. Your answer may be demonstrably wrong. If so, admit it and get on with the interview.

**15) Do not dwell at length on your present job**

The opening question may relate to your present assignment. Answer the question but do not go into an extended discussion. You are being examined for a *new* job, not your present one. As a matter of fact, try to phrase ALL your answers in terms of the job for which you are being examined.

*Basis of Rating*

Probably you will forget most of these "do's" and "don'ts" when you walk into the oral interview room. Even remembering them all will not ensure you a passing grade. Perhaps you did not have the qualifications in the first place. But remembering them will help you to put your best foot forward, without treading on the toes of the board members.

Rumor and popular opinion to the contrary notwithstanding, an oral board wants you to make the best appearance possible. They know you are under pressure – but they also want to see how you respond to it as a guide to what your reaction would be under the pressures of the job you seek. They will be influenced by the degree of poise you display, the personal traits you show and the manner in which you respond.

## ABOUT THIS BOOK

This book contains tests divided into Examination Sections. Go through each test, answering every question in the margin. At the end of each test look at the answer key and check your answers. On the ones you got wrong, look at the right answer choice and learn. Do not fill in the answers first. Do not memorize the questions and answers, but understand the answer and principles involved. On your test, the questions will likely be different from the samples. Questions are changed and new ones added. If you understand these past questions you should have success with any changes that arise. Tests may consist of several types of questions. We have additional books on each subject should more study be advisable or necessary for you. Finally, the more you study, the better prepared you will be. This book is intended to be the last thing you study before you walk into the examination room. Prior study of relevant texts is also recommended. NLC publishes some of these in our Fundamental Series. Knowledge and good sense are important factors in passing your exam. Good luck also helps. So now study this Passbook, absorb the material contained within and take that knowledge into the examination. Then do your best to pass that exam.

# EXAMINATION SECTION

# READING COMPREHENSION
## UNDERSTANDING WRITTEN MATERIALS

### COMMENTARY

The ability to read and understand written materials – texts, publications, newspapers, orders, directions, expositions – is a skill basic to a functioning democracy and to an efficient business or viable government.

That is why almost all examinations – for beginning, middle, and senior levels – test reading comprehension, directly or indirectly.

The reading test measures how well you understand what you read. This is how it is done: You read a passage followed by several statements. From these statements, you choose the *one* statement, or answer, that is *BEST* supported by, or *BEST* matches, what is said in the paragraph. *PRINT THE LETTER OF THE CORRECT ANSWER IN THE SPACE AT THE RIGHT.*

# SAMPLE QUESTIONS

DIRECTIONS:   Answer Questions 1 to 2 *only* according to the information given in the following passage.

When a fingerprint technician inks and takes rolled impressions of a subject's fingers, the degree of downward pressure the technician applies is important. The correct pressure may best be determined through experience and observation. It is quite important, however, that the subject be cautioned to relax and not help the fingerprint technician by also applying pressure, as this prevents the fingerprint technician from gaging the amount needed. A method which is helpful in getting the subject to relax his hand is to instruct him to look at some distant object and not to look at his hands.

1.  According to this passage, the technician tries to relax the subject's hands by          1._____

    A.   instructing him to let his hands hang loosely
    B.   telling him that being fingerprinted is painless
    C.   asking him to look at his hand instead of some distant object
    D.   asking him to look at something other than his hand

2.  The subject is asked *NOT* to press down on his fingers while being fingerprinted because          2._____

    A.   the impressions taken become rolled
    B.   the subject may apply too little downward pressure and spoil the impressions
    C.   the technician cannot tell whether he is applying the right degree of pressure
    D.   he doesn't have the experience to apply the exact amount of pressure

*CORRECT ANSWERS*
1.   D
2.   C

―――――――

# EXAMINATION SECTION
## TEST 1

Questions 1-3.

DIRECTIONS:   The following three questions relate to the information given in the paragraph below.

Thermostats should be tested in hot water for proper opening. A bucket should be filled with sufficient water to cover the thermostat and fitted with a thermometer suspended in the water so that the sensitive bulb portion does not rest directly on the bucket. The water is then heated on a stove. As the temperature of the water passes the 160-165° range, the thermostat should start to open and should be completely opened when the temperature has risen to 185-190°. Lifting the thermostat into the air should cause a pronounced closing action and the unit should be closed entirely within a short time.

1.   The thermostat described above is a device which opens and closes with changes in the          1.____

    A.   position       B.   pressure       C.   temperature    D.   surroundings

2.   According to the above paragraph, the closing action of the thermostat should be tested          2.____
    by

    A.   working the thermostat back and forth
    B.   permitting the water to cool gradually
    C.   adding cold water to the bucket
    D.   removing the thermostat from the bucket

3.   The bulb of the thermometer should not rest directly on the bucket because          3.____

    A.   the bucket gets hotter than the water
    B.   the thermometer might be damaged in that position
    C.   it is difficult to read the thermometer in that position
    D.   the thermometer might interfere with operation of the thermostat

———

# TEST 2

Questions 1-3.

DIRECTIONS:   Questions 1 to 3 inclusive are to be answered in accordance with information given in the paragraph below.

All idle pumps should be turned daily by hand, and should be run under power at least once a week. Whenever repairs are made on a pump, a record should be kept so that it will be possible to judge the success with which the pump is performing its functions. If a pump fails to deliver liquid there may be an obstruction in the suction line, the pump's parts may be badly worn, or the packing defective.

1.  According to the above paragraph, pumps                                                          1.____

    A.   in use should be turned by hand every day
    B.   which are not in use should be run under power every day
    C.   which are in daily use should be run under power several times a week
    D.   which are not in use should be turned by hand every day

2.  According to the above paragraph, the reason for keeping records of repairs made on       2.____
    pumps is to

    A.   make certain that proper maintenance is being performed
    B.   discover who is responsible for improper repairs
    C.   rate the performance of the pumps
    D.   know when to replace worn parts

3.  The one of the following causes of pump failure which is NOT mentioned in the above         3.____
    paragraph is

    A.   excessive suction lift              B.   clogged lines
    C.   bad packing                         D.   worn parts

_____

# TEST 3

DIRECTIONS:    Answer Questions 1 through 5 *SOLELY* on the basis of the information contained in the following passage.

Floors in warehouses, storerooms, and shipping rooms must be strong enough to stay
level under heavy loads. Unevenness of floors may cause boxes of materials to topple and
fall. Safe floor load capacities and maximum heights to which boxes may be stacked should
be posted conspicuously so all can notice it. Where material in boxes, containers, or cartons
of the same weight is regularly stored, it is good practice to paint a horizontal line on the wall
indicating the maximum height to which the material may be piled. A qualified expert should
determine floor load capacity from the building plans, the age and condition of the floor sup-
ports, the type of floor, and other related information.

Working aisles are those from which material is placed into and removed from storage.
Working aisles are of two types: transportation aisles, running the length of the building, and
cross aisles, running across the width of the building. Deciding on the number, width, and
location of working aisles is important. While aisles are necessary and determine boundaries
of storage areas, they reduce the space actually used for storage.

1.   According to the passage above, how should safe floor load capacities be made known      1._____
     to employees? They should be

     A.   given out to each employee
     B.   given to supervisors only
     C.   printed in large red letters
     D.   posted so that they are easily seen

2.   According to the passage above, floor load capacities should be determined by      2._____

     A.   warehouse supervisors        B.   the fire department
     C.   qualified experts            D.   machine operators

3.   According to the above passage, transportation aisles      3._____

     A.   run the length of the building
     B.   run across the width of the building
     C.   are wider than cross aisles
     D.   are shorter than cross aisles

4.   According to the above passage, working aisles tend to      4._____

     A.   take away space that could be used for storage
     B.   add to space that could be used for storage
     C.   slow down incoming stock
     D.   speed up outgoing stock

5.   According to the passage above, unevenness of floors may cause      5._____

     A.   overall warehouse deterioration
     B.   piles of stock to fall
     C.   materials to spoil
     D.   many worker injuries

_____

# TEST 4

DIRECTIONS:   Questions 1 to 3 are to be answered *SOLELY* on the basis of the information
contained in the following paragraph.

In a retail establishment, any overweight means a distinct loss to the merchant, and even
an apparently inconsequential overweight on a single package or sale, when multiplied by the
total number of transactions, could run into large figures. In addition to the use of reliable
scales and weights, and their maintenance in proper condition, there must be proper supervision of the selling force. Such supervision is a difficult matter, particularly on the score of
carelessness, as the depositing of extra amounts of material on the scale and failure to
remove the same when it overbalances the scale may become a habit. In case of under-
weight, either in the weighing or by the use of fraudulent scales and weights, the seller soon
will hear of it, but there is no reason why the amount weighed out should be in excess of what
the customer pays for. Checking sales records against invoices and inventories can supply
some indication of the tendency of the sales force to become careless in this field.

1. Of the following, the *MOST* valid implication of the above paragraph is that       1._____

   A.   all overweights which occur in retail stores are in small amounts
   B.   even-arm and uneven-arm balances and weights which are unreliable lead more
        often to underweights than to overweights
   C.   overweights due to errors of salesclerks necessarily lead to large losses by a
        retailer
   D.   supervision to prevent overweights is more important to a retailer than remedial
        measures after their occurrence

2. Of the following, the *MOST* valid implication of the above paragraph is that       2._____

   A.   depositing of insufficient amounts of commodities on scales and failure to add to
        them may become a habit with salesclerks
   B.   salesclerks should be trained in understanding and maintenance of scale mecha-
        nisms
   C.   supervision of salesclerks to prevent careless habits in weighing must depend
        upon personal observation
   D.   training and supervision of salesclerks in proper estimation of the amount asked
        for by the customer can eliminate errors of overweight

3. According to the above paragraph, the *MOST* accurate of the following statements is:       3._____

   A.   For the most part, the ideas expressed in the paragraph do not apply to wholesale
        establishments.
   B.   Inventories of commodities prepacked in the store are the only ones which can be
        used in checking losses due to overweight.
   C.   Invoices which give the value and weight of merchandise received are useful in
        checking losses due to overweights.
   D.   The principal value of inventories is to indicate losses due to overweights.

# TEST 5

Questions 1-5.

DIRECTIONS: Read *the* information below carefully. Then answer Questions 1 to 5 *SOLELY* on the basis of this information.

### TITANIC AIR COMPRESSOR

*Valves:* The compressors are equipped with Titanic plate valves which are automatic in operation. Valves are so constructed that an entire valve assembly can readily be removed from the head. The valves provide large port areas with short lift and are accurately guided to Insure positive seating.

*Starting Unloader:* Each compressor (or air end) is equipped with a centrifugal governor which is bolted directly to the compressor crank shaft. The governor actuates cylinder relief valves so as to relieve pressure from the cylinders during starting and stopping. The motor is never required to start the compressor tinder load.

*Air Strainer:* Each cylinder air inlet connection is fitted with a suitable combination air strainer and muffler.

*Pistons:* Pistons are light-weight castings, ribbed internally to secure strength, and are accurately turned and ground. Each piston is fitted with four (4) rings, two of which are oil control rings. Piston pins are hardened and tempered steel of the full floating type. Bronze bushings are used between piston pin and piston.

*Connecting Rods:* Connecting rods are of solid bronze designed for maximum strength, rigidity and wear. Crank pins are fitted with renewable steel bushings. Connecting rods are of the one-piece type, there being no bolts, nuts, or cotter pins which can come loose. With this type of construction, wear is reduced to a negligible amount, and adjustment of wrist pin and crank pin bearings is unnecessary .

*Main Bearings:* Main bearings are of the ball type and are securely held in position by spacers. This type of bearing entirely eliminates the necessity of frequent adjustment or attention. The crank shaft is always in perfect alignment.

*Crank Shaft:* The crank shaft is a one-piece heat-treated forging of best quality open-hearth steel, of rugged design and of sufficient size to transmit the motor power and any additional stresses which may occur in service. Each crank shaft is counter-balanced Cdynamically balanced) to reduce vibration to a minimum, and is accurately machined to properly receive the ball-bearing races, crank pin bushing, flexible coupling, and centrifugal governor. Suitable provision is made to insure proper lubrication of all crank shaft bearings and bushings with the minimum amount of attention.

*Coupling:* Compressor and motor shafts are connected through a Morse Chain Company all-metal enclosed flexible coupling. This coupling consists of two sprockets, one mounted on, and keyed to, each shaft; the sprockets are wrapped by a single Morse Chain, the entire assembly being enclosed in a split aluminum grease-packed cover.

1. The crank pin of the connecting rod is fitted with a renewable bushing made of          1.\_\_\_\_

   A. solid bronze
   B. steel
   C. a light-weight casting
   D. ball bearings

2. When the connecting rod is of the one-piece type,          2.\_\_\_\_

   A. the wrist pins require frequent adjustment
   B. the crank pins require frequent adjustment

   C.   the cotter pins frequently will come loose
   D.   wear is reduced to a negligible amount

3.   The centrifugal governor is bolted *directly* to the          3._____

   A.   compressor crank shaft         B.   main bearing
   C.   piston pin                  D.   muffler

4.   The *number* of oil control rings required for each piston is       4._____

   A.   one        B.   two        C.   three        D.   four

5.   The compressor and motor shafts are connected through a flexible coupling. These cou-   5._____
   plings are

   A.   keyed to the shafts
   B.   brazed to the shafts
   C.   soldered to the shafts
   D.   press-fit to the shafts

# TEST 6

Questions 1-6.

DIRECTIONS: Answer Questions 1 to 6 *only* according to the information given in the paragraph below.

Perhaps the strongest argument the mass transit backer has is the advantage in efficiency that mass transit has over the automobile in the urban traffic picture. It has been estimated that given comparable location and construction conditions, the subway can carry four times as many passengers per hour and cost half as much to build as urban highways. Yet public apathy regarding the mass transportation movement in the 1960's resulted in the building of more roads. Planned to provide 42,000 miles of highways in the period from 1956-72, including 7500 miles within cities, the Federal Highway System project is now about two-thirds completed. The Highway Trust Fund supplies 90 percent of the cost of the System, with state and local sources putting up the rest of the money. By contrast, a municipality has had to put up the bulk of the cost of a rapid transit system. Although the System and its Trust Fund have come under attack in the past few years from environmentalists and groups opposed to the continued building of urban freeways – considered to be the most expensive, destructive, and inefficient segments of the System – a move by them to get the Trust Fund transformed into a general transportation fund at the expiration of the present program in 1972 seems to be headed nowhere.

1. Given similar building conditions and location, a city that builds a subway instead of a highway can expect to receive for each dollar spent                                          1._____

    A. half as much transport value
    B. twice as much transport value
    C. four times as much transport value
    D. eight times as much transport value

2. The general attitude of the public in the past ten years toward the mass transportation movement has been                                          2._____

    A. favorable                          B. indifferent
    C. enthusiastic                       D. unfriendly

3. The number of miles of highways still to be completed in the Federal Highway System project is, most nearly,                                          3._____

    A. 2,500          B. 5,000          C. 14,000          D. 28,000

4. *What* do certain groups who object to some features of the Federal Highway System program want to do with the Highway Trust Fund after 1972?                                          4._____

    A. Extend it in order to complete the project
    B. Change it so that the money can be used for all types of transportation
    C. End it even if the project is not completed
    D. Change it so that the money will be used only for urban freeways

5. *Which one* of the following statements is a *VALID* conclusion based on the facts in the above passage?                                          5._____

A.  The advantage of greater efficiency is the only argument that supporters of the mass transportation movement can offer.
B.  It was easier for cities to build roads rather than mass transit systems in the last 15 years because of the large financial contribution made by the Federal Government.
C.  Mass transit systems cause as much congestion and air pollution in cities as automobiles.
D.  In 1972, the Highway Trust Fund becomes a general transportation fund.

6.  The *MAIN* idea or theme of the above passage is that the          6.____

A.  cost of the Federal Highway System is shared by the federal, state, and local governments
B.  public is against spending money for building mass transportation facilities in the cities
C.  cities would benefit more from expansion and improvement of their mass transit systems than from the building of more highways
D.  building of mass transportation facilities has been slowed by the Highway Trust Fund

———————

# TEST 7

DIRECTIONS: Answer Questions 1 to 5 *ONLY* according to the information given in the paragraph below.

    The use of role-playing as a training technique was developed during the past decade by social scientists, particularly psychologists, who have been active in training experiments. Originally, this technique was applied by clinical psychologists who discovered that a patient appears to gain understanding of an emotionally disturbing situation when encouraged to act out roles in that situation. As applied in government and business organizations, the purpose of role-playing is to aid employees to understand certain work problems involving interpersonal relations and to enable observers to evaluate various reactions to them. Thus, for example, on the problem of handling grievances, two individuals from the group might be selected to act out extemporaneously the parts of subordinate and supervisor. When this situation is enacted by various pairs among the class and the techniques and results are discussed, the members of the group are presumed to reach conclusions about the most effective means of handling similar situations. Often the use of role reversal, where participants take parts different from their actual work roles, assists individuals to gain more insight into other people's problems and viewpoints. Although role-playing can be a rewarding training device, the trainer must be aware of his responsibilities. If this technique is to be successful, thorough briefing of both actors and observers as to the situation in question, the participants' roles, and what to look for, is essential.

1. The role-playing technique was *FIRST* used for the purpose of     1._____

    A. measuring the effectiveness of training programs
    B. training supervisors in business organizations
    C. treating emotionally disturbed patients
    D. handling employee grievances

2. When role-playing is used in private business as a training device, the *CHIEF* aim is to     2._____

    A. develop better relations between supervisor and subordinate in the handling of grievances
    B. come up with a solution to a specific problem that has arisen
    C. determine the training needs of the group
    D. increase employee understanding of the human-relation factors in work situations

3. From the above passage, it is *MOST* reasonable to conclude that when role-playing is used, it is preferable to have the roles acted out by     3._____

    A. only one set of actors
    B. no more than two sets of actors
    C. several different sets of actors
    D. the trainer or trainers of the group

4. It can be *inferred* from the above passage that a limitation of role-play as a training method is that     4._____

    A. many work situations do not lend themselves to role-play
    B. employees are not experienced enough as actors to play the roles realistically
    C. only trainers who have psychological training can use it successfully
    D. participants who are observing and not acting do not benefit from it

5. To obtain *good* results from the use of role-play in training, a trainer should give partici-      5._____
   pants

   A. a minimum of information about the situation so that they can act spontaneously
   B. scripts which illustrate the best method for handling the situation
   C. a complete explanation of the problem and the roles to be acted out
   D. a summary of work problems which involve interpersonal relations

---

# KEY (CORRECT ANSWERS)

| **TEST 1** | **TEST 2** | **TEST 3** | **TEST 4** |
|---|---|---|---|
| 1.  C | 1.  A | 1.  D | 1.  D |
| 2.  D | 2.  C | 2.  C | 2.  C |
| 3.  A | 3.  A | 3.  A | 3.  C |
|  |  | 4.  A |  |
|  |  | 5.  B |  |

| **TEST 5** | **TEST 6** | **TEST 7** |
|---|---|---|
| 1.  B | 1.  D | 1.  C |
| 2.  D | 2.  B | 2.  D |
| 3.  A | 3.  C | 3.  C |
| 4.  B | 4.  B | 4.  A |
| 5.  A | 5.  B | 5.  C |
|  | 6.  C |  |

---

# READING COMPREHENSION
## UNDERSTANDING AND INTERPRETING WRITTEN MATERIAL
## EXAMINATION SECTION
## TEST 1

DIRECTIONS: All questions are to be answered *SOLELY* on the basis of the information contained in the passage. Each question or incomplete statement is followed by several suggested answers or completions. Select the one that *BEST* answers the question or completes the statement. *PRINT THE LETTER OF THE CORRECT ANSWER IN THE SPACE AT THE RIGHT.*

Questions 1-3.

The equipment in a mail room may include a mail-metering machine. This machine simultaneously stamps, postmarks, seals, and counts letters as fast as the operator can feed them. It can also print the proper postage directly on a gummed strip to be affixed to bulky items. It is equipped with a meter which is removed from the machine and sent to the postmaster to be set for a given number of stampings of any denomination. The setting of the meter must be paid for in advance. One of the advantages of metered mail is that it bypasses the cancellation operation and, thereby, facilitates handling by the post office. Mail metering also makes the pilfering of stamps impossible, but does not prevent the passage of personal mail in company envelopes through the meters unless there is established a rigid control or censorship over outgoing mail.

1.  According to this statement, the postmaster

    A.  is responsible for training new clerks in the use of mail-metering machines
    B.  usually recommends that both large and small firms adopt the use of mail metering machines
    C.  is responsible for setting the meter to print a fixed number of stampings
    D.  examines the mail-metering machines to see that they are properly installed in the mail room

1.\_\_\_\_

2.  According to this statement, the use of mail-metering machines

    A.  requires the employment of more clerks in a mail room than does the use of postage stamps
    B.  interferes with the handling of large quantities of out-going mail
    C.  does not prevent employees from sending their personal letters at company expense
    D.  usually involves smaller expenditures for mail-room equipment than does the use of postage stamps

2.\_\_\_\_

3.  On the basis of this statement, it is MOST accurate to state that

    A.  mail-metering machines are often used for opening envelopes
    B.  postage stamps are generally used when bulky packages are to be mailed
    C.  the use of metered mail tends to interfere with rapid mail handling by the post office
    D.  mail-metering machines can seal and count letters at the same time

3.\_\_\_\_

Questions 4-8.

It is the Housing Administration's policy that all tenants, whether new or transferring from one housing development to another, shall be required to pay a standard security deposit of one month's rent based on the rent at the time of admission. There are, however, certain exceptions to this policy. Employees of the Administration shall not be required to pay a security deposit if they secure an apartment in an Administration development. Where the payment of a full security deposit may present a hardship to a tenant, the development's manager may allow a tenant to move into an apartment upon payment of only part of the security deposit. In such cases, however, the tenant must agree to gradually pay the balance of the deposit. If a tenant transfers from one apartment to another within the same project, the security deposit originally paid by the tenant for his former apartment will be acceptable for his new apartment, even if the rent in the new apartment is greater than the rent in the former one. Finally, tenants who receive public assistance need not pay a security deposit before moving into an apartment if the appropriate agency states, in writing, that it will pay the deposit. However, it is the responsibility of the development's manager to make certain that payment shall be received within one month of the date that the tenant moves into the apartment.

4. According to the above passage, when a tenant transfers from one apartment to another in the same development, the Housing Administration will

    A. *accept* the tenant's old security deposit as the security deposit for his new apartment regardless of the new apartment's rent
    B. *refund* the tenant's old security deposit and not requires him to pay a new deposit
    C. *keep* the tenant's old security deposit and require him to pay a new deposit
    D. *require* the tenant to pay a new security deposit based on the difference between his old rent and his new rent

4.\_\_\_\_

5. On the basis of the above passage, it is INCORRECT to state that a tenant who receives public assistance may move into an Administration development if

    A. he pays the appropriate security deposit
    B. the appropriate agency gives a written indication that it will pay the security deposit before the tenant moves in
    C. the appropriate agency states, by telephone, that it will pay the security deposit
    D. he appropriate agency writes the manager to indicate that the security deposit will be paid within one month but not less than two weeks from the date the tenant moves into the apartment

5.\_\_\_\_

6. On the basis of the above passage, a tenant who transfers from an apartment In one development to an apartment in a different development will

    A. forfeits his old security deposit and be required to pay another deposit
    B. have his old security deposit refunded and not have to pay a new deposit
    C. pays the difference between his old security deposit and the new one
    D. has to pay a security deposit based on the new apartment's rent 2

6.\_\_\_\_

7. The Housing Administration will NOT require payment of a Security deposit if a tenant　　7.____

    A. is, an Administration employee
    B. is receiving public assistance
    C. claims that payment will present a hardship
    D. indicates, in writing, that he will be responsible for any damage done to his apartment

8. Of the following, the BEST title for the above passage is:　　8.____

    A. Security Deposits - Transfers
    B. Security Deposits - Policy
    C. Exemptions and Exceptions - Security Deposits
    D. Amounts - Security Deposits

Questions 9-11.

Terrazzo flooring will last a very long time if it is cared for properly. Lacquers, shellac or varnish preparations should never be used on terrazzo. Soap cleaners are not recommended, since they dull the appearance of the floor. Alkaline solutions are harmful, so neutral cleaner or non-alkaline synthetic detergents will give best results. If the floor is very dirty, it may be necessary to scrub it. The same neutral cleaning solution should be used for scrubbing as for mopping. Scouring powder may be sprinkled at particularly dirty spots. Do not use steel wool for scrubbing. Small pieces of steel filings left on the floor will rust and discolor the terrazzo. Non-woven nylon or open-mesh fabric abrasive pads are suitable for scrubbing terrazzo floors.

9. According to the passage above, the BEST cleaning agent for terrazzo flooring is a(n)　　9.____

    A. soap cleaner
    C. neutral cleaner
    B. varnish preparation
    D. alkaline solution

10. According to the passage above, terrazzo floors should NOT be scrubbed with　　10.____

    A. non-woven nylon abrasive pads
    C. open-mesh fabric abrasive pads
    B. steel wool
    D. scouring powder

11. As used in the passage above, the word *discolor* means, most nearly,　　11.____

    A. crack
    C. dissolve
    B. scratch
    D. stain

Questions 12-15.

Planning for the unloading of incoming trucks is not easy since generally little or no advance notice of truck arrivals is received. The height of the floor of truck bodies and loading platforms sometimes are different; this makes necessary the use of special unloading methods. When available, hydraulic ramps compensate for the differences in platform and truck floor levels. When hydraulic ramps are not available, forklift equipment can sometimes be used, if the truck springs are strong enough to support such equipment. In a situation like this, the unloading operation does not differ much from unloading a railroad box car In the cases where the forklift truck or a hydraulic pallet jack cannot be used inside the truck, a pallet dolly should be placed inside the truck, so that the empty pallet can be loaded close to the truck contents and rolled easily to the truck door and platform.

12. According to the passage above, unloading trucks are          12._____

    A. easy to plan since the time of arrival is usually known beforehand
    B. the same as loading a railroad box car
    C. hard to plan since trucks arrive without notice
    D. a very normal thing to do

13. According to the above passage, which materials-handling equipment can make up for   13._____
the difference in platform and truck floor levels?

    A. Hydraulic jacks                 B. Hydraulic ramps
    C. Forklift trucks                 D. Conveyors

14. According to the passage above, what materials-handling equipment can be used when   14._____
a truck cannot support the weight of forklift equipment?

    A. A pallet dolly                 B. A hydraulic ramp
    C. Bridge plates                D. A warehouse tractor

15. Which is the BEST title for the above passage?          15._____

    A. Unloading Railroad Box Cars       B. Unloading Motor Trucks
    C. Loading Rail Box             D. Loading Motor Trucks

Questions 16-19.

Ventilation, as used in fire-fighting operations, means opening up a building or structure in which a fire is burning to release the accumulated heat, smoke, and gases. Lack of knowledge of the principles of ventilation on the part of firemen may result in unnecessary punishment due to ventilation being neglected or improperly handled. While ventilation itself extinguishes no fires, when used in an intelligent manner, it allows firemen to get at the fire more quickly, easily, and with less danger and hardship.

16. According to the above paragraph, the MOST important result of failure to apply the prin-   16._____
ciples of ventilation at a fire may be

    A. loss of public confidence       B. disciplinary action
    C. waste of water              D. excessive use of equipment
    E. injury to firemen

17. It may be inferred from the above paragraph that the CHIEF advantage of ventilation is   17._____
that it

    A. eliminates the need for gas masks
    B. reduces smoke damage
    C. permits firemen to work closer to the fire
    D. cools the fire
    E. enables firemen to use shorter hose lines

18. Knowledge of the principles of ventilation, as defined in the above paragraph, would be   18._____
LEAST important in a fire in a

    A. tenement house         B. grocery store
    C. ship's hold            D. lumberyard
    E. office building

19. We may conclude from the above paragraph that, for the well-trained and equipped fire-man, ventilation is
19.____

    A. a simple matter
    C. relatively unimportant
    E. sometimes a handicap

    B. rarely necessary
    D. a basic tool

Questions 20-22.

Many public service and industrial organizations are becoming increasingly insistent that supervisors at the work level be qualified instructors. The reason for this is that technological improvements and overall organizational growth require the acquisition of new skills and knowledge by workers. These skills and knowledge can be acquired in two ways. They can be gained either by absorption-rubbing shoulders with the job or through planned instruction. Permitting the acquisition of new skills and knowledge is to be haphazard and uncertain is too costly. At higher supervisory levels, the need for instructing subordinates is not so obvious, but it is just as important as at the lowest work level. A high-ranking supervisor accomplishes the requirements of his position only if his subordinate supervisors perform their work efficiently. Regardless of one's supervisory position, the ability to instruct easily and efficiently helps to insure well-qualified and thoroughly-trained subordinates. There exists an unfounded but rather prevalent belief that becoming a competent instructor is a long, arduous, and complicated process. This belief arises partially as a result of the requirement of a long period of college preparation involved in preparing teachers for our school system. This time is necessary because teachers must learn a great deal of subject matter. The worker who advances to a supervisory position generally has superior skill and knowledge; therefore, he has only to learn the techniques by which he can impart his knowledge in order to become a competent instructor.

20. According to the above paragraph, a prolonged period of preparation for instructing is NOT generally necessary for a worker who is advanced to a supervisory position because
20.____

    A. he may already possess some of the requirements of a competent instructor
    B. his previous job knowledge is generally sufficient to enable him to begin instructing immediately
    C. in his present position there is less need for the specific job knowledge of the ordinary worker
    D. the ability to instruct follows naturally from superior skill and knowledge

21. According to the above paragraph, it is important for the higher-level supervisor to be a good instructor because
21.____

    A. at this level there is a tendency to overlook the need for instruction of both subordinate supervisors and workers
    B. good training practices will then be readily adopted by lower-level supervisors
    C. the need for effective training is more critical at the higher levels of responsibility
    D. training can be used to improve the supervisory performance of his subordinate supervisors

22. According to the above paragraph, the acquisition of new skills and knowledge by work-   22.____
ers is BEST accomplished when

    A. the method of training allows for the use of absorption
    B. organizational growth and technological improvement indicate a need for further training
    C. such training is the result of careful planning
    D. the cost factor involved in training can be readily justified

Questions 23-25.

The organization of any large agency falls into three broad general zones: top manage-ment, middle management, and rank-and-file operations. The normal task of middle manage-ment is to supervise, direct and control the performance of operations within the scope of law, policy, and regulations already established. Where policy is settled and well defined, middle management is basically a set of standard operations, although they may call for high-devel-oped skills. Where, however, policy is not clearly stated, is ambiguous, or is rapidly shifting, middle management is likely to have an important influence upon emergency policy trends. Persons working in the zone of middle management usually become specialists. They need specialist knowledge of law, rules and regulations, and court decisions governing their organi-zation if they are to discharge their duties effectively. They will also have acquired specialist knowledge of relationships and sequences in the normal flow of business. Further, their attention is brought to bear on a particular administrative task, in a particular jurisdiction, with a particular clientele. The importance of middle management is obviously great. The reasons for such importance are not difficult to find: Here it is that the essential action of government in behalf of citizens is taken; here it is that citizens deal with government when they pass beyond their first contacts; here is a training ground from which a considerable part of top management emerges; and here also it is that the spirit and temper of the public service and its reputation are largely made,

23. According to the above paragraph, the critical importance of middle management is due   23.____
to the fact that it is at this level that

    A. formal executive training can be most useful
    B. the greatest amount of action is taken on the complaints of the general public
    C. the official actions taken have the greatest impact on general attitudes towards the public service
    D. the public most frequently comes in contact with governmental operations and agencies

24. According to the above paragraph, the one of the following statements which is NOT   24.____
offered as an explanation of the tendency for middle management responsibility to pro-duce specialists is that

    A. middle-management personnel frequently feel that their work is the most important in an organization
    B. specialized knowledge is acquired during the course of everyday work
    C. specialized knowledge is necessary for effective job performance
    D. their work assignments are directed to specific problems in specific situations

25. According to the above paragraph, the GREATEST impact of middle management in policy determination would be likely to be felt in the situation in which   25.____
    A. middle management possesses highly developed operational skills
    B. several policy directives from top management are subject to varying interpretations
    C. the authority of middle management to supervise, direct, and control operations has been clearly established
    D. top management has neglected to consider the policy views of middle management

———

# KEYS (CORRECT ANSWERS)

| | | | |
|---|---|---|---|
| 1. | C | 11. | D |
| 2. | C | 12. | C |
| 3. | D | 13. | B |
| 4. | A | 14. | A |
| 5. | C | 15. | B |
| 6. | D | 16. | E |
| 7. | A | 17. | C |
| 8. | B | 18. | D |
| 9. | C | 19. | D |
| 10. | B | 20. | A |

| | |
|---|---|
| 21. | D |
| 22. | C |
| 23. | C |
| 24. | A |
| 25. | B |

———

# TEST 2

Metal spraying is used for many purposes. Worn bearings on shafts and spindles can be readily restored to original dimensions with any desired metal or alloy. Low-carbon steel shafts may be supplied with high-carbon steel journal surfaces, which can then be ground to size after spraying. By using babbitt wire, bearings can be lined or babbitted while rotating. Pump shafts and impellers can be coated with any desired metal to overcome wear and corrosion. Valve seats may be re-surfaced. Defective castings can be repaired by filling in blow-holes and checks. The application of metal spraying to the field of corrosion resistance is growing, although the major application in this field is in the use of sprayed zinc. tin, lead, and aluminum have been used considerably. The process is used for structural and tank applications in the field as well as in the shop.

1. According to the above paragraph, worn bearing surfaces on shafts are metal-sprayed in order to   1.____

   A. prevent corrosion of the shaft
   B. fit them into larger-sized impellers
   C. returns them to their original sizes
   D. replaces worn babbitt metal

2. According to the above paragraph, rotating bearings can be metal-sprayed using   2.____

   A. babbitt wire             B. high-carbon steel
   C. low-carbon steel       D. any desired metal

Questions 3-5.

The method of cleaning which should generally be used is the space assignment method. Under this method, the buildings to be cleaned are divided into different sections. Within each section, each crew of Custodial Assistants is assigned to do one particular cleaning job. For example, within a section, one crew may be assigned to cleaning offices, another to scrubbing floors, a third to collecting trash, and so on. Other methods which may be used are the post-assignment method and the gang-cleaning method. Under the post-assignment method, a Custodial Assistant is assigned to one area of a building and performs all cleaning jobs in that area. This method is seldom used except where buildings are so small and distant from each other that it is not economical to use the space-assignment method. Under the gang-cleaning method, a Custodial Foreman takes a number of Custodial Assistants through a section of the building. These Custodial Assistants work as a group and complete the various cleaning jobs as they go. This method is generally used only where the building contains very large open areas.

3. According to the passage above, under the space-assignment method, each crew   3.____
   *generally*

   A. works as a group and does a variety of different cleaning jobs
   B. is assigned to one area and performs all cleaning jobs in that area
   C. does one particular cleaning job within a section of a building
   D. follows the Custodial Foreman through a building containing large, open areas

4. According to the passage above, the post-assignment method is used mostly where the buildings to be cleaned are

    A. *large* in size and situated *close together*
    B. *small* in size and situated *close together*
    C. *large* in size and situated *far apart*
    D. *small* in size and situated *far apart*

4.\_\_\_\_

5. As used in the passage above, the word *economical* means, most nearly,

    A. thrifty               B. agreed
    C. unusual            D. wasteful

5.\_\_\_\_

Questions 6-9.

The desirability of complete refuse collection by municipalities is becoming generally accepted. In many cases, however, such ideal service is economically impractical and certain limits must be imposed. Some municipal authorities find it necessary to regulate the quantity of refuse, by weight or volume, which will be collected from a single residence or place of business at one collection. The purpose of the regulations is twofold: First, to maintain the degree of service rendered on a somewhat uniform basis; and, second, to insure a more or less constant collection from week to week. If left unregulated, careless producers might permit large quantities of refuse to accumulate on their premises over long periods and place abnormal amounts out for collection at irregular intervals, thus upsetting the collection schedule. Regulation is especially applied to large wholesale, industrial, and manufacturing enterprises which, in the great majority of cases, are required to dispose of all or part of their refuse themselves, at their own expense. The maximum quantities permitted by regulation should obviously be sufficient to take care of a normal accumulation at a household over the established interval between regular collections. In commercial districts, the maximum quantity limitations are often fixed on arbitrary bases rather than on normal production.

6. According to the above paragraph, many municipalities do not have complete refuse collections because

    A. it costs too much           B. it is difficult to regulate
    C. it is not a municipal function    D. they don't consider it desirable

6.\_\_\_\_

7. According to the above paragraph, regulation by municipalities of the amount of refuse collected per collection from any one place of business does NOT contribute to

    A. accumulation of refuse by careless producers
    B. maintenance of collection schedules
    C. steady collection from one week to the next
    D. uniform service

7.\_\_\_\_

8. According to the above paragraph, regulations by municipalities of refuse collection from certain enterprises helps to cut down

    A. accumulation of refuse for private collection
    B. the amount of refuse produced
    C. variation in the volume of refuse produced
    D. variation in collection service

8.\_\_\_\_

9. According to the above paragraph, municipalities limit the amount of refuse collected in commercial districts on an arbitrary basis rather than on the basis of a normal accumulation. This is *probably* done because      9.____

    A. arbitrary standards are easy to establish and enforce
    B. normal accumulation is different for each district
    C. normal accumulation would require the collection of too much refuse
    D. there is no such thing as a normal accumulation

Questions 10-13.

Modern office methods, geared to ever higher speeds and aimed at ever greater efficiency, are largely the result of the typewriter. The typewriter is a substitute for handwriting and, in the hands of a skilled typist, not only turns out letters and other documents at least three times faster than a penman can do the work, but turns out the greater volume more uniformly and legibly. With the use of carbon paper and onionskin paper, identical copies can be made at the same time.

The typewriter, besides its effect on the conduct of business and government, has had a very important effect on the position of women. The typewriter has done much to bring women into business and government and today there are vastly more women than men typists. Many women have used the keys of the typewriter to climb the ladder to responsible managerial positions.

The typewriter, as its name implies, employs type to make an ink impression on paper. For many years, the manual typewriter was the standard machine used. Today, the electric typewriter is dominant, and completely automatic typewriters are coming into wider use.

The mechanism of the office manual typewriter includes a set of keys arranged systematically in rows; a semicircular frame of type, connected to the keys by levers; the carriage, or paper carrier; a rubber roller, called a platen, against which the type strikes; and an inked ribbon which makes the impression of the type character when the key strikes it.

10. The passage mentions a number of good features of the combination of a skilled typist and a typewriter of the following, the feature which is NOT mentioned in the passage is      10.____

    A. speed                B. uniformity
    C. reliability          D. legibility

11. According to the passage, a skilled typist can      11.____

    A. turn out at least five carbon copies of typed matter
    B. type at least three times faster than a penman can write
    C. type more than 80 words a minute
    D. readily move into a managerial position

12. According to the passage, which of the following is NOT part of the mechanism of a manual typewriter?      12.____

    A. Carbon paper         B. Paper carrier
    C. Platen               D. Inked ribbon

13. According to the passage, the typewriter has helped      13.\_\_\_\_

    A. men more than women in business
    B. women in career advancement into management
    C. men and women equally, but women have taken better advantage of it
    D. more women than men, because men generally dislike routine typing work

Questions 14-18.

Reductions in pipe size of a building heating system are made with eccentric fittings and are pitched downward. The ends of mains with gravity return shall be at least 18" above the water line of the boiler. As condensate flows opposite to the steam, run outs are one size larger than the vertical pipe and are pitched upward. In a one-pipe system, an automatic air vent must be provided at each main to relieve air pressure and to let steam enter the radiator. As steam enters the radiator, a *thermal* device causes the vent to close, thereby holding the steam. Steam mains should not be less than two inches in diameter. The end of the steam main should have a minimum size of one-half of its greatest diameter. Small steam systems should be sized for a 2-oz. pressure drop. Large steam systems should be sized for a 4-oz. pressure drop.

14. The word *thermal*, as used in the above paragraph, means, most nearly,      14.\_\_\_\_

    A. convector                    B. heat
    C. instrument                D. current

15. According to the above paragraph, the one of the following that is one size larger than the vertical pipe is the      15.\_\_\_\_

    A. steam main               B. valve
    C. water line                D. run out

16. According to the above paragraph, small steam systems should be sized for a pressure drop of      16.\_\_\_\_

    A. 2 oz                    B. 3 oz
    C. 4 oz                    D. 5 oz

17. According to the above paragraph ends of mains with gravity return shall be *at least*      17.\_\_\_\_

    A. 18" above the water line of the boiler
    B. one-quarter of the greatest diameter of the main
    C. twice the size of the vertical pipe in the main
    D. 18" above the steam line of the boiler

18. According to the above paragraph, the one of the following that is provided at each main to relieve air pressure is a (n)      18.\_\_\_\_

    A. gravity return             B. convector
    C. eccentric                D. vent

Questions 19-21.

The bearings of all electrical equipment should be subjected to careful inspection at scheduled periodic intervals in order to secure maximum life. The newer type of sleeve bearings requires very little attention since the oil does not become contaminated and oil leakage is negligible. Maintenance of the correct oil level is frequently the only upkeep required for years of service with this type of bearing.

19. According to the above paragraph, the MAIN reason for making periodic inspections of electrical equipment is to

    A. reduce waste of lubricants
    B. prevent injury to operators
    C. make equipment last longer
    D. keeps operators "on their toes"

19._____

20. According to the above paragraph, the bearings of electrical equipment should be inspected

    A. whenever the equipment isn't working properly
    B. whenever there is time for inspections
    C. at least once a year
    D. at regular times

20._____

21. According to the above paragraph, when using the newer type of sleeve bearings,

    A. oil leakage is slight
    B. the oil level should be checked every few years
    C. oil leakage is due to carelessness
    D. oil soon becomes dirty

21._____

Questions 22-25.

There is hardly a city in the country that is not short of fire protection in some areas within its boundaries. These municipalities have spread out and have re-shuffled their residential, business and industrial districts without readjusting the existing protective fire forces; or creating new protection units. Fire stations are still situated according to the needs of earlier times and have not been altered or improved to house modern fire-fighting equipment. They are neither efficient for carrying out their tasks nor livable for the men who must occupy them.

22. Of the following, the title which BEST describes the central idea of the above paragraph is:

    A. The Dynamic Nature of Contemporary Society
    B. The Cost of Fire Protection
    C. The Location and Design of Fire Stations
    D. The Design and Use of Fire-Fighting Equipment
    E. The Growth of American Cities

22._____

23. According to the above paragraph, fire protection is inadequate in the United States in

    A. most areas of some cities       B. some areas of most cities
    C. some areas in all cities         D. all areas in some cities
    E. most areas in most cities

23._____

24. The one of the following criteria for planning of fire stations which is NOT mentioned in the above paragraph is: 24.____

    A. Comfort of firemen     B. Proper location
    C. Design for modern equipment     D. Efficiency of operation
    E. Cost of construction

25. Of the following suggestions for improving the fire service, the *one* which would BEST deal with the problem discussed in the paragraph above would involve 25.____

    A. specialized training in the use of modern fire apparatus
    B. replacement of obsolete fire apparatus
    C. revision of zoning laws
    D. longer basic training for probationary firemen
    E. reassignment of fire districts

Questions 26-30.

Stopping, standing, and parking of motor vehicles is regulated by law to keep the public highways open for a smooth flow of traffic, and to keep stopped vehicles from blocking inter-sections, driveways, signs, fire hydrants, and other areas that must be kept clear. These established regulations apply in all situations, unless otherwise indicated by signs. Other local restrictions are posted in the areas to which they apply. Three examples of these other types of restrictions, which may apply singly or in combination with one another are:
NO STOPPING - This means that a driver may not stop a vehicle for any purpose except when necessary to avoid interference with other vehicles, or in compliance with directions of a police officer or signal.
NO STANDING - This means that a driver may stop a vehicle only temporarily to actually receive or discharge passengers.
NO PARKING - This means that a driver may stop a vehicle only temporarily to actually load or unload merchandise or passengers. When stopped, it is advisable to turn on warning flashers if equipped with them. However, one should never use a directional signal for this purpose, because it may confuse other drivers. Some NO PARKING signs prohibit parking between certain hours on certain days. For example, the sign may read NO PARKING 8 a.m. to 11 a.m., MONDAY, WEDNESDAY, FRIDAY. These signs are usually utilized on streets where cleaning operations take place on alternate days.

26. The parking regulation that applies to fire hydrants is an example of 26.____

    A. local regulations     B. established regulations
    C. posted regulations     D. temporary regulations

27. When stopped in a NO PARKING zone, it is advisable to 27.____

    A. turn on the right directional signal to indicate to other drivers that you will remain stopped
    B. turn on the left directional signal to indicate to other drivers that you may be leaving the curb after a period of time
    C. turn on the warning flashers if your car is equipped with them
    D. put the vehicle in reverse so that the backup lights will be on to warn approaching cars that you have temporarily stopped

28. You may stop a vehicle temporarily to discharge passengers in an area under the restriction of a    28.____

    A.   NO STOPPING - NO STANDING zone
    B.   NO STANDING - NO PARKING zone
    C.   NO PARKING - NO STOPPING zone
    D.   NO STOPPING - NO STANDING - NO PARKING zone

29. A sign reads "NO PARKING 8 a.m. to 11 a.m., MONDAY, WEDNESDAY, FRIDAY." Based on this sign, an enforcement agent would issue a summons to a car that is parked on a    29.____

    A.   Tuesday at 9:30 a.m.        B.   Wednesday at 12:00.a.m.
    C.   Friday at 10:30 a.m.          D.   Saturday at 8:00 a.m.

30. NO PARKING signs prohibiting parking between certain hours, on certain days, are usually utilized on streets where    30.____

    A.   vehicles frequently take on and discharge passengers
    B.   cleaning operations take place on alternate days
    C.   NO STOPPING signs have been ignored
    D.   commercial vehicles take on and unload merchandise

---

# KEYS (CORRECT ANSWERS)

| | | | |
|---|---|---|---|
| 1. | C | 16. | A |
| 2. | A | 17. | A |
| 3. | C | 18. | D |
| 4. | D | 19. | C |
| 5. | A | 20. | D |
| 6. | A | 21. | A |
| 7. | A | 22. | C |
| 8. | D | 23. | B |
| 9. | C | 24. | E |
| 10. | C | 25. | E |
| 11. | B | 26. | B |
| 12. | A | 27. | C |
| 13. | B | 28. | B |
| 14. | B | 29. | C |
| 15. | D | 30. | B |

---

# READING COMPREHENSION
## UNDERSTANDING AND INTERPRETING WRITTEN MATERIAL
# EXAMINATION SECTION
# TEST 1

DIRECTIONS:    Each question or incomplete statement is followed by several suggested answers or completions. Select the one that BEST answers the question or completes the statement. *PRINT THE LETTER OF THE CORRECT ANSWER IN THE SPACE AT THE RIGHT.*

Questions 1-2.

DIRECTIONS:    Questions 1 and 2 are to be answered SOLELY on the basis of the following paragraph.

When fixing an upper sash cord, you must also remove the lower sash. To do this, the parting strip between the sash must be removed. Now remove the cover from the weight box channel, cut off the cord as before, and pull it over the pulleys. Pull your new cord over the pulleys and down into the channel where it may be fastened to the weight. The cord for an upper sash is cut off 1" or 2" below the pulley with the weight resting on the floor of the pocket and the cord held taut. These measurements allow for slight stretching of the cord. When the cord is cut to length, it can be pulled up over the pulley and tied with a single common knot in the end to fit into the socket in the sash groove. If the knot protrudes beyond the face of the sash, tap it gently to flatten. In this way, it will not become frayed from constant rubbing against the groove.

1.    When repairing the upper sash cord, the FIRST thing to do is to      1._____
    A.   remove the lower sash
    B.   cut the existing sash cord
    C.   remove the parting strip
    D.   measure the length of new cord necessary

2.    According to the above paragraph, the rope may become frayed if the      2._____
    A.   pulley is too small      B.   knot sticks out
    C.   cord is too long      D.   weight is too heavy

Questions 3-4.

DIRECTIONS:    Questions 3 and 4 are to be answered SOLELY on the basis of the following paragraph.

Repeated burning of the same area should be avoided. Burning should not be done on impervious, shallow, unstable, or highly erodible soils, or on steep slopes—especially in areas subject to heavy rains or rapid snowmelt. When existing vegetation is likely to be killed or seriously weakened by the fire, measures should be taken to assure prompt revegetation of the burned area. Burns should be limited to relatively small proportions of a watershed unit so that the stream channels will be able to carry any increased flows with a minimum of damage.

3. According to the above paragraph, planned burning should be limited to small areas of the watershed because                                                   3._____
    A. the fire can be better controlled
    B. existing vegetation will be less likely to be killed
    C. plants will grow quicker in small areas
    D. there will be less likelihood of damaging floods

4. According to the above paragraph, burning USUALLY should be done on soils that                                                   4._____
    A. readily absorb moisture
    B. have been burnt before
    C. exist as a thin layer over rock
    D. can be flooded by nearby streams

Questions 5-11.

DIRECTIONS:    Questions 5 through 11 are to be answered SOLELY on the basis of the following paragraph.

### FUSE INFORMATION

Badly bent or distorted fuse clips cannot be permitted. Sometimes, the distortion or bending is so slight that it escapes notice, yet it may be the cause for fuse failures through the heat that is developed by the poor contact. Occasionally, the proper spring tension of the fuse clips has been destroyed by overheating from loose wire connections to the clips. Proper contact surfaces must be maintained to avoid faulty operation of the fuse. Maintenance men should remove oxides that form on the copper and brass contacts, check the clip pressure, and make sure that contact surfaces are not deformed or bent in any way. When removing oxides, use a well-worn file and remove only the oxide film. Do not use sandpaper or emery cloth as hard particles may come off and become embedded in the contact surfaces. All wire connections to the fuse holders should be carefully inspected to see that they are tight.

5. Fuse failure because of poor clip contact or loose connections is due to the resulting                                                   5._____
    A. excessive voltage          B. increased current
    C. lowered resistance         D. heating effect

6. Oxides should be removed from fuse contacts by using                                                   6._____
    A. a dull file          B. emery cloth
    C. fine sandpaper       D. a sharp file

7. One result of loose wire connections at the terminal of a fuse clip is stated in the above paragraph to be                                                   7._____
    A. loss of tension in the wire
    B. welding of the fuse to the clip
    C. distortion of the clip
    D. loss of tension of the clip

28

8. Simple reasoning will show that the oxide film referred to is undesirable 8._____
   CHIEFLY because it
   A. looks dull
   B. makes removal of the fuse difficult
   C. weakens the clips
   D. introduces undesirable resistance

9. Fuse clips that are bent very slightly 9._____
   A. should be replaced with new clips
   B. should be carefully filed
   C. may result in blowing of the fuse
   D. may prevent the fuse from blowing

10. From the fuse information paragraph, it would be reasonable to conclude that 10._____
    fuse clips
    A. are difficult to maintain
    B. must be given proper maintenance
    C. require more attention than other electrical equipment
    D. are unreliable

11. A safe practical way of checking the tightness of the wire connection to the 11._____
    fuse clips of a live 120-volt lighting circuit is to
    A. feel the connection with your hand to see if it is warm
    B. try tightening with an insulated screwdriver or socket wrench
    C. see if the circuit works
    D. measure the resistance with an ohmmeter

Questions 12-13.

DIRECTIONS:     Questions 12 through 13 are to be answered SOLELY on the basis
                of the following paragraph.

For cast iron pipe lines, the middle ring or sleeve shall have *beveled* ends and
shall be high quality cast iron. The middle ring shall have a minimum wall thickness of
3/8" for pipe up to 8", 7/16" for pipe 10" to 30", and 1/2" for pipe over 30", nominal
diameter. Minimum length of middle ring shall be 5" for pipe up to 10", 6" for pipe 10" to
30", and 10" for pipe 30" nominal diameter and larger. The middle ring shall not have a
center pipe stop, unless otherwise specified.

12. As used in the above paragraph, the word *beveled* means MOST NEARLY 12._____
    A. straight    B. slanted    C. curved    D. rounded

13. In accordance with the above paragraph, the middle ring of a 24" nominal 13._____
    diameter pipe would have a minimum wall thickness and length of _____
    thick and _____ long.
    A. 3/8"; 5:              B. 3/8"; 6"
    C. 7/16"; 6"             D. 1/2"; 6"

Questions 14-17.

DIRECTIONS:     Questions 14 through 17 are to be answered SOLELY on the basis
                of the following paragraph.

Operators spotting loads with long booms and working around men need the smooth, easy operation and positive control of uniform pressure swing clutches. There are no jerks or grabs with these large disc-type clutches because there is always even pressure over the entire clutch lining surface. In the conventional band-type swing clutch, the pressure varies between dead and live ends of the band. The uniform pressure swing clutch has excellent provision for heat dissipation. The driving elements, which are always rotating, have a great number of fins cast in them. This gives them an impeller or blower action for cooling, resulting in longer life and freedom from frequent adjustment.

14. According to the above paragraph, it may be said that conventional band-type swing clutches have     14._____
    A. even pressure on the clutch lining
    B. larger contact area
    C. smaller contact area
    D. uneven pressure on the clutch lining

15. According to the above paragraph, machines equipped with uniform pressure swing clutches will     15._____
    A. give better service under all conditions
    B. require no clutch adjustment
    C. give positive control of hoist
    D. provide better control of swing

16. According to the above paragraph, it may be said that the rotation of the driving elements of the uniform pressure swing clutch is ALWAYS     16._____
    A. continuous         B. constant
    C. varying            D. uncertain

17. According to the above paragraph, freedom from frequent adjustment is due to the     17._____
    A. operator's smooth, easy operation
    B. positive control of the clutch
    C. cooling effect of the rotating fins
    D. larger contact area of the bigger clutch

Questions 18-22.

DIRECTIONS:    Questions 18 through 22 are to be answered SOLELY on the basis of the following paragraphs.

Exhaust valve clearance adjustment on diesel engines is very important for proper operation of the engine. Insufficient clearance between the exhaust valve stem and the rocker arm causes a loss of compression and, after a while, burning of the valves and valve seat inserts. On the other hand, too much valve clearance will result in noisy operation of the engine.

Exhaust valves that are maintained in good operating condition will result in efficient combustion in the engine. Valve seats must be true and unpitted, and valve stems must work smoothly within the valve guides. Long valve life will result from proper maintenance and operation of the engine.

Engine operating temperatures should be maintained between 160°F and 185°F. Low operating temperatures result in incompl ete combustion and the deposit of fuel lacquers on valves.

18. According to the above paragraphs, too much valve clearance will cause the engine to operate
    A.  slowly    B.  noisily    C.  smoothly    D.  cold

18._____

19. On the basis of the information given in the above paragraphs, operating temperatures of a diesel engine should be between
    A.  125°F and 130°F    B.  140°F and 150°F
    C.  160°F and 185°F    D.  190°F and 205°F

19._____

20. According to the above paragraphs, the deposit of fuel lacquers on valves is caused by
    A.  high operating temperatures
    B.  insufficient valve clearance
    C.  low operating temperatures
    D.  efficient combustion

20._____

21. According to the above paragraphs, for efficient operation of the engine, valve seats must
    A.  have sufficient clearance
    B.  be true and unpitted
    C.  operate at low temperatures
    D.  be adjusted regularly

21._____

22. According to the above paragraphs, a loss of compression is due to insufficient clearance between the exhaust valve stem and the
    A.  rocker arm    B.  valve seat
    C.  valve seat inserts    D.  valve guides

22._____

Questions 23-25.

DIRECTIONS:    Questions 23 through 25 are to be answered SOLELY on the basis of the following excerpt:

## A SPECIFICATION FOR ELECTRIC WORK FOR THE CITY

Breakers shall be equipped with magnetic blowout coils...Handles of breakers shall be trip-free...Breakers shall be designed to carry 100% of trip rating continuously; to have inverse time delay tripping above 100% of trip rating...

23. According to the above paragraph, the breaker shall have provision for
    A.  resetting    B.  arc quenching
    C.  adjusting trip time    D.  adjusting trip rating

23._____

24. According to the above paragraph, the breaker
    A.  shall trip easily at exactly 100% of trip rating
    B.  shall trip instantly at a little more than 100% of trip rating
    C.  should be constructed so that it shall not be possible to prevent it from opening on overload or short circuit by holding the handle in the ON position
    D.  shall not trip prematurely at 100% of trip rating

24._____

25. According to the above paragraph, the breaker shall trip                    25._____
    A. instantaneously as soon as 100% of trip rating is reached
    B. instantaneously as soon as 100% of trip rating is exceeded
    C. more quickly the greater the current, once 100% of trip rating is exceeded
    D. after a predetermined fixed time lapse, once 100% of trip rating is reached

_____

## KEY (CORRECT ANSWERS)

| | | | | |
|---|---|---|---|---|
| 1. | C | | 11. | B |
| 2. | B | | 12. | B |
| 3. | D | | 13. | C |
| 4. | A | | 14. | D |
| 5. | D | | 15. | D |
| 6. | A | | 16. | A |
| 7. | D | | 17. | C |
| 8. | D | | 18. | B |
| 9. | C | | 19. | C |
| 10. | B | | 20. | C |

| | |
|---|---|
| 21. | B |
| 22. | A |
| 23. | B |
| 24. | C |
| 25. | C |

_____

# TEST 2

DIRECTIONS:    Each question or incomplete statement is followed by several suggested answers or completions. Select the one that BEST answers the question or completes the statement. *PRINT THE LETTER OF THE CORRECT ANSWER IN THE SPACE AT THE RIGHT.*

Questions 1-4.

DIRECTIONS:    Questions 1 through 4 are to be answered SOLELY on the basis of the following paragraph.

A low pressure hot water boiler shall include a relief valve or valves of a capacity such that with the heat generating equipment operating at maximum, the pressure cannot rise more than 20 percent above the maximum allowable working pressure (set pressure) if that is 30 p.s.i. gage or less, nor more than 10 percent if it is more than 30 p.s.i. gage. The difference between the set pressure and the pressure at which the valve is relieving is known as *over-pressure or accumulation.* If the steam relieving capacity in pounds per hour is calculated, it shall be determined by dividing by 1,000 the maximum BTU output at the boiler nozzle obtainable from the heat generating equipment, or by multiplying the square feet of heating surface by five.

1. In accordance with the above paragraph, the capacity of a relief valve should be computed on the basis of    1._____
    - A. size of boiler
    - B. maximum rated capacity of generating equipment
    - C. average output of the generating equipment
    - D. minimum capacity of generating equipment

2. In accordance with the above paragraph, with a set pressure of 30 p.s.i. gage, the overpressure should not be more than _____ p.s.i.    2._____
    - A. 3    B. 6    C. 33    D. 36

3. In accordance with the above paragraph, a relief valve should start relieving at a pressure equal to the    3._____
    - A. set pressure
    - B. over pressure
    - C. over pressure minus set pressure
    - D. set pressure plus over pressure

4. In accordance with the above paragraph, the steam relieving capacity can be computed by    4._____
    - A. *multiplying* the maximum BTU output by 5
    - B. *dividing* the pounds of steam per hour by 1,000
    - C. *dividing* the maximum BTU output by the square feet of heating surface
    - D. *dividing* the maximum BTU output by 1,000

Questions 5-8.

DIRECTIONS:     Questions 5 through 8 are to be answered SOLELY on the basis of
the following paragraph.

Air conditioning units requiring a minimum rate of flow of water in excess of
one-half (1/2) gallon per minute shall be metered. Air conditioning equipment with a
refrigeration unit which has a definite rate of capacity in tons or fractions thereof, the
charge will be at the rate of $30 per annum per ton capacity from the date installed to
the date when the supply is metered. Such units, when equipped with an approved
water-conserving device, shall be charged at the rate of $4.50 per annum per ton
capacity from the date installed to the date when the supply is metered.

5.   A man who was in the market for air conditioning equipment was considering          5._____
three different units. Unit 1 required a flow of 28 gallons of water per hour; Unit
2 required 30 gallons of water per hour; Unit 3 required 32 gallons of water per
hour. The man asked the salesman which units would require the installation of
a water meter. According to the above passage, the salesman SHOULD
answer:
     A.   All three units require meters
     B.   Units 2 and 3 require meters
     C.   Unit 3 only requires a meter
     D.   None of the units require a meter

6.   Suppose that air conditioning equipment with a refrigeration unit of 10 tons          6._____
was put in operation on October 1; and in the following year on July 1, a meter
was installed. According to the above passage, the charge for this period
would be _____ the annual rate.
     A.   twice                    B.   equal to
     C.   three-fourths            D.   one-fourth

7.   The charge for air conditioning equipment which has no refrigeration unit          7._____
     A.   is $30 per year
     B.   is $25.50 per year
     C.   is $4.50 per year
     D.   cannot be determined from the above passage

8.   The charge for air conditioning equipment with a seven-ton refrigeration unit          8._____
equipped with an approved water-conserving device
     A.   is $4.50 per year
     B.   is $25.50 per year
     C.   is $31.50 per year
     D.   cannot be determined from the above passage

Questions 9-14.

DIRECTIONS:     Questions 9 through 14 are to be answered SOLELY on the basis of
the following paragraph.

The city makes unremitting efforts to keep the water free from pollution. An
inspectional force under a sanitary expert is engaged in patrolling the watersheds to
see that the department's sanitary regulations are observed. Samples taken daily from
various points in the water supply system are examined and analyzed at the three

laboratories maintained by the department. All water before delivery to the distribution mains is treated with chlorine to destroy bacteria. In addition, some water is aerated to free it from gases and, in some cases, from microscopic organisms. Generally, microscopic organisms which develop in the reservoirs and at times impart an unpleasant taste and odor to the water, though in no sense harmful to health, are destroyed by treatment with copper sulfate and by chlorine dosage. None of the supplies is filtered, but the quality of the water supplied by the city is excellent for all purposes, and it is clear and wholesome.

9. According to the above paragraph, microscopic organisms are removed from the water supplied to the city by means of
   A. chlorine alone
   B. chlorine, aeration, and filtration
   C. chlorine, aeration, filtration, and sampling
   D. copper sulfate, chlorine, and aeration

9._____

10. Microscopic organisms in the water supply GENERALLY are
   A. a health menace          B. impossible to detect
   C. not harmful to health    D. not destroyed in the water

10._____

11. The MAIN function of the inspectional force, as described in the above paragraph, is to
   A. take samples of water for analysis
   B. enforce sanitary regulations
   C. add chlorine to the water supply
   D. inspect water-use meters

11._____

12. According to the above paragraph, chlorine is added to water before entering the
   A. watersheds          B. reservoirs
   C. distribution mains  D. run-off areas

12._____

13. Of the following suggested headings or titles for the above paragraph, the one that BEST tells what the paragraph is about is
   A. QUALITY OF WATER   B. CHLORINATION OF WATER
   C. TESTING OF WATER   D. BACTERIA IN WATER

13._____

14. The MOST likely reason for taking samples of water for examination and analysis from various points in the water supply system is:
   A. The testing points are convenient to the department's laboratories
   B. Water from one part of the system may be made undrinkable by a local condition
   C. The samples can be distributed equally among the three laboratories
   D. The hardness or softness of water varies from place to place

14._____

Questions 15-17.

DIRECTIONS:    Questions 15 through 17 are to be answered SOLELY on the basis of the following paragraph.

A building measuring 200' x 100' at the street is set back 20' on all sides at the 15th floor, and an additional 10' on all sides at the 30th floor. The building is 35 stories high.

15.  The **floor area** of the 16th floor is MOST NEARLY _____ sq. ft.          15._____
     A.   20,000     B.     14,400     C.   9,600     D.     7,500

16.  The floor area of the 35th floor is MOST NEARLY _____ sq. ft.          16._____
     A.   20,000     B.     13,900     C.   7,500     D.     5,600

17.  The floor area of the 16th floor, compared to the floor area of the 2nd floor, is     17._____
     MOST NEARLY _____ as much.
     A.   three-fourths (3/4)          B.   two-thirds (2/3)
     C.   one-half (1/2)               D.   four-tenths (4/10)

Question 18.

DIRECTIONS:     Question 18 is to be answered SOLELY on the basis of the following
                paragraph.

Experience has shown that, in general, a result of the installation of meters on
services not previously metered is to reduce the amount of water consumed, but is not
necessarily to reduce the peak load on plumbing systems. The permissible head loss
through meters at their rated maximum flow is 20 p.s.i. The installation of a meter may
therefore appreciably lower the pressures available in fixtures on a plumbing system.

18.  According to the above paragraph, a water meter may          18._____
     A.   limit the flow in the plumbing system of 20 p.s.i.
     B.   reduce the peak load on the plumbing system
     C.   increase the overall amount of water consumed
     D.   reduce the pressure in the plumbing system

Question 19.

DIRECTIONS:     Question 19 is to be answered SOLELY on the basis of the following
                paragraph.

Spring comes without trumpets to a city. The asphalt is a wilderness that does
not quicken overnight; winds blow gritty with cinders instead of merry with the smells of
earth and fertilizer. Women wear their gardens on their hats. But spring is a season in
the city, and it has its own harbingers, constant as daffodils. Shop windows change
their colors, people walk more slowly on the streets, what one can see of the sky has a
bluer tone. Pulitzer prizes awake and sing and matinee tickets go-a-begging. But gayer
than any of these are the carousels, which are already in sheltered places, beginning to
turn with the sound of springtime itself. They are the earliest and the truest and the
oldest of all the urban signs.

19.  In the passage above, the word *harbingers* means          19._____
     A.   storms     B.   truths     C.   virtues     D.   forerunners

Questions 20-22.

DIRECTIONS:     Questions 20 through 22 are to be answered SOLELY on the basis
                of the following paragraph.

Gas heaters include manually operated, automatic, and instantaneous heaters. Some heaters are equipped with a thermostat which controls the fuel supply so that when the water falls below a predetermined temperature, the fuel is automatically turned on. In some types, the hot-water storage tank is well-insulated to economize the use of fuel. Instantaneous heaters are arranged so that the opening of a faucet on the hot-water pipe will increase the flow of fuel, which is ignited by a continuously burning pilot light to heat the water to from 120° to 130°F. The possibility that the pilot light will die out offers a source of danger in the use of automatic appliances which depend on a pilot light. Gas and oil heaters are dangerous, and they should be designed to prevent the accumulation, in a confined space within the heater, of a large volume of an explosive mixture.

20. According to the above passage, the opening of a hot-water faucet on a hot-water pipe connected to an instantaneous hot-water heater will the pilot light.
    A. *increase* the temperature of
    B. *increase* the flow of fuel to
    C. *decrease* the flow of fuel to
    D. *have a marked effect* on

20._____

21. According to the above passage, the fuel is automatically turned on in a heater equipped with a thermostat whenever
    A. the water temperature drops below 120°F
    B. the pilot light is lit
    C. the water temperature drops below some predetermined temperature
    D. a hot water supply is opened

21._____

22. According to the above passage, some hot-water storage tanks are well-insulated to
    A. accelerate the burning of the fuel
    B. maintain the water temperature between 120° and 130°F
    C. prevent the pilot light from being extinguished
    D. minimize the expenditure of fuel

22._____

Question 23.

DIRECTIONS:    Question 23 is to be answered SOLELY on the basis of the following paragraph.

Breakage of the piston under high-speed operation has been the commonest fault of disc piston meters. Various techniques are adopted to prevent this, such as *throttling* the meter, cutting away the edge of the piston, or reinforcing it, but these are simply makeshifts.

23. As used in the above paragraph, the word *throttling* means MOST NEARLY
    A. enlarging          B. choking
    C. harnessing         D. dismantling

23._____

Questions 24-25.

DIRECTIONS:    Questions 24 and 25 are to be answered SOLELY on the basis of the following paragraph.

One of the most common and objectionable difficulties occurring in a drainage system is trap seal loss. This failure can be attributed directly to inadequate ventilation of the trap and the subsequent negative and positive pressures which occur. A trap seal may be lost either by siphonage and/or back pressure. Loss of the trap seal by siphonage is the result of a negative pressure in the drainage system. The seal content of the trap is forced by siphonage into the waste piping of the drainage system through exertion of atmospheric pressure on the fixture side of the trap seal.

24. According to the above paragraph, a positive pressure is a direct result of  24._____
  A. siphonage      B. unbalanced trap seal
  C. poor ventilation    D. atmospheric pressure

25. According to the above paragraph, the water in the trap is forced into the drain 25._____
  pipe by
  A. atmospheric pressure  B. back pressure
  C. negative pressure   D. back pressure on fixture side of seal

_____

## KEY (CORRECT ANSWERS)

| | | | | |
|---|---|---|---|---|
| 1. | B | | 11. | B |
| 2. | B | | 12. | C |
| 3. | D | | 13. | A |
| 4. | D | | 14. | B |
| 5. | C | | 15. | C |
| | | | | |
| 6. | C | | 16. | D |
| 7. | D | | 17. | C |
| 8. | C | | 18. | D |
| 9. | D | | 19. | B |
| 10. | C | | 20. | B |

| | |
|---|---|
| 21. | C |
| 22. | D |
| 23. | B |
| 24. | C |
| 25. | A |

_____

# ARITHMETICAL REASONING
# EXAMINATION SECTION
# TEST 1

DIRECTIONS: Each question or incomplete statement is followed by several suggested answers or completions. Select the one that BEST answers the question or completes the statement. *PRINT THE LETTER OF THE CORRECT ANSWER IN THE SPACE AT THE RIGHT.*

1. A supplier quotes a list price of $172.00 less 15 and 10 percent for twelve tools. The actual cost for these twelve tools is MOST NEARLY

    A.  $146        B.  $132        C.  $129        D.  $112

1._____

2. If the diameter of a circular piece of sheet metal is 1 1/2 feet, the area, in square inches, is MOST NEARLY

    A.  1.77        B.  2.36        C.  254        D.  324

2._____

3. The sum of 5'6", 7'3", 9'3 1/2", and 3'7 1/4" is

    A.  19'8 1/2"        B.  22' 1/2"        C.  25'7 3/4"        D.  28'8 3/4"

3._____

4. If the floor area of one shop is 15' by 21'3" and the size of an adjacent shop is 18' by 30'6", then the TOTAL floor area of these two shops is _____ square feet.

    A.  1127.75        B.  867.75        C.  549.0        D.  318.75

4._____

5. The fraction which is equal to 0.875 is

    A.  7/16        B.  5/8        C.  3/4        D.  7/8

5._____

6. The sum of 1/2, 2 1/32, 4 3/16, and 1 7/8 is MOST NEARLY

    A.  9.593        B.  9.625        C.  9.687        D.  10.593

6._____

7. If the base of a right triangle is 9" and the altitude is 12", the length of the third side will be

    A.  13"        B.  14"        C.  15"        D.  16"

7._____

8. If a steel bar 1" in diameter and 12' long weighs 32 lbs., then the weight of a piece of this bar 5'9" long is MOST NEARLY _____ lbs.

    A.  15.33        B.  15.26        C.  16.33        D.  15.06

8._____

9. The diameter of a circle whose circumference is 12" is MOST NEARLY

    A.  3.82"        B.  3.72"        C.  3.62"        D.  3.52"

9._____

10. A dimension of 39/64 inches converted to decimals is MOST NEARLY

    A.  .600"        B.  .609"        C.  .607"        D.  .611"

10._____

11. A farm worker was paid a weekly wage of $415.20 for a 44-hour work week. As a result of a new labor contract, he is paid $431.40 a week for a 40-hour work week with time and one-half pay for time worked in excess of 40 hours in any work week.
    If he continues to work 44 hours weekly under the new contract, the amount by which his average hourly rate for a 44-hour work week under the new contract exceeds the hourly rate previously paid him lies between _____ and _____, inclusive.

    11.____

    A.  80¢; $1.00
    C.  $1.25; $1.45

    B.  $1.00; $1.20
    D.  $1.50; $1.70

12. The sum of 4 feet 3 1/4 inches, 7 feet 2 1/2 inches, and 11 feet 1/4 inch is _____ feet _____ inches.

    12.____

    A.  21; 6 1/4       B.  22; 6       C.  23; 5       D.  24; 5 3/4

13. The number 0.038 is read as

    13.____

    A.  38 tenths
    C.  38 thousandths

    B.  38 hundredths
    D.  38 ten-thousandths

14. Assume that an employee is paid at the rate of $10.86 per hour with time and a half for overtime past 40 hours in a week.
    If he works 43 hours in a week, his gross weekly pay is

    14.____

    A.  $434.40       B.  $438.40       C.  $459.18       D.  $483.27

15. The sum of the following dimensions: 3'2 1/4", 8 7/8", 2'6 3/8", 2'9 3/4", and 1'0" is

    15.____

    A.  16'7 1/4"       B.  10'7 1/4"       C.  10'3 1/4"       D.  9'3 1/4"

16. Two gears are meshed together and have a gear ratio of 6 to 1.
    If the small gear rotates 120 revolutions per minute, the large gear rotates at

    16.____

    A.  20       B.  40       C.  60       D.  720

17. The vacuum side of a compound gage reads 14 inches of vacuum. The barometer reading is 29.76 inches of mercury. The equivalent absolute pressure of the compound gage reading, in inches of mercury, is MOST likely

    17.____

    A.  15.06       B.  15.76       C.  43.06       D.  43.76

18. The fraction 5/8 expressed as a decimal is

    18.____

    A.  0.125       B.  0.412       C.  0.625       D.  0.875

19. If 300 feet of a certain size pipe weighs 450 pounds, the number of pounds that 100 feet will weigh is

    19.____

    A.  1,350       B.  150       C.  300       D.  250

20. As an oiler, you work for a facility that has automobiles that use, on the average, 600 quarts of one grade of lubricating oil every month.
    The number of one-gallon cans of the above oil that should be ordered each month to meet this requirement is

    20.____

    A.  100       B.  125       C.  140       D.  150

21. The inside dimensions of a rectangular oil gravity tank are: height 15", width 9", length 10".
The amount of oil in the tank, in gallons, (231 cu.in. = 1 gallon), when the oil level is 9" high, is MOST NEARLY

    A.  2.3          B.  3.5          C.  5.2          D.  5.8

21.____

22. If 30 gallons of oil cost $76.80, 45 gallons of oil at the same rate will cost

    A.  $91.20       B.  $115.20      C.  $123.20      D.  $131.20

22.____

23. If an oiler earns $18,000 in the first six months of a year and receives a 10% raise in salary for the next six months of the same year, his TOTAL earnings for the year will be

    A.  $36,000      B.  $37,500      C.  $37,800      D.  $39,600

23.____

24. If the cost of lubricating oil increases 15%, then a gallon of oil which used to cost $10.00 will now cost MOST NEARLY

    A.  $10.50       B.  $11.00       C.  $11.50       D.  $12.00

24.____

25. The sum of 7/8", 3/4", 1/2", and 3/8" is

    A.  2 1/8"       B.  2 1/4"       C.  2 3/8"       D.  2 1/2"

25.____

---

# KEY (CORRECT ANSWERS)

| | | | |
|---|---|---|---|
| 1. | B | 11. | A |
| 2. | C | 12. | B |
| 3. | C | 13. | C |
| 4. | B | 14. | D |
| 5. | D | 15. | C |
| 6. | A | 16. | A |
| 7. | C | 17. | B |
| 8. | A | 18. | C |
| 9. | A | 19. | B |
| 10. | B | 20. | D |

| | |
|---|---|
| 21. | B |
| 22. | B |
| 23. | C |
| 24. | C |
| 25. | D |

---

# SOLUTIONS TO PROBLEMS

1. Actual cost = ($172)(,85)(.90) = $131.58 $\approx$ $132

2. Radius = .75', then area = (3.14)(.75)$^2$ $\approx$ 1.77 sq.ft.
   Since 1 sq.ft. = 144 sq.in., the area $\approx$ 254 sq.in.

3. 5'6" + 7'3" + 9'3 1/2" + 3'7 1/4" = 24'19 3/4" = 25'7 3/4"

4. Total area = (15)(21.25) + (18)(30.5) = 867.75 sq.ft.

5. .875 = 875/1000 =7/8

6. 1 1/2 + 2 1/32 +4 3/16 +1 7/8 = 8 51/32 = 9 19/32 = 9.593

7. Third side = $\sqrt{9^2+12^2} = \sqrt{225} = 15"$

8. Let x = weight. Then, 12/32 = 5.75/x . Solving, x $\approx$ 15.33 lbs.

9. 12" = (3.14)(diameter), so diameter $\approx$ 3.82"

10. $\dfrac{39}{64}$ " = .609375" $\approx$ .609"

11. Under his new contract, the weekly wage for 44 hours can be found by first determining his hourly rate for the first 40 hours = $431.40 $\div$ 40 $\approx$ $10.80. Now, his time and one-half pay will =($10.80)(1.5) = $16.20. His weekly wage for the new contract = $431.40 + (4)($16.20) = $496,20. His new hourly rate for 44 hours = $496.20 $\div$ 44 $\approx$ $10.34. Under the old contract, his hourly rate for 44 hours was $415.20 $\div$ 44 = $9.44. His hourly rate increase = $10.34 - $9.44 = $0.90. (Answer key: between $0.80 and $1.00)

12. 4'3 1/4" + 7'2 1/2" + 11' 1/4" = 22'6"

13. .038 = 38 thousandths

14. ($10.86)(40) + ($16.29)(3) = $483.27

15. 3'2 1/4" + 8 7/8" + 2'6 3/8" + 2'9 3/4" + 1'0" = 8'25 18/8" = 10'3 1/4"

16. The gear ratio is inversely proportional to the gear size. Let x = large gear's rpm. Then, 6/1 = 120/x . Solving, x = 20

17. Subtract 14 from 29.76

18. 5/8 = .625

19. Let x = number of pounds. Then, 300/450 = 100/x . Solving, x = 150

20. 600 quarts = 150 gallons, since 4 quarts = 1 gallon

21. (9")(9")(10") = 810 cu.in.  Then, 810 ÷ 231 ≈ 3.5

22. Let x = unknown cost. Then, 30/$76.80 = 45/x. Solving, x = $115.20

23. $18,000 + ($18,000)(1.10) = $37,800

24. ($10.00)(1.15) = $11.50

25. 7/8" + 3/4" + 1/2" + 3/8" = 20/8" = 2 1/2"

———————

# TEST 2

DIRECTIONS: Each question or incomplete statement is followed by several suggested answers or completions. Select the one that BEST answers the question or completes the statement. *PRINT THE LETTER OF THE CORRECT ANSWER IN THE SPACE AT THE RIGHT.*

1. A sheet metal plate has been cut in the form of a right triangle with sides of 5, 12, and 13 inches.
The area of this plate, in square inches, is

   A. 30          B. 32 1/2          C. 60          D. 78

   1.____

2. If steel weighs 480 lbs. per cubic foot, the weight of an 18" x 18" x 2" steel base plate is _____ lbs.

   A. 180          B. 216          C. 427          D. 648

   2.____

3. By trial, it is found that by using 2 cubic feet of sand, a 5 cubic foot batch of concrete is produced.
Using the same proportions, the amount of sand, in cubic feet, required to produce 2 cubic yards of concrete is MOST NEARLY

   A. 7          B. 22          C. 27          D. 45

   3.____

4. The total number of cubic yards of earth to be removed to make a trench 3'9" wide, 25'0" long, and 4'3" deep is MOST NEARLY

   A. 53.1          B. 35.4          C. 26.6          D. 14.8

   4.____

5. A large number of 2 x 4 studs, some 10'5" long and some 6'5 1/2" long, are required for a job.
To minimize waste, it would be PREFERABLE to order lengths of _____ feet.

   A. 16          B. 17          C. 18          D. 19

   5.____

6. A 6" pipe is connected to a 4" pipe through a reducer. If 100 cubic feet of water is flowing through the 6" pipe per minute, the flow, in cubic feet, per minute through the 4" pipe is

   A. 225          B. 100          C. 66.6          D. 44.4

   6.____

7. If steel weighs 0.28 pounds per cubic inch, then the weight, in pounds, of a 2" square steel bar 120" long is MOST NEARLY

   A. 115          B. 125          C. 135          D. 155

   7.____

8. A three-inch diameter steel bar two feet long weighs MOST NEARLY (assume steel weighs 480 lbs./cu.ft.) _____ lbs.

   A. 48          B. 58          C. 68          D. 78

   8.____

9. The area of a circular plate will be reduced by 5% if a sector removed from it has an angle of _____ degrees.

   A. 18          B. 24          C. 32          D. 60

   9.____

10. If a 4 1/16 inch shaft wears six thousandths of an inch, the NEW diameter will be _____ inches.    10.____

    A.  4.0031        B.  4.0565        C.  4.0578        D.  4.0605

11. A set of mechanical plan drawings is drawn to a scale of 1/8" = 1 foot.    11.____
If a length of pipe measures 15 7/16" on the drawing, the ACTUAL length of the pipe is _____ feet.

    A.  121.5        B.  122.5        C.  123.5        D.  124.5

12. An electrical drawing is drawn to a scale of 1/4" = 1'. If a length of conduit on the drawing measures 7 3/8", the actual length of the conduit, in feet, is    12.____

    A.  7.5        B.  15.5        C.  22.5        D.  29.5

13. Assume that you have assigned 6 mechanics to do a job that must be finished in 4 days.    13.____
At the end of 3 days, your men have completed only two-thirds of the job. In order to complete the job on time and because the job is such that it cannot be speeded up, you should assign a MINIMUM of _____ extra men.

    A.  3        B.  4        C.  5        D.  6

14. Assume that a trench is 42" wide, 5' deep, and 100' long. If the unit price of excavating the trench is $105 per cubic yard, the cost of excavating the trench is MOST NEARLY    14.____

    A.  $6,805        B.  $15,330        C.  $21,000        D.  $63,000

15. If the scale on a shop drawing is 1/4 inch to the foot, then the length of a part which measures 2 3/8 inches long on the drawing is ACTUALLY _____ feet.    15.____

    A.  9 1/2        B.  8 1/2        C.  7 1/4        D.  4 1/4

16. It is necessary to pour a new concrete floor for a shop. If the dimensions of the concrete slab for the floor are to be 27' x 18' x 6", then the number of cubic yards of concrete that must be poured is    16.____

    A.  9        B.  16        C.  54        D.  243

17. The jaws of a vise move 1/4" for each complete turn of the handle.    17.____
The number of complete turns necessary to open the jaws 2 3/4" is

    A.  9        B.  10        C.  11        D.  12

18. Assume that a jobbing shop is to submit a price for a contract involving 300 pieces of work. Assume that material costs 50 cents per piece, labor costs $7.50 an hour, and a lathe operator can complete 5 pieces in an hour.    18.____
If overhead is 40% of material and labor costs and the profit is 10% of all costs, the submitted price for the entire job will be

    A.  $630.24        B.  $872.80        C.  $900.00        D.  $924.00

19. The following formula is used in connection with the three-wire method of measuring pitch diameters of screw threads: $G = \dfrac{0.57735}{N}$ , where G = wire size and N = number of threads per inch.
According to this formula, the proper size of wire for a 1"-8NC thread is MOST NEARLY

    A.  .0722"        B.  .7217"        C.  .0072"        D.  .0074"

19.____

20. A millimeter is 1/25.4 of an inch and there are 10 millimeters to a centimeter.
If a piece of stock measures 127 centimeters long, the length of the stock, in feet and inches, would be MOST NEARLY

    A.  2'1"        B.  4'2"        C.  8'4"        D.  41'8"

20.____

21. For a certain job, you will need 25 steel bars 1 inch in diameter and 4"6" long.
If these bars weigh 3 pounds per foot of length, then the TOTAL weight for all 25 bars is _____ pounds.

    A.  13.5        B.  75.0        C.  112.5        D.  337.5

21.____

22. If steel weighs 0.30 pounds per cubic inch, then the weight of a 2 inch square steel bar 90 inches long is _____ pounds.

    A.  27        B.  54        C.  108        D.  360

22.____

23. A concrete wall is 36' long, 9' high, and 1 1/2' thick. The number of cubic yards of concrete that were needed to make this wall is

    A.  14        B.  18        C.  27        D.  36

23.____

24. If the scale on a shop drawing is 1/2 inch to the foot, then the length of a part which measures 41/4 inches long on the drawing has a length of APPROXIMATELY _____ feet.

    A.  2 1/8        B.  4 1/4        C.  8 1/2        D.  10 3/4

24.____

25. If the allowable load on a wooden scaffold is 60 pounds per square foot and the scaffold surface area is 3 feet by 12 feet, then the MAXIMUM total distributed load that is permitted on the scaffold is _____ pounds.

    A.  720        B.  1,800        C.  2,160        D.  2,400

25.____

# KEY (CORRECT ANSWERS)

| | | | | |
|---|---|---|---|---|
| 1. | A | | 11. | C |
| 2. | A | | 12. | D |
| 3. | B | | 13. | A |
| 4. | D | | 14. | A |
| 5. | B | | 15. | A |
| | | | | |
| 6. | B | | 16. | A |
| 7. | C | | 17. | C |
| 8. | A | | 18. | D |
| 9. | A | | 19. | A |
| 10. | B | | 20. | B |

21. D
22. C
23. B
24. C
25. C

———————————

# SOLUTIONS TO PROBLEMS

1. Area = (1/2)(base)(height) = (1/2)(5")(12") = 30 sq.in.

2. Volume = (18" ) (18") (2" ) = 648 cu.in. = 648/1720 cu.ft.
   Then, (480)(648/1720) = $\approx$ 180 lbs.

3. 2 cu.yds. = 54 cu.ft. Let x = required cubic feet of sand. Then, 2/5 = x/54. Solving, x = 21.6 (or about 22)

4. (3.75')(25')(4.25') = 398.4375 cu.ft. $\approx$ 14.8 cu.yds.

5. 10'5" + 6'5 1/2" = 16'10 1/2", so lengths of 17 feet are needed

6. The amount of water flowing through each pipe must be equal.

7. (2")(2")(120") = 480 cu. in. Then, (480)(.28) $\approx$ 135 lbs.

8. Volume = $(\pi)$ (.125 ')$^2$ (2) $\approx$ .1 cu.ft. Then, (.1)(480) = 48 lbs.

9. (360°)(.05) - 18°

10. 4 1/16 - .006 = 4.0625 - .006 = 4.0565

11. 15 7/16" $\div$ 1/8" = 247/16 . 8/1 = 123.5. Then, (123.5)(1 ft.) = 123.5 ft.

12. 7 3/8" $\div$ 1/4" = 59/8 . 4/1 = 29.5 Then, (29.5)(1 ft.) = 29.5 ft.

13. (6)(4) = 24 man-days normally required. Since after 3 days only the equivalent of (2/3)(24) = 16 man-days of work has been 1 done, 8 man-days of work is still left. 16 $\div$ 3 = 5 1/3, which means the crew is equivalent to only 5 1/3 men. To do the 8 man-days of work, it will require at least 8 - 5 1/3 = 2 2/3 = 3 additional men.

14. (3.5')(5')(100') = 1750 cu.ft. $\approx$ 64.8 cu.yds. Then, (64.8)($105) $\approx$ $6805

15. 2 3/8" $\div$ 1/4" = 19/8 . 4/1 = 9 1/2 Then, (9 1/2)(1 ft.) = 9 1/2 feet

16. (27')(18')(1/2') = 243 cu.ft. = 9 cu.yds. (1 cu.yd. = 27 cu.ft.)

17. 2 3/4" $\div$ 1/4" = 11/4 . 4/1 = 11

18. Material cost = (300)($.50) = $150. Labor cost = ($7.50)(300/5) = $450. Overhead = (.40)($150+$450) = $240. Profit = .10($150+$450+$240) = $84. Submitted price = $150 + $450 + $240 + $84 = $924

19. 6 = .57735" $\div$ 8 = .0722"

20. 127 cm = 1270 mm = 1270/25.4" $\approx$ 50" = 4.2"

21. (25)(4.5') = 112.5'  Then, (112.5X3) = 337.5 lbs.

22. (2")(2")(90") = 360 cu.in.  Then, (360)(30) = 108 lbs.

23. (36')(9')(1 1/2') = 486 cu.ft. = 18 cu.yds. (1 cu.yd. = 27 cu.ft.)

24. 4 1/4" $\div$ 1/2" = 17/4 . 2/1 = 8 1/2.  Then, (8 1/2)(1 ft.) = 8 1/2 ft.

25. (12')(3') = 36 sq.ft.  Then, (36)(60) = 2160 lbs.

———————

# TEST 3

DIRECTIONS:   Each question or incomplete statement is followed by several suggested answers or completions. Select the one that BEST answers the question or completes the statement. *PRINT THE LETTER OF THE CORRECT ANSWER IN THE SPACE AT THE RIGHT.*

1.  A right triangular metal sheet for a roofing job has sides of 36 inches and 4 feet. The length of the remaining side is

    A.  7 feet
    C.  60 inches
    B.  6 feet
    D.  90 inches

1.____

2.  A U.S. Standard Gauge thickness is given as 0.15625.
This thickness, in fractions of an inch, is MOST NEARLY _____ inches.

    A.  1/8      B.  4/32      C.  5/32      D.  3/64

2.____

3.  The weight per 100 of sheet metal fasteners is given as 2/3 pound.
The APPROXIMATE number of fasteners in a 2-pound package is

    A.  166      B.  200      C.  300      D.  266

3.____

4.  The decimal equivalent of 27/32 is MOST NEARLY

    A.  0.813      B.  0.828      C.  0.844      D.  0.859

4.____

5.  If a scaled measurement of 1'3" on the drawing of a sheet metal layout represents an actual length of 10"0", then the drawing has been made to a scale of _____ inch to the foot.

    A.  3/4      B.  1 1/4      C.  1 1/2      D.  1 3/4

5.____

6.  Two and two-thirds tees can be made from one sheet of steel.
If 24 tees must be made, then the number of sheets required is

    A.  6      B.  7      C.  8      D.  9

6.____

7.  A main duct 20 inches in diameter discharges into two branch ducts. The sum of the areas of the branches is to be equal to the area of the main duct. One branch is 12 inches in diameter.
The diameter of the other branch is _____ inches.

    A.  16      B.  12      C.  10      D.  8

7.____

8.  If steel weighs 480 lbs. per cubic foot, the weight of 10 sheets, each 6 feet by 3 feet by 1/32 inch, is _____ lbs.

    A.  2,700      B.  1,237      C.  270      D.  225

8.____

9.  The area, in square inches, of a right triangle that has sides of 12 1/2, 10, and 7 1/2 inches is

    A.  18 1/4      B.  37 1/2      C.  75      D.  60

9.____

10. In making a container to hold 1 gallon (231 cu.in.) and to be 6 inches in diameter at the top and 8 inches in diameter at the bottom, the height must be, in inches,

    A. 10.0       B. 8.2       C. 4.6       D. 6

10.____

11. A sheet metal worker is given a job to make a transition piece from a 8 1/2" diameter duct to an 11 1/4" diameter duct. If the length of the transition piece is 5 1/2" for each inch change in diameter, then the length of the transition piece is

    A. 14 7/8"       B. 15"       C. 15 1/8"       D. 15 1/4"

11.____

12. A duct layout is drawn to a scale of 3/8" to a foot. If the length of a run shown on the drawing scales 7 1/2", then the ACTUAL length of the run is

    A. 19'6"       B. 19'9"       C. 20'0"       D. 20'3"

12.____

13. An 18" x 24" duct is to be connected to a 24" x 24" duct by means of an eccentric transition piece (3 sides flush). If the taper is to be 1" in 4", then the length of the transition piece is

    A. 6"       B. 12"       C. 18"       D. 24"

13.____

14. Twenty-seven pairs of 3/8" diameter rods each 3'3 1/2" long are needed to support a duct.
If the available rods are ten feet long, then the MINIMUM number of rods that will be needed to make the twenty-seven sets is

    A. 9       B. 12       C. 15       D. 18

14.____

15. A rectangular sheet metal air duct with open ends is 12 feet long and 15" x 20" in cross-section. If one square foot of the sheet metal weighs 1/2 pound, then the TOTAL weight of the duct is _____ lbs.

    A. 10       B. 17 1/2       C. 35       D. 150

15.____

16. The sum of 1/12 and 1/4 is

    A. 1/3       B. 5/12       C. 7/12       D. 3/8

16.____

17. The product of 12 and 2 1/3 is

    A. 27       B. 28       C. 29       D. 30

17.____

18. If 4 1/2 is subtracted from 7 1/5, the remainder is

    A. 3 7/10       B. 2 7/10       C. 3 3/10       D. 2 3/10

18.____

19. The number of cubic yards in 47 cubic feet is MOST NEARLY

    A. 1.70       B. 1.74       C. 1.78       D. 1.82

19.____

20. A wall 8'0" high by 12'6" long has a window opening 4'0" high by 3'6" wide. The net area of the wall (allowing for the window opening) is, in square feet,

    A. 86       B. 87       C. 88       D. 89

20.____

21. A worker's hourly rate is $11.36.
    If he works 11 1/2 hours, he should receive

    A. $129.84　　　B. $130.64　　　C. $131.48　　　D. $132.24

    21.____

22. The number of cubic feet in 3 cubic yards is

    A. 81　　　B. 82　　　C. 83　　　D. 84

    22.____

23. At an annual rate of $.40 per $100, what is the fire insurance premium for one year on a house that is insured for $80,000?

    A. $120　　　B. $160　　　C. $240　　　D. $320

    23.____

24. A meter equals approximately 1.09 yards.
    How much longer, in yards, is a 100-meter dash than a 100-yard dash?

    A. 6　　　B. 8　　　C. 9　　　D. 12

    24.____

25. A train leaves New York City at 8:10 A.M. and arrives in Buffalo at 4:45 P.M. on the same day. How long, in hours and minutes, does it take the train to make the trip?
    _____ hours, _____ minutes.

    A. 6; 22　　　B. 7; 16　　　C. 7; 28　　　D. 8; 35

    25.____

---

# KEY (CORRECT ANSWERS)

| | | | |
|---|---|---|---|
| 1. | C | 11. | C |
| 2. | C | 12. | C |
| 3. | C | 13. | D |
| 4. | C | 14. | D |
| 5. | C | 15. | C |
| 6. | D | 16. | A |
| 7. | A | 17. | B |
| 8. | D | 18. | B |
| 9. | B | 19. | B |
| 10. | D | 20. | A |

| | |
|---|---|
| 21. | B |
| 22. | A |
| 23. | D |
| 24. | C |
| 25. | D |

# SOLUTIONS TO PROBLEMS

1. Let x = remaining side. Converting to inches, $x^2 = 36^2 + 48^2$ So, $x^2 = 3600$. Solving, $x = 60$ inches.

2. $.15625 = \dfrac{15,625}{100,000} = \dfrac{5}{32}$

3. $2 \div 2/3 = 3$. Then, $(3)(100) = 300$ fasteners

4. $27/32 = .84375 \approx .844$

5. $1'3" \div 10 = 15" \div 10 = 1\ 1/2"$

6. $24 \div 2\ 2/3 = 24/1.3/8 = 9$

7. Area of main duct = $(\pi)(10^2) = 100\ \pi$. One of the branches has an area of $(\pi)(6^2) = 36\ \pi$. Thus, the area of the 2nd branch = $100\ \pi - 36\ \pi = 64\ \pi$. The 2nd branch's radius must be 8" and its diameter must be 16".

8. Volume = $(1/384')(6')(3') = .046875$ cu.ft. Then, 10 sheets have a volume of .46875 cu.ft. Now, $(.46875)(480) = 225$ lbs.

9. Note that $(7\ 1/2)^2 + (10)^2 = (12\ 1/2)^2$, so that this is a right triangle. Area = $(1/2)(10")(7\ 1/2")$ = 371/2 sq.in.

10. $231 = \dfrac{h}{3}[(\pi)(3)^2 + (\pi)(4)^2 + \sqrt{(9\pi)(16\pi)}]$, where h = required height. Then,

    $231 = \dfrac{h}{3}(9\pi + 16\pi + 12\pi)$. Simplifying, $231 = 37\ \pi\ h/3$.
    Solving, h ~ 5.96" or 6"

11. $11\ 1/4 - 8\ 1/2 = 2\ 3/4$. Then, $(2\ 3/4)(5\ 1/2) = 11/4 .11/2 = 15\ 1/8$

12. $7\ 1/2\ " \div 3/8" = 15/2 .8/3 = 20$ Then, $(20)(1\ \text{ft.}) = 20$ feet

13. $24" - 18" = 6"$ Then, $(6")(4) = 24"$

14. $3'3\ 1/2" = 39.5"$. Now, $(27)(2)(39.5") = 2133"$. 10 ft. = 120".
    Finally, $2133 \div 120 = 17.775$, so 18 rods are needed.

15. Surface area = $(2)(12')(1\ 1/4') + (2)(12')(1\ 2/3') = 70$ sq.ft.
    Then, $(70)(1/2\ \text{lb.}) - 35$ lbs.

16. $1/12 + 1/4 = 4/12 = 1/3$

17.  (12)(2 1/3) = 12/1 . 7/3 = 28

18.  7 1/5 - 4 1/2 = 7 2/10 - 4 5/10 = 6 12/10 - 4 5/10 = 2 7/10

19.  47 cu.ft. = 47/27 cu.yds. = 1.74 cu.yds.

20.  (8')(12.5') - (4')(3.5') = 86 sq.ft.

21.  ($11.36)(11.5) = $130.64

22.  1 cu.yd. = 27 cu.ft., so 3 cu.yds. = 81 cu.ft.

23.  $80,000 ÷ $100 = 800. Then, (800)($.40) = $320

24.  100 meters = 109 yds. Then, 109 - 100 = 9 yds.

25.  4:45 P.M. - 8:10 AM. = 8 hrs. 35 min.

_____

# SPATIAL RELATIONS
## EXAMINATION SECTION
## TEST 1

DIRECTIONS: In each of questions 1 to 16 the front and top views of an object are given. Of the views labelled 1, 2, 3 and 4, select the one that CORRECTLY represents the right side view of each object for third angle projection.

1.

1._____

A.  1          B.  2          C.  3          D.  4

2.

2._____

A.  1          B.  2          C.  3          D.  4

3.

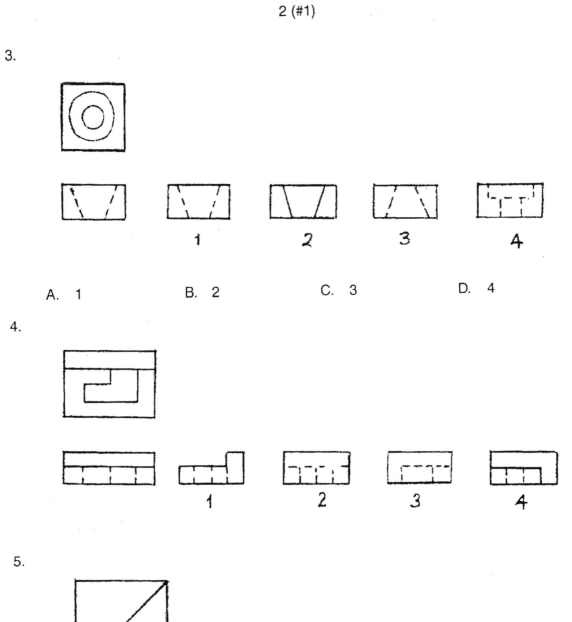

A. 1     B. 2     C. 3     D. 4

4.

5.

A. 1     B. 2     C. 3     D. 4

6.

A.  1          B.  2          C.  3          D.  4

7.

A.  1          B.  2          C.  3          D.  4

8.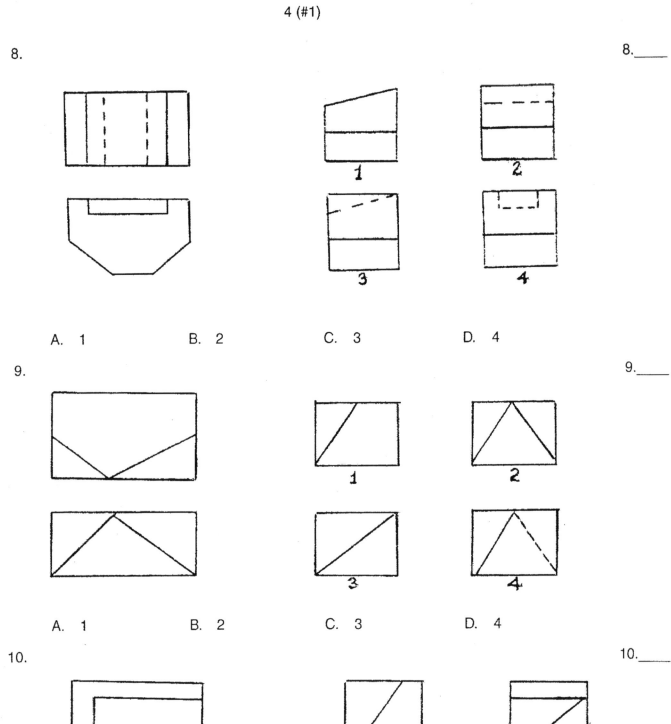

A. 1  B. 2  C. 3  D. 4

9.

A. 1  B. 2  C. 3  D. 4

10.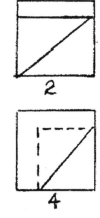

A. 1  B. 2  C. 3  D. 4

11.                                                                                                    11.____

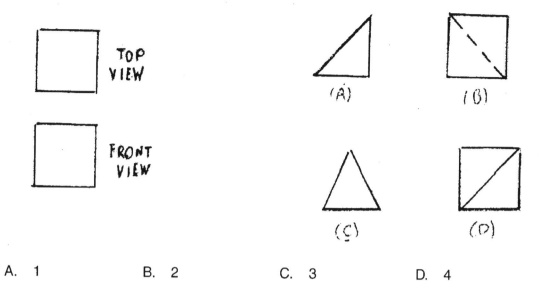

A.  1                    B.  2                    C.  3                    D.  4

Questions 12 - 16

DIRECTIONS:   In each of questions 12 to 16 inclusive, two views of an object are given. Of the
              views labelled 1, 2, 3, and 4, select the one that CORRECTLY represents the
              right side view of each object.

12.                                                                                                    12.____

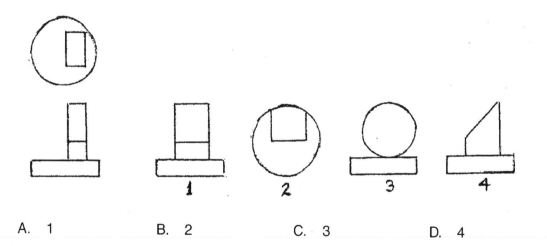

A.  1                    B.  2                    C.  3                    D.  4

13.

A.  1          B.  2          C.  3          D.  4

14.

A.  1          B.  2          C.  3          D.  4

15.

15._____

A. 1          B. 2          C. 3          D. 4

16.

16._____

A. 1          B. 2          C. 3          D. 4

17.

17._____

A. 1          B. 2          C. 3          D. 4

18.

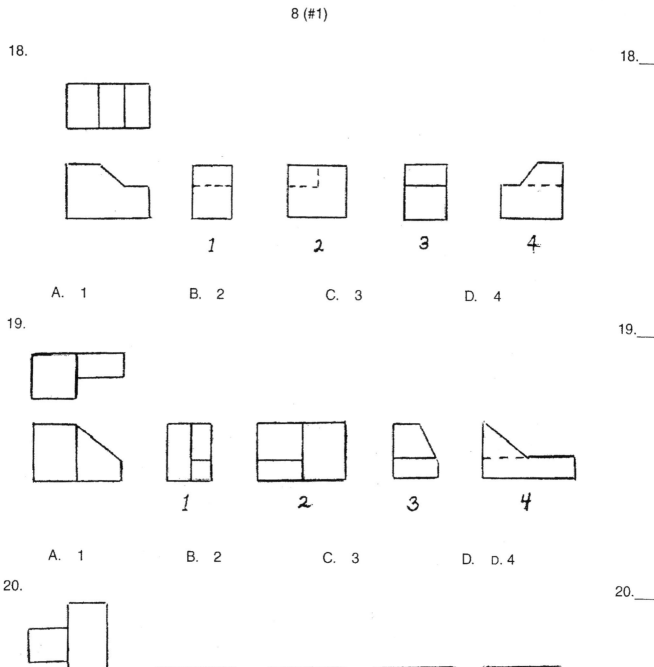

A.  1             B.  2             C.  3             D.  4

19.

A.  1             B.  2             C.  3             D.  D. 4

20.

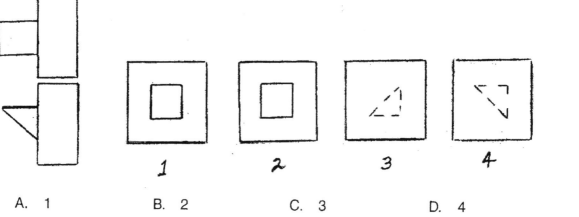

A.  1             B.  2             C.  3             D.  4

21.

A.  1      B.  2      C.  3      D.  4

22.

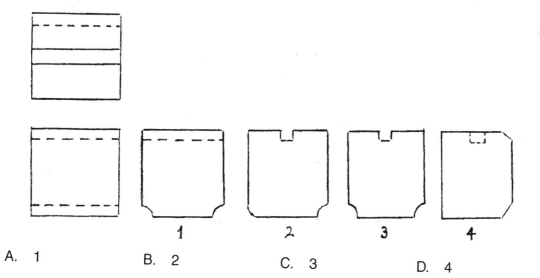

A.  1      B.  2      C.  3      D.  4

23.

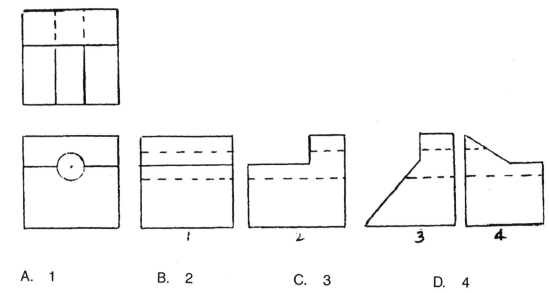

A. 1 B. 2 C. 3 D. 4

24.

A. 1 B. 2 C. 3 D. 4

25.

25.____

A. 1          B. 2          C. 3          D. 4

DIRECTIONS:    In questions 26 through 30 which follow, the plan and front elevation of an object are shown on the left, and on the right are shown four figures one of which, and only one, represents the right side elevation. Mark in the space at the right the letter which represents the right aide elevation. In the sample below, which figure correctly represents the right side elevation?

A. 1          B. 2          C. 3          D. 4

The correct answer is A

## Sample Question

26.

    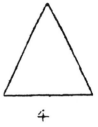

1          2          3          4

A.  1          B.  2          C.  3          D.  4

26.____

27.

1          2          3          4

A.  1          B.  2          C.  3          D.  4

27.____

28.

A. 1 B. 2 C. 3 D. 4

29.

A. 1 B. 2 C. 3 D. 4

30.

30._____

2   3   4.

A. 1        B. 2        C. 3        D. 4

# KEY (CORRECT ANSWERS)

| | | | |
|---|---|---|---|
| 1. | B | 16. | B |
| 2. | D | 17. | D |
| 3. | A | 18. | C |
| 4. | A | 19. | A |
| 5. | C | 20. | B |
| 6. | B | 21. | C |
| 7. | D | 22. | B |
| 8. | C | 23. | A |
| 9. | A | 24. | B |
| 10. | A | 25. | A |
| 11. | A | 26. | B |
| 12. | D | 27. | A |
| 13. | C | 28. | B |
| 14. | C | 29. | A |
| 15. | B | 30. | C |

# TEST 2

DIRECTIONS: Questions 1 through 10 deal with relationships between sets of figures. For each question, select that choice (A, or B, or C, or D) which has the SAME relationship to Figure 3 that Figure 2 has to Figure 1.

SAMPLE: Study Figures 1 and 2 in the SAMPLE. Notice that Figure 1 has been turned clockwise 1/4 of a turn to get Figure 2. Taking Figure 3 and turning it clockwise 1/4 of a turn, we get choice A, the correct answer.

DIRECTIONS: Questions 11 through 16 show the top view of an object in the first column, the front view of the same object in the second column and four drawings in the third column, one of which correctly represents the RIGHT side view of the object.

Select the CORRECT right side view.

As a guide, the first one is an illustrative example, the correct answer of which is C.

| TOP VIEW | FRONT VIEW | RIGHT SIDE VIEW |
|----------|------------|-----------------|

DIRECTIONS: Each question or incomplete statement is followed by several suggested answers or completions. Select the one that *BEST* answers the question or completes the statement. *PRINT THE LETTER OF THE CORRECT ANSWER IN THE SPACE AT THE RIGHT.*

Questions 17 - 20

DIRECTIONS: In each of the following groups of drawings, the top view and front elevation of an object are shown on the left. At the right are four drawings, one of which represents the end elevation of the object as seen from the right. Select the drawing which represents the correct end elevation and mark in the answer space the letter of this drawing

The first group is shown as an example only.
The correct answer in this group is C.

17.                                                                                                              17._____

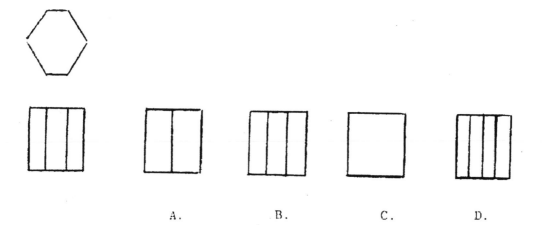

18.

A.      B.      C.      D.

19.

A.      B.      C.      D.

20.

A.       B.       C.       D.

---

# KEY (CORRECT ANSWERS)

| | | | | |
|---|---|---|---|---|
| 1. | C | | 11. | C |
| 2. | B | | 12. | A |
| 3. | D | | 13. | C |
| 4. | A | | 14. | B |
| 5. | B | | 15. | B |
| 6. | C | | 16. | C |
| 7. | A | | 17. | A |
| 8. | B | | 18. | C |
| 9. | B | | 19. | D |
| 10. | D | | 20. | A |

---

# ABSTRACT REASONING

## SPATIAL RELATIONS

### COMMENTARY

Since intelligence exists in many forms or phases and the theory of differential aptitudes is now firmly established in testing, other manifestations and measurements of intelligence than verbal or purely arithmetical must be identified and measured.

The spatial relations test, including that phase designated as spatial perception, involves and measures the ability to solve problems, drawn up in the form of outlines or pictures, which are concerned with the shapes of objects or the interrelationship of their parts. While, concededly, little is known about the nature and scope of this aptitude, it appears that this ability is required in science, mathematics, engineering, and drawing courses and curricula. Accordingly, tests of spatial perception involving the reconstruction of three-dimensional patterns, are presented in this section.

It is to be noted that the relationships expressed in spatial tests are geometric, definitive, and exact. Keeping these basic characteristics in mind, the applicant is to proceed to solve the spatial perception problems in his own way. There is no set method of solving these problems. The examinee may find that there are different methods for different types of spatial problems. Therefore, the BEST way to prepare for this type of test is to *TAKE* and study the work-practice problems in three-dimensional patterns provided in this section.

———

# EXAMINATION SECTION

## PART/1

For questions 1 through 15 you are to examine the four INTERIOR angles and rank each in terms of degrees from SMALL TO LARGE. Choose the alternative that has the correct ranking.

**EXAMPLE:** (Do not mark these on the answer sheet)

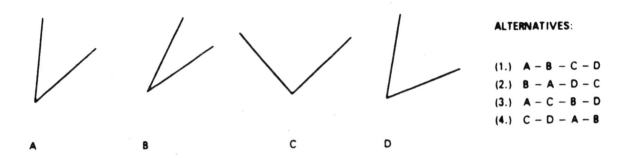

**ALTERNATIVES:**

(1.) A – B – C – D
(2.) B – A – D – C
(3.) A – C – B – D
(4.) C – D – A – B

The correct ranking of the angles from small to large is B – A – D – C; therefore, alternative (2) is correct. Now, proceed to the questions marking the correct alternative on your answer sheet.

**PROCEED TO QUESTIONS**

1.

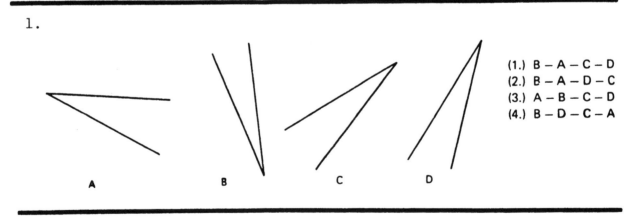

(1.) B – A – C – D
(2.) B – A – D – C
(3.) A – B – C – D
(4.) B – D – C – A

2.

(1.) B – D – A – C
(2.) D – C – B – A
(3.) A – B – C – D
(4.) C – B – A – D

3.

   A           B     C         D

(1.) C - A - D - B
(2.) A - C - D - B
(3.) A - C - B - D
(4.) C - B - A - D

4.

   A           B     C         D

(1.) D - C - B - A
(2.) B - D - A - C
(3.) B - D - C - A
(4.) D - B - C - A

5.

   A           B     C     D

(1.) C - A - D - B
(2.) A - D - C - B
(3.) C - D - B - A
(4.) C - A - B - D

6.

  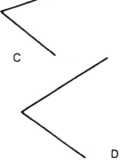

   A           B         C     D

(1.) C - A - B - D
(2.) A - C - B - D
(3.) C - A - D - B
(4.) A - C - D - B

7.

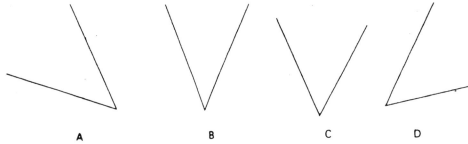

A         B         C         D

(1.) B – A – C – D
(2.) B – A – D – C
(3.) A – B – C – D
(4.) B – D – C – A

8.

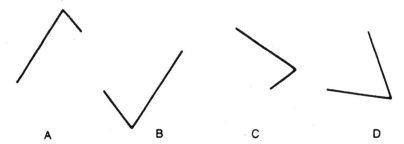

A         B         C         D

(1.) C · B · D · A
(2.) D · C · B · A
(3.) C · D · A · B
(4.) D · A · C · B

9.

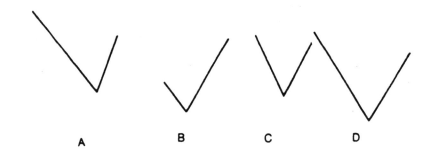

A         B         C         D

(1.) C · A · B · D
(2.) A · C · B · D
(3.) C · A · D · B
(4.) A · C · D · B

10.

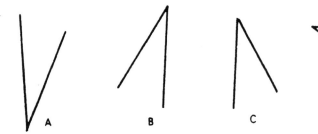

A         B         C         D

(1.) C · A · D · B
(2.) A · C · D · B
(3.) A · B · C · D
(4.) C · A · B · D

11.

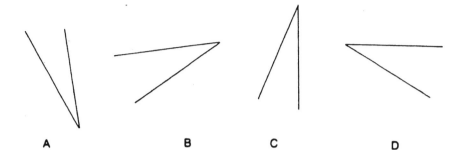

A      B      C      D

(1.)   C · A · D · B
(2.)   A · C · D · B
(3.)   A · C · B · D
(4.)   C · B · A · D

12.

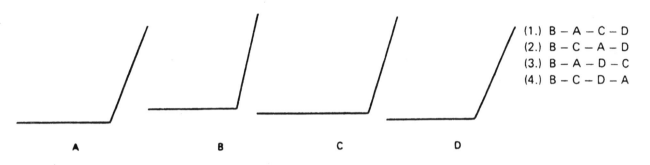

A      B      C      D

(1.)   B – A – C – D
(2.)   B – C – A – D
(3.)   B – A – D – C
(4.)   B – C – D – A

13.

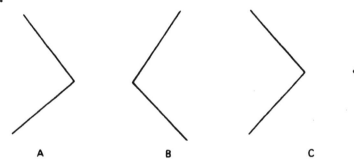

A      B      C      D

(1.)   D – A – B – C
(2.)   A – D – C – B
(3.)   D – A – C – B
(4.)   A – D – B – C

14.

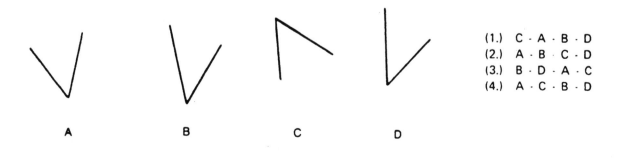

A      B      C      D

(1.)   C · A · B · D
(2.)   A · B · C · D
(3.)   B · D · A · C
(4.)   A · C · B · D

15.

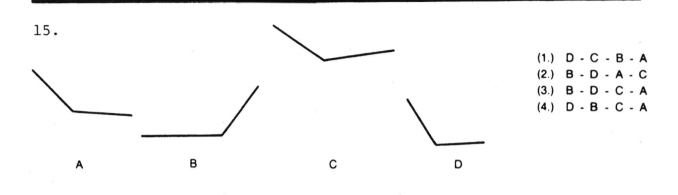

A                    B                    C                    D

(1.)  D - C - B - A
(2.)  B - D - A - C
(3.)  B - D - C - A
(4.)  D - B - C - A

**DO NOT STOP – READ DIRECTIONS FOR PART 2 AND CONTINUE**

# PART /2

For questions **16** through **30**

The pictures that follow are top, front, and end views of various solid objects. The views are without perspective. That is, the points in the viewed surface are viewed along parallel lines of vision. The projection of the object looking DOWN on it is shown in the upper left-hand corner (TOP VIEW). The projection looking at the object from the FRONT is shown in the lower left-hand corner (FRONT VIEW). The projection looking at the object from the END is shown in the lower right-hand corner.(END VIEW). These views are ALWAYS in the same positions and are labeled accordingly.

If there were a hole in the block, the views would look like this:

Note that lines that cannot be seen on the surface in some particular view are DOTTED in that view.

In the problems that follow, two views will be shown, with four alternatives to complete the set. You are to select the correct one and mark its number on the answer sheet.

**EXAMPLE**:   Choose the correct END VIEW.

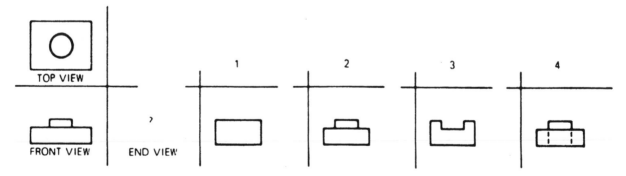

The front view shows that there is a smaller block on the base and that there is no hole. The top view shows that the block is round and in the center of the base. The answer, therefore, must be number 2.

In the problems that follow, it is not always the end view that must be selected, sometimes it is the top view or front view that is missing. Now, proceed to the questions marking the number of the correct view on your answer sheet.

**PROCEED TO QUESTIONS**

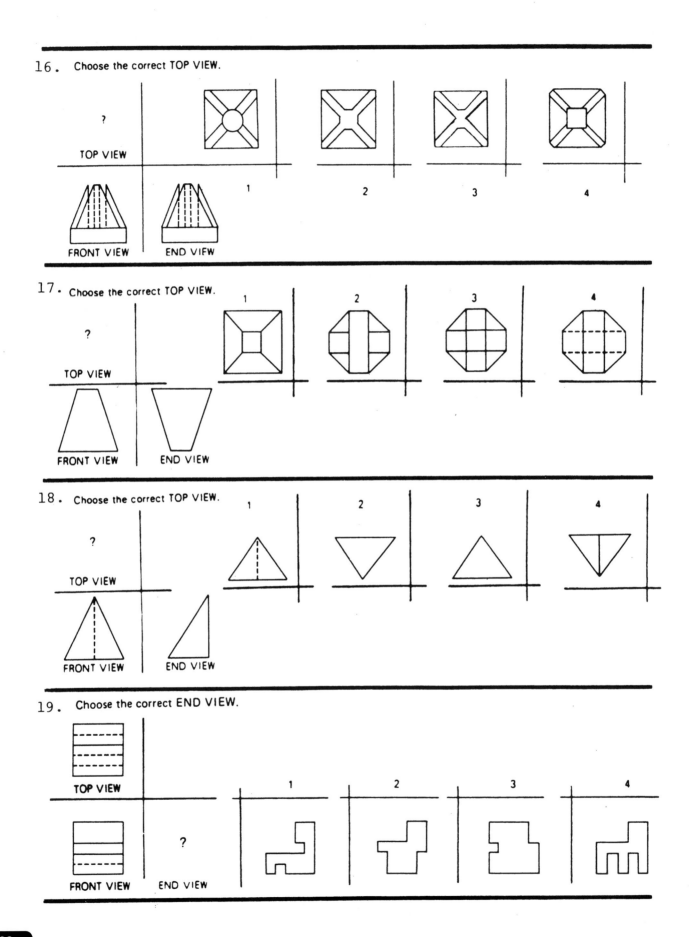

16. Choose the correct TOP VIEW.

?

TOP VIEW

FRONT VIEW    END VIEW

1    2    3    4

17. Choose the correct TOP VIEW.

1    2    3    4

?

TOP VIEW

FRONT VIEW    END VIEW

18. Choose the correct TOP VIEW.

1    2    3    4

?

TOP VIEW

FRONT VIEW    END VIEW

19. Choose the correct END VIEW.

TOP VIEW

FRONT VIEW    END VIEW

?

1    2    3    4

82

**20.** Choose the correct **FRONT VIEW**

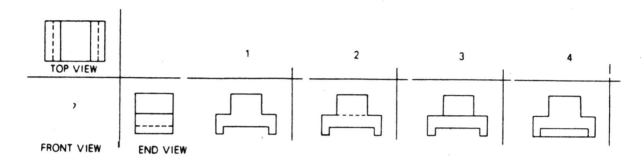

**21.** Choose the correct END VIEW.

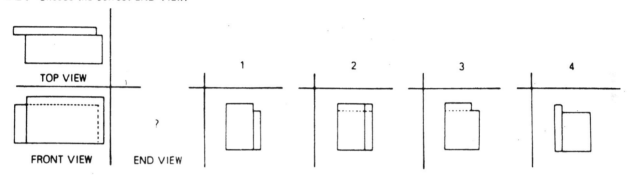

**22.** Choose the correct END VIEW.

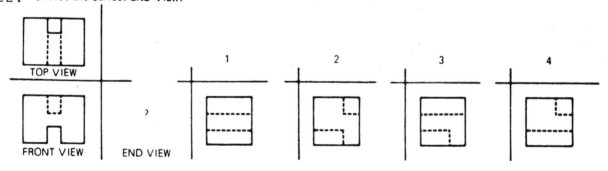

**23.** Choose the correct END VIEW.

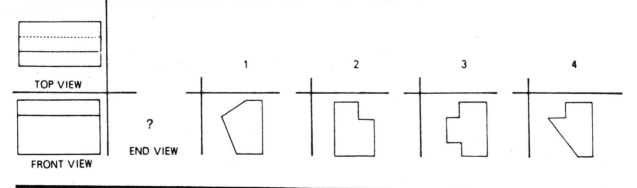

**24.** Choose the correct TOP VIEW.

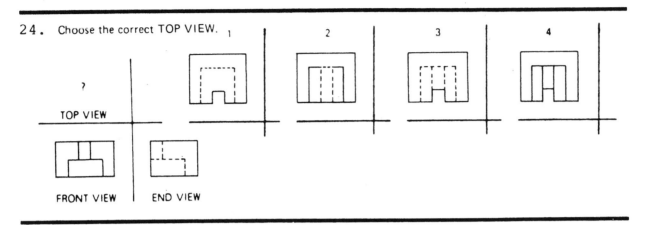

**25.** Choose the correct END VIEW.

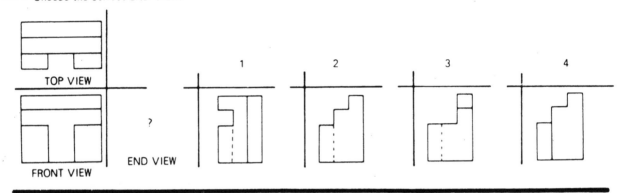

**26.** Choose the correct END VIEW.

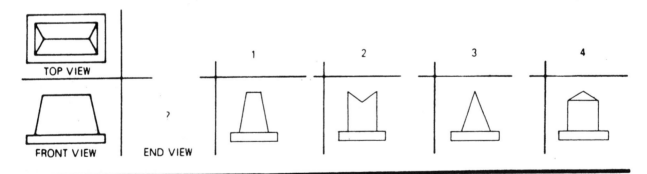

**27.** Choose the correct END VIEW.

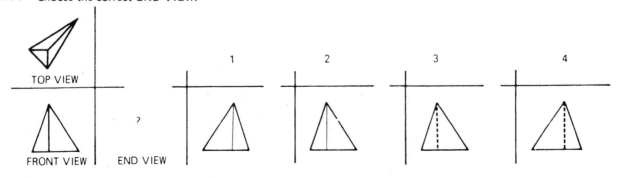

28. Choose the correct TOP VIEW.

1    2    3    4

?

TOP VIEW

FRONT VIEW    END VIEW

29. Choose the correct FRONT VIEW

TOP VIEW

1    2    3    4

?

FRONT VIEW    END VIEW

30. Choose the correct TOP VIEW.

TOP VIEW

?

1    2    3    4

FRONT VIEW    END VIEW

**DO NOT STOP — READ DIRECTIONS FOR PART 3 AND CONTINUE**

# PART/3

Each group of cubes has been made by cementing together cubes of the same size. After being cemented together, each group was PAINTED ON ALL EXPOSED SIDES EXCEPT THE BOTTOM ON WHICH IT IS RESTING.

For questions 31 through 42 you are to examine each figure closely and then determine HOW MANY CUBES have:

one of their exposed sides painted.
two of their exposed sides painted.
three of their exposed sides painted.
four of their exposed sides painted.
five of their exposed sides painted.

**Note:** There are no problems for which the answer zero (0) is a correct answer.

**Example:** (Do not mark these on the answer sheet)

PROBLEM Z                                                                                 ANSWERS:

In Figure Z how many cubes have

702. two of their exposed sides painted?
703. four of their exposed sides painted?
704. five of their exposed sides painted?

FIGURE Z

702.    1
703.    2
704.    1

Now, proceed to the questions. Mark on your answer sheet the number of cubes that have the different number of exposed sides painted. Remember, after being cemented together, each group was PAINTED ON ALL EXPOSED SIDES EXCEPT THE BOTTOM.

PROCEED TO QUESTIONS

PROBLEM A

In Figure A how many cubes have

31. two of their exposed sides painted?
32. four of their exposed sides painted?

FIGURE A

## PROBLEM B

In Figure B how many cubes have

FIGURE B

33. two of their exposed sides painted?
34. three of their exposed sides painted?

## PROBLEM C

In Figure C how many cubes have

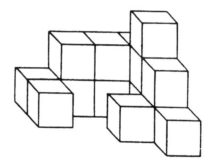

FIGURE C

35. two of their exposed sides painted?
36. three of their exposed sides painted?
37. four of their exposed sides painted?

## PROBLEM D

In Figure D how many cubes have

FIGURE D

38. two of their exposed sides painted?
39. three of their exposed sides painted?

## PROBLEM E

In Figure E how many cubes have

40. one of their exposed sides painted?
41. two of their exposed sides painted?
42. three of their exposed sides painted?

FIGURE E

---

**DO NOT STOP — READ DIRECTIONS FOR PART 4 AND CONTINUE**

# PART/4

For questions 43 through 60

This visualization test consists of a number of items similar to the sample below. A three-dimensional object is shown at the left. This is followed by outlines of five apertures or openings.

In each item the task is exactly the same. *First*, you are to imagine how the object looks from *all* directions (rather than from a single direction as shown). *Then*, pick from the five apertures outlined, the opening through which the object could pass directly if the proper side were inserted first. *Finally*, mark on your answer sheet (after the number of the item) the letter corresponding to the answer you have chosen.

Here are the rules:

1. Prior to passing through the aperture, the irregular solid object may be turned in any direction. It may be started through the aperture on a side not shown.

2. Once the object is started through the aperture, it may not be twisted or turned. It must pass completely through the opening. The opening is always the exact shape of the appropriate external outline of the object.

3. Both objects and apertures are drawn to the same scale. Thus it is possible for an opening to be the correct shape but too small for the object. In all cases, however, differences are large enough to judge by eye.

4. There are no irregularities in any hidden portion of the object. However, if the figure has symmetric indentations, the hidden portion is symmetric with the part shown.

5. For each object there is only one correct aperture.

EXAMPLE: (Do not mark these on the answer sheet)

The correct answer is 3 since the object would pass through this aperture if the side at the left were introduced first.

PROCEED TO QUESTIONS

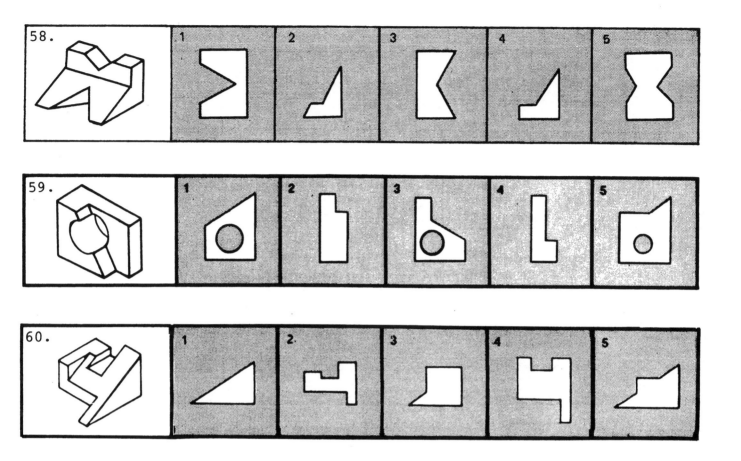

# KEY (CORRECT ANSWERS)

| | | | |
|---|---|---|---|
| 1. 4 | 16. 2 | 31. 3 | 46. 1 |
| 2. 3 | 17. 4 | 32. 4 | 47. 1 |
| 3. 3 | 18. 3 | 33. 3 | 48. 1 |
| 4. 3 | 19. 1 | 34. 8 | 49. 5 |
| 5. 1 | 20. 1 | 35. 5 | 50. 4 |
| | | | |
| 6. 3 | 21. 1 | 36. 3 | 51. 2 |
| 7. 2 | 22. 4 | 37. 5 | 52. 5 |
| 8. 2 | 23. 4 | 38. 4 | 53. 4 |
| 9. 3 | 24. 1 | 39. 5 | 54. 3 |
| 10. 3 | 25. 2 | 40. 2 | 55. 3 |
| | | | |
| 11. 3 | 26. 3 | 41. 3 | 56. 3 |
| 12. 2 | 27. 3 | 42. 6 | 57. 4 |
| 13. 3 | 28. 4 | 43. 3 | 58. 4 |
| 14. 3 | 29. 2 | 44. 1 | 59. 2 |
| 15. 4 | 30. 2 | 34. 2 | 60. 5 |

———

# ABSTRACT REASONING

## CLASSIFICATION INVENTORY SECTION
## INCOMPLETE PATTERNS (NINE FIGURES)

The tests of incomplete patterns that follow consist of items which involve the visualization of nine figures arranged in sequence.

An incomplete pattern only is given. The candidate is to select from the five-lettered choices the correct figure for the last or ninth space.

DIRECTIONS:   Each item in this test consists of an incomplete pattern. The complete pattern would be made up of nine figures arranged in sequence. The candidate is to determine the correct figure for the last or ninth space from the five-lettered choices given.

### SAMPLE QUESTIONS AND EXPLANATIONS

QUESTIONS

EXPLANATIONS: In question 1 notice how the figures change as they go across each row of the pattern. They become darker. As they go down, the figures become larger. Therefore, the CORRECT figure for space IX is large and dark. Answer choice D is the CORRECT answer.

In question 2 the figures acquire more dots as they go across the top row. As they go down, the point of the figure is rotated a quarter of a turn to the right. Therefore, the CORRECT figure for space IX has three dots and its point is directed toward the bottom of the page. Answer choice C is the CORRECT answer.

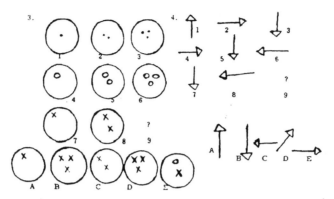

3. The correct answer is D. Each of the rows of circles has, exclusively, a number of ., o, or x's in ascending order. (Note that B is incorrect since the circle is larger than the given circles. )

4. The correct answer is A. Note that in row 1, two of the arrows (1, 2) are turned to the right, and one (3) is turned to the left. In row two, one of the arrows (4) is turned to the right, and two (5,6) are turned to the left. In row three, two arrows are turned to the left (7, 8). Therefore, one arrow (9) must be turned to the right in a similar way (answer A).

# TESTS IN INCOMPLETE PATTERNS

## TEST 1

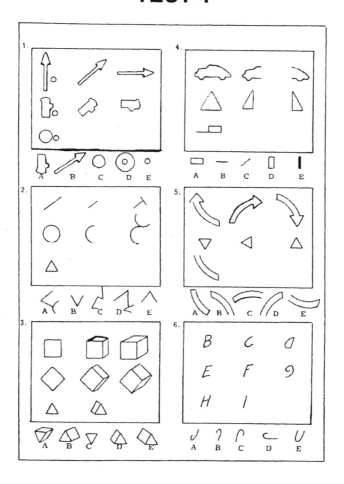

---

# KEY (CORRECT ANSWERS)

1. C
2. C
3. E
4. A
5. B
6. C

---

# TEST 2

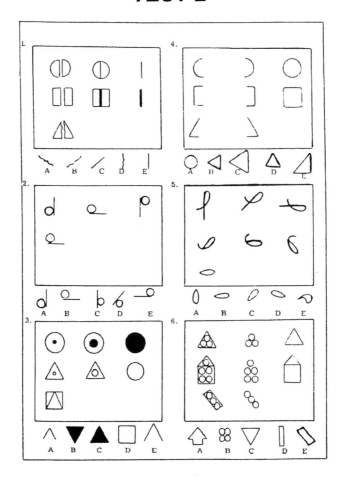

---

# KEY (CORRECT ANSWERS)

1. D
2. A
3. E
4. C
5. A
6. E

---

# TEST 3

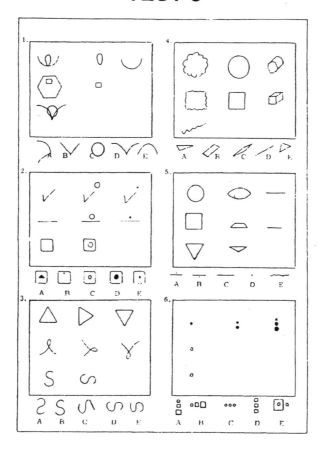

---

# KEY (CORRECT ANSWERS)

1. D
2. E
3. B
4. C
5. C
6. A

---

6

# TEST 4

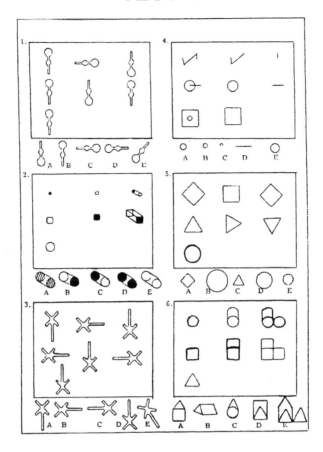

---

# KEY (CORRECT ANSWERS)

1. A
2. B
3. A
4. B
5. D
6. E

---

# TEST 5

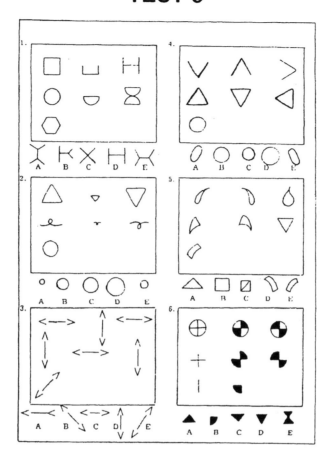

---

# KEY (CORRECT ANSWERS)

1. E
2. C
3. E
4. B
5. B
6. B

---

# PATTERN ANALYSIS (RIGHT SIDE ELEVATION)

## SAMPLE QUESTION

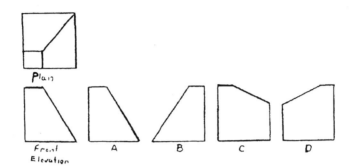

5.  In the sample shown above, which figure *CORRECTLY* represents the right side elevation?     5.____

    1.   A              2.   B              3.   C              4.   D

The *CORRECT* answer is 1.

# TEST 1

Questions 1-5.

DIRECTIONS:   In questions 1 through 5 which follow, the plan and front elevation of an object are shown on the left, and on the right are shown four figures one of which, and ONLY one, represents the right side elevation. Mark on your answer sheet the number which represents the right side elevation.

    1.  1. A              2.   B              3. C              4.   D

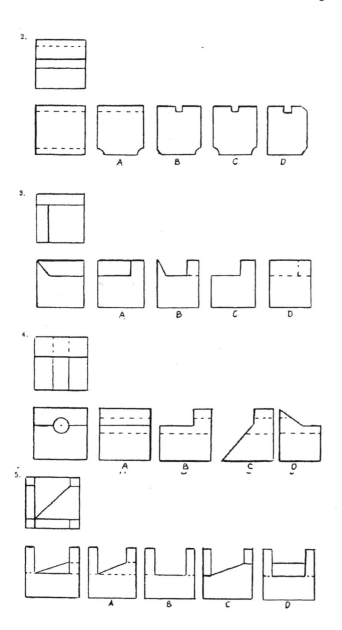

---

## KEY (CORRECT ANSWERS)

1.  4
2.  3
3.  3
4.  2
5.  2

---

# PATTERN ANALYSIS (END ELEVATION)

Questions 1-5.

DIRECTIONS:  In each of the following groups of drawings the top view and front elevation of
an object are shown at the left. At the right are four drawings, one of which
represents the end elevation of the object as seen from the right. Select the
drawing which represents the CORRECT end elevation. The first group is
shown as a sample ONLY. Which drawing represents the CORRECT end elevation? 1. A 2.B 3. C 4. D The CORRECT answer is 3.

**SAMPLE QUESTION**

Top View

Front View    A    B    C    D

## TEST 1

1.

A    B    C    D

2.

A    B    C    D

3.

4.

5.

---

# KEY (CORRECT ANSWERS)

1. 4
2. 3
3. 2
4. 1
5. 1

---

# PATTERN ANALYSIS (RIGHT SIDE VIEW)

# TEST 1

Questions 1-5.

DIRECTIONS: In each of questions 1 to 5 inclusive, two views of an object are given. Of the views labelled A, B, C, and D, select the one that *CORRECTLY* represents the right side view of each object.

Which view represents the right side view? 1. A  2. B  3. C  4. D

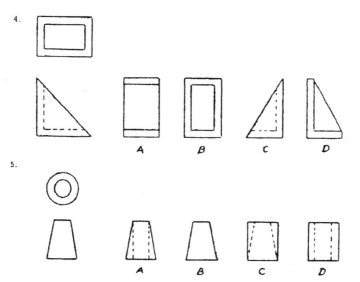

4.

A    B    C    D

5.

A    B    C    D

---

## KEY (CORRECT ANSWERS

1.  4
2.  3
3.  3
4.  2
5.  2

---

# SURVEY OF OTHER TYPES OF
# PATTERN ANALYSIS QUESTIONS

## SOLID FIGURE TURNING

Questions 1-3.

The following questions represent figures made up of cubes or other forms glued together. Select the ONE of the four figures lettered A, B, C, D, which is the figure at the left turned in a different position and mark the correct space on the answer sheet. (Note: You are permitted to turn over the figures, to turn them around, and to turn them both over and around.)

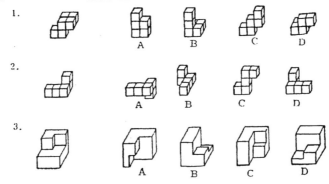

## TOUCHING CUBES

Questions 4-7.
Questions 4 and 5 are based on the group of touching cubes at the left, and questions 6 and 7 on the group at the right.

All the cubes are exactly the same size, and there are only enough hidden cubes to support the ones you can see. The question number is on a cube in the group. You are to find how many cubes in that group touch the numbered cube. Note: A cube is considered to touch the numbered cube if ANY part, EVEN A CORNER, touches. Mark the answer sheet to show how many cubes touch the numbered cube by blackening space

A. if the answer is 1 or 6 or 11 cubes
B. if the answer is 2 or 7 or 12 cubes
C. if the answer is 3 or 8 or 13 cubes
D. if the answer is 4 or 9 or 14 cubes
E. if the answer is 5 or 10 or 15 cubes

# CUBE TURNING

Questions 8-9

In each of the following questions, the drawing at the left represents a cube. There is a different design on each of the six faces of the cube. At the right are four other drawings of cubes lettered A, B, C, and D.

Select the ONE of the four which is actually the cube on the left turned to a different position and blacken the appropriate space on the answer sheet. (Note: The cube at the left may have been turned <u>over</u>, it may have been turned <u>around</u>, or it may have been turned <u>both</u> over and around, and faces not seen in the drawing on the left may have become visible.)

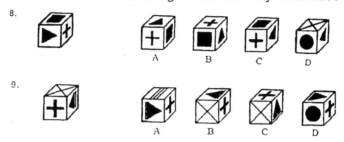

## CUBE COUNTING

Questions 10-15.

In each of the following questions, count the number of boxes or cubes represented in the drawing and blacken the appropriate space on the answer sheet.

_____

# KEY (CORRECT ANSWERS)

| | | |
|---|---|---|
| 1. D | 6. B(7) | 11. A |
| 2. B | 7. E(10) | 12. B |
| 3. D | 8. B | 13. D |
| 4. C(3) | 9. A | 14. A |
| 5. A(6) | 10. C | 15. A |

_____

# MECHANICAL APTITUDE

## EXAMINATION SECTION
## TEST 1

## MECHANICAL COMPREHENSION

DIRECTIONS:  Questions 1 to 4 test your ability to understand general mechanical devices. Pictures are shown and questions asked about the mechanical devices shown in the picture. Read each question and study the picture. Each question is followed by four choices. For each question, choose the one BEST answer (A, B, C, or D). Then *PRINT THE LETTER OF THE CORRECT ANSWER IN THE SPACE AT THE RIGHT.*

1.  The reason for crossing the belt connecting these wheels is to

1.____

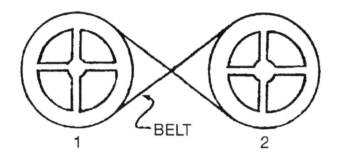

A.  make the wheels turn in opposite directions
B.  make wheel 2 turn faster than wheel 1
C.  save wear on the belt
D.  take up slack in the belt

2.  The purpose of the small gear between the two large gears is to

2.____

A.  increase the speed of the larger gears
B.  allow the larger gears to turn in different directions
C.  decrease the speed of the larger gears
D.  make the larger gears turn in the same direction

3.  Each of these three-foot-high water cans have a bottom with an area of-one square foot.    3._____
    The pressure on the bottom of the cans is

A        B        C

A.  least in A          B.  least in B
C.  least in C          D.  the same in all

4.  The reading on the scale should be                                    4._____

6 lb
rod

10 lbs.          10 lbs

A.  zero
B.  10 pounds
C.  13 pounds
D.  26 pounds

_____

# KEY (CORRECT ANSWERS)

1. A
2. D
3. D
4. D

_____

# TEST 2

DIRECTIONS: Questions 1 to 6 test knowledge of tools and how to use them. For each question, decide which one of the four things shown in the boxes labeled A, B, C, or D normally is used with or goes best with the thing in the picture on the left. Then *PRINT THE LETTER OF THE CORRECT ANSWER IN THE SPACE AT THE RIGHT.*

NOTE: All tools are NOT drawn to the same scale.

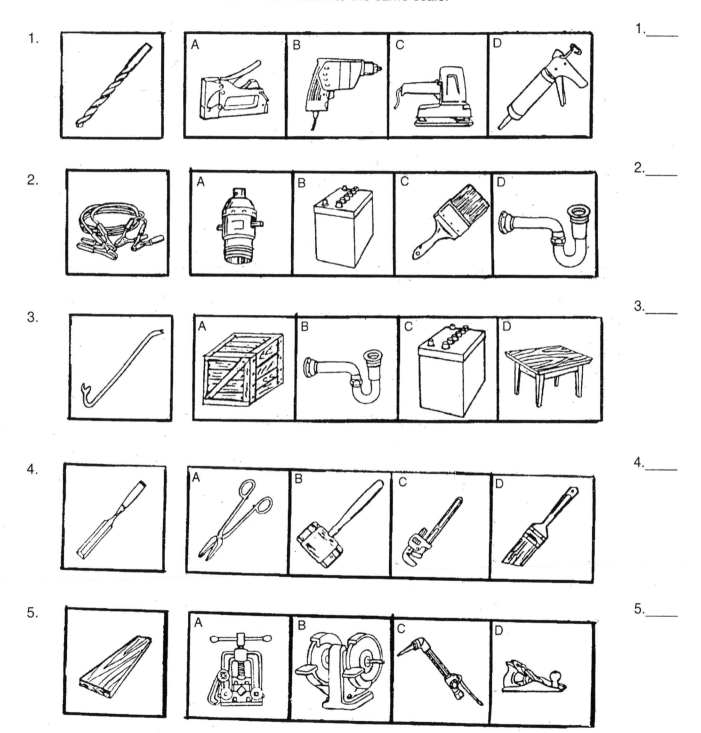

1.

2.

3.

4.

5.

1.____

2.____

3.____

4.____

5.____

6.

6._____

---

# KEY (CORRECT ANSWERS)

| | | | | |
|---|---|---|---|---|
| 1. | B | | 4. | B |
| 2. | B | | 5. | D |
| 3. | A | | 6. | B |

---

# EXAMINATION SECTION
## TEST 1

DIRECTIONS: Each question or incomplete statement is followed by several suggested answers or completions. Select the one that BEST answers the question or completes the statement. *PRINT THE LETTER OF THE CORRECT ANSWER IN THE SPACE AT THE RIGHT.*

1. A bit is held in a hand drill by means of a(n)　　　　　　　　　　　　　1.＿＿＿

    A. arbor　　　　　　B. chuck　　　　　　C. collet　　　　　　D. clamp

2. The type of screw that MOST often requires a countersunk hole is a ＿＿＿＿ head.　　2.＿＿＿

    A. flat　　　　　　B. round　　　　　　C. fillister　　　　　　D. hexagon

3. Instead of using the ordinary 1 piece screwdriver, a screwdriver bit is MOST often used with a brace because of the　　3.＿＿＿

    A. increased length of the brace　　　　B. different types of bits available
    C. increased leverage of the brace　　　　D. ability to work in tight corners

4. A thread gage is usually used to measure the　　　　　　　　　　　4.＿＿＿

    A. thickness of a thread　　　　B. diameter of a thread
    C. number of threads per inch　　D. height of a thread

5. The wheel of a glass cutter is BEST lubricated with　　　　　　　　5.＿＿＿

    A. kerosene　　　　　　B. linseed oil
    C. varnolene　　　　　　D. diesel oil

6. A nail set is a　　　　　　　　　　　　　　　　　　　　6.＿＿＿

    A. group of nails of the same size and type
    B. group of nails of different sizes but the same type
    C. tool used to extract nails
    D. tool used to drive nails below the surface of wood

7. To test for leaks in a gas line, it is BEST to use　　　　　　　　7.＿＿＿

    A. a match　　　　　　B. soapy water
    C. a colored dye　　　　D. ammonia

8. Routing is the process of cutting a　　　　　　　　　　　　8.＿＿＿

    A. strip out of sheet metal　　　　B. groove in wood
    C. chamfer on a shaft　　　　　　D. core out of concrete

9. A hacksaw frame has a wing nut mainly to　　　　　　　　　　9.＿＿＿

    A. make it easier to replace blades
    B. increase the strength of the frame
    C. prevent vibration of the blade
    D. adjust the length of the frame

10. A mitre box is usually used with a _____ saw.　　　　　　　　　　10._____

    A. hack　　　　　B. crosscut　　　　C. rip　　　　　　D. back

11. A continuous flexible saw blade is MOST often used on a _____ saw.　　11._____

    A. radial　　　　B. band　　　　　C. swing　　　　　D. table

12. A pipe reamer is used to　　　　　　　　　　　　　　　　　　　　　12._____

    A. clean out a length of pipe
    B. thread pipe
    C. remove burrs from the ends of pipe
    D. seal pipe joints

13. To lay out a straight cut on a piece of wood at the same angle as the cut on a second　　13._____
piece of wood, the PROPER tool to use is a

    A. bevel　　　　B. cope　　　　　C. butt gauge　　D. clevis

14. Before drilling a hole in a piece of metal, an indentation should be made with a _____　　14._____
punch.

    A. pin　　　　　B. taper　　　　　C. center　　　　D. drift

15. Curved cuts in wood are BEST made with a _____ saw.　　　　　　　15._____

    A. jig　　　　　B. veneer　　　　C. radial　　　　D. swing

16. A face plate is generally used to　　　　　　　　　　　　　　　　　16._____

    A. hold material while working with it on a lathe
    B. smooth out irregularities in a metal plate
    C. protect the finish on a metal plate
    D. locate centers of holes to be drilled on a drill press

17. A die would be used to　　　　　　　　　　　　　　　　　　　　　17._____

    A. gage the groove in a splined shaft
    B. cut a thread on a metal rod
    C. hold a piece to be machined on a milling machine
    D. control the depth of a hole to be drilled in a piece of metal

18. Before using a ladle to scoop up molten solder, you should make sure that the ladle is　　18._____
dry.
This is done to prevent

    A. the solder from sticking to the ladle
    B. impurities from getting into the solder
    C. injuries due to splashing solder
    D. cooling of the solder

19. To PROPERLY adjust the gap on a spark plug, you should use a(n)    19.____

    A. inside caliper               B. center gauge
    C. wire type feeler gauge     D. micrometer

20. The length of the MOST common type of folding wood rule is _____ feet.    20.____

    A. 4          B. 5          C. 6          D. 7

21. A four-foot mason's level is usually used to determine whether the top of a wall is level    21.____
and whether it is

    A. square       B. plumb       C. rigid       D. in line

22. To match a tongue in a board, the matching board MUST have a    22.____

    A. rabbet       B. chamfer       C. bead       D. groove

23. When driving screws in close quarters, the BEST type of screwdriver to use is a(n)    23.____

    A. Phillips       B. offset       C. butt       D. angled

24. The term 12-24 refers to a _____ screw.    24.____

    A. wood               B. lag
    C. sheet metal       D. machine

25. To measure the length of a curved line on a drawing or plan, the PROPER tool to use in    25.____
addition to a ruler is(are)

    A. dividers            B. calipers
    C. surface gage      D. radius gage

26. For the standard machine screw, the diameter of a tap drill is generally    26.____

    A. *equal* to the diameter of the shaft of the screw at the base of the threads (the root diameter)
    B. *larger* than the root diameter, but smaller than the diameter of the screw
    C. *equal* to the diameter of the screw
    D. *larger* than the diameter of the screw

27. In order to drill a 1" hole accurately with a drill press, you should    27.____

    A. drill at high speeds
    B. use very little pressure on the drill
    C. drill partway down, release pressure on the drill, and then continue drilling
    D. drill a pilot hole first

28. Before taking apart an electric motor to repair, punch marks are sometimes placed on    28.____
the casing near each other.
The MOST probable reason for doing this is to

    A. make sure the parts lock together on reassembly
    B. properly line up the parts that are next to each other
    C. keep track of the number of parts in the assembly
    D. identify all the parts as coming from the one motor

29. To locate a point on a floor directly under a point on the ceiling, the PROPER tool to use    29._____
    is a

    A.  square                               B.  line level
    C.  height gage                     D.  plumb bob

Question 30.

DIRECTIONS:   Question 30 is based on the diagram appearing below.

P

200 lb

30. In the above diagram, the full P required to lift the weight a distance of four feet is MOST    30._____
    NEARLY _____ lbs.

    A.  50              B.  67             C.  75             D.  100

31. The EASIEST tool to use to determine whether the edge of a board is at right angles to    31._____
    the face of the board is a

    A.  rafter square                     B.  try square
    C.  protractor                       D.  marking gage

32. *Whetting* refers to    32._____

    A.  tempering of tools by dipping them in water
    B.  annealing of tools by heating and slow cooling
    C.  brazing of carbide tips on tools
    D.  sharpening of tools

33. The MOST difficult part of a plank to plane is the    33._____

    A.  face           B.  side           C.  end           D.  back

34. To prevent wood from splitting when drilling with an auger, it is BEST to    34._____

    A.  use even pressure on the bit
    B.  drill at a slow speed
    C.  hold the wood tightly in a vise
    D.  back up the wood with a piece of scrap wood

35. The term *dressing a grinding wheel* refers to  35.____

    A. setting up the wheel on the arbor
    B. restoring the sharpness of a wheel face that has become clogged
    C. placing flanges against the sides of the wheel
    D. bringing the wheel up to speed before using it

36. Heads of rivets are BEST cut off with a  36.____

    A. hacksaw                     B. cold chisel
    C. fly cutter                 D. reamer

37. A *V-block* is especially useful to  37.____

    A. prevent damage to work held in a vise
    B. hold round stock while a hole is being drilled into it
    C. prevent rolling of round stock stored on the ground
    D. shim up the end of a machine so that it is level

38. A full set of taps for a given size usually consists of a _____ tap.  38.____

    A. taper and bottoming
    B. taper and plug
    C. plug and bottoming
    D. taper, plug, and bottoming

39. Round thread cutting dies are usually held in stock by means of  39.____

    A. wing nuts      B. clamps      C. set screws      D. bolts

40. The one of the following diagrams that shows the plan view and the elevation of a counterbored hole is  40.____

A.

B.

C.

D.

41. With regard to pipe, *I.D.* usually means  41.____

    A. inside diameter          B. inside dressed
    C. invert diameter          D. installation date

42. A compression fitting is MOST often used to

    A.  lubricate a wheel
    B.  join two pieces of tubing
    C.  reduce the diameter of a hole
    D.  press fit a gear to a shaft

42.____

43. The shape of a mill file is basically

    A.  flat        B.  half round        C.  triangular        D.  square

43.____

44. Of the following, the ratio of tin to lead that will produce the solder with the LOWEST melting point is

    A.  30-70        B.  40-60        C.  50-50        D.  60-40

44.____

45. A safe edge on a file is one that

    A.  is smooth and can not cut
    B.  has a finer cut than the face of the file
    C.  is rounded to prevent scratches
    D.  has a coarser cut than the face of the file

45.____

46. The MOST frequent use of a file card is to _____ files.

    A.  sort out                B.  clean
    C.  prevent damage to      D.  prevent clogging of

46.____

47. The BEST way of determining whether a grinding wheel has an internal crack is to

    A.  run the wheel at high speed, stop it, and examine the wheel
    B.  spray lubricating oil on the sides of the wheel and check the amount of absorption of the oil
    C.  hit the wheel with a rubber hammer and listen to the sound
    D.  drop the wheel sharply on a table and then check the wheel

47.____

48. If a grinding wheel has worn to a smaller diameter, the BEST practice to follow is to

    A.  discard the wheel
    B.  continue using the wheel as before
    C.  use the wheel, but at a faster speed
    D.  use the wheel, but at a slower speed

48.____

49. With respect to the ordinary awl,

    A.  only the tip is hardened
    B.  the entire blade is hardened
    C.  the tip is tempered, and the rest of the blade is hardened
    D.  the entire blade is tempered

49.____

50. To prevent overheating of drills, it is BEST to use _____ oil.

    A.  cutting                B.  lubricating
    C.  penetrating          D.  heating

50.____

# KEY (CORRECT ANSWERS)

| | | | | | | | | | |
|---|---|---|---|---|---|---|---|---|---|
| 1. | B | 11. | B | 21. | B | 31. | B | 41. | A |
| 2. | A | 12. | C | 22. | D | 32. | D | 42. | B |
| 3. | C | 13. | A | 23. | B | 33. | C | 43. | A |
| 4. | C | 14. | C | 24. | D | 34. | D | 44. | D |
| 5. | A | 15. | A | 25. | A | 35. | B | 45. | A |
| 6. | D | 16. | A | 26. | B | 36. | B | 46. | B |
| 7. | B | 17. | B | 27. | D | 37. | B | 47. | C |
| 8. | B | 18. | C | 28. | B | 38. | D | 48. | C |
| 9. | A | 19. | C | 29. | D | 39. | C | 49. | A |
| 10. | D | 20. | C | 30. | D | 40. | A | 50. | A |

# TEST 2

DIRECTIONS:   Each question or incomplete statement is followed by several suggested answers or completions. Select the one that BEST answers the question or completes the statement. *PRINT THE LETTER OF THE CORRECT ANSWER IN THE SPACE AT THE RIGHT.*

1.  Crocus cloth is commonly used to

    A.  protect finely machined surfaces from damage while the machines are being repaired
    B.  remove rust from steel
    C.  protect floors and furniture while painting walls
    D.  wipe up oil and grease that has spilled

1.____

2.  Before using a new paint brush, the FIRST operation should be to

    A.  remove loose bristles
    B.  soak the brush in linseed oil
    C.  hang the brush up overnight
    D.  clean the brush with turpentine

2.____

3.  When sharpening a hand saw, the FIRST operation is to

    A.  file the teeth down to the same height
    B.  shape the teeth to the proper profile
    C.  bend the teeth over to provide clearance when sawing
    D.  clean the gullies with a file

3.____

4.  To prevent solder from dripping when soldering a vertical seam, it is BEST to

    A.  hold a waxed rag under the soldering iron
    B.  use the soldering iron in a horizontal position
    C.  tin the soldering iron on one side only
    D.  solder the seam in the order from bottom to top

4.____

5.  If a round nut has two holes in the face, the PROPER type wrench to use to tighten this nut is a(n)

    A.  Stillson       B.  monkey       C.  spanner       D.  open end

5.____

6.  A box wrench is BEST used on

    A.  pipe fittings              B.  flare nuts
    C.  hexagonal nuts         D.  Allen screws

6.____

7.  To prevent damage to fine finishes on metal work that is to be held in a vise, you should

    A.  clamp the work lightly
    B.  use brass inserts on the vise
    C.  wrap the work with cloth before inserting it in the vise
    D.  substitute a smooth face plate for the serrated plate on the vise

7.____

8. The MOST frequent use for a turnbuckle is to      8.____

    A. tighten a guy wire
    B. adjust shims on a machine
    C. bolt a bracket to a wall
    D. support electric cable from a ceiling

9. To form the head of a tinner's rivet, the PROPER tool to use is a rivet      9.____

    A. anvil      B. plate      C. set      D. brake

10. A socket speed handle MOST closely resembles a      10.____

    A. screwdriver      B. brace      C. spanner      D. spin grip

11. Tips of masonry drills are usually made of      11.____

    A. steel      B. carbide      C. corundum      D. monel

12. The BEST flux to use for soldering galvanized iron is      12.____

    A. resin                  B. sal ammoniac
    C. borax                D. muriatic acid

13. The one of the following that is NOT a common type of oilstone is      13.____

    A. silicon carbide        B. aluminum oxide
    C. hard Arkansas       D. pumice

14. A method of joining metals using temperatures intermediate between soldering and welding is      14.____

    A. corbelling      B. brazing      C. annealing      D. lapping

15. When an unusually high degree of accuracy is required with woodwork, lines should be marked with a      15.____

    A. pencil ground to a chisel point
    B. pencil line over a crayon line
    C. sharp knife point
    D. scriber

16. The MOST important difference between pipe threads and V threads on bolts is that pipe threads are usually      16.____

    A. longer               B. sharper
    C. tapered           D. more evenly spaced

17. A street elbow differs from the ordinary elbow in that the street elbow has      17.____

    A. different diameter threads at each end
    B. male threads at one end and female threads at the other
    C. female threads at both ends
    D. male threads at both ends

18. Water hammer in a pipe line can MOST often be stopped by the installation of a(n)      18.____

    A. pressure reducing valve       B. expansion joint
    C. flexible coupling            D. air chamber

19. If water is leaking from the top part of a bibcock, the part that should be replaced is MOST likely the      19.____

     A. bibb washer             B. packing
     C. seat                     D. bibb screw

20. When joining electric wires together in a fixture box, the BEST thing to use are wire      20.____

     A. connectors      B. couplings      C. clamps      D. bolts

21. If the name plate of a motor indicates that it is a split phase motor, it is LIKELY that this motor      21.____

     A. is a universal motor
     B. operates on DC only
     C. operates on AC only
     D. operates either on DC at full power or on AC at reduced power

22. To make driving of a screw into hard wood easier, it is BEST to lubricate the threads of the screw with      22.____

     A. varnoline             B. penetrating oil
     C. beeswax            D. cutting oil

23. Assume that a thermostatically controlled oil heater fails to operate.
To determine whether it is the thermostat that is at fault, you should      23.____

     A. check the circuit breaker
     B. connect a wire across the terminals of the thermostat
     C. replace the contacts on the thermostat
     D. put an ammeter on the line

24. The function of the carburetor on a gasoline engine is to      24.____

     A. mix the air and gasoline properly
     B. filter the fuel
     C. filter the air to engine
     D. pump the gasoline into the cylinder

25. If a car owner complains that the battery in his car is constantly running dry, the item that should be checked FIRST is the      25.____

     A. fan belt              B. generator
     C. voltage regulator     D. relay

26. On MOST modern automobiles, foot brake pressure is transmitted to the brake drums by      26.____

     A. air pressure         B. mechanical linkage
     C. hydraulic fluid       D. electro-magnetic force

27. Assume that the engine of a car remains cold even though it is run for a period of time. The part that is MOST likely at fault is the      27.____

     A. heat by-pass valve     B. thermostat
     C. heater control        D. choke

28. To permit easy stripping of concrete forms, they should be    28.____

    A. dried      B. oiled      C. wet down      D. cleaned

29. To prevent honey combing in concrete, the concrete should be    29.____

    A. vibrated                    B. cured
    C. heated in cold weather      D. protected from the rain

30. The MAIN reason for using wire mesh in connection with concrete work is to    30.____

    A. strain the impurities from the sand
    B. increase the strength of the concrete
    C. hold the forms together
    D. protect the concrete till it hardens

31. Segregation of concrete is MOST often caused by pouring concrete    31.____

    A. in cold weather
    B. from too great a height
    C. too rapidly
    D. into a form in which the concrete has already begun to harden

32. Headers in carpentry are MOST closely associated with    32.____

    A. trimmers             B. cantilevers
    C. posts                 D. newels

33. Joists are very often supported by    33.____

    A. suspenders         B. base plates
    C. anchor bolts       D. bridal irons

34. At outside corners, the type of joint MOST frequently used on a baseboard is the    34.____

    A. plowed                B. mitered
    C. mortise and tenon    D. butt

35. The vehicle used with latex paints is usually    35.____

    A. linseed oil         B. shellac
    C. varnish            D. water

36. *Boxing* of paint refers to the _____ of paints.    36.____

    A. mixing      B. storage      C. use      D. canning

37. When painting wood, nail holes should be puttied    37.____

    A. *before* applying the prime coat
    B. *after* applying the prime coat but before the second coat
    C. *after* applying the second coat but before the third coat
    D. *after* applying the third coat

38. In laying up a brick wall, you find that at the end of the wall there is not enough space for    38.____
a full brick.
You should use a

    A. stretcher      B. bat      C. corbel      D. bull nose

39. Pointing a brick wall is the same as

    A. truing up the wall
    B. topping the wall with a waterproof surface
    C. repairing the mortar joints in the wall
    D. providing a foundation for the wall

40. The pigment MOST often used in a prime coat of paint on steel to prevent rusting is

    A. lampblack          B. calcimine
    C. zinc oxide         D. red lead

41. If you find a co-worker lying unconscious across an electric wire, the FIRST thing you should do is

    A. get him off the wire      B. call the foreman
    C. get a doctor              D. shut off the power

42.

The area of the metal plate shown above, minus the hole area, is MOST NEARLY _____ square inches.

A. 8.5          B. 8.9          C. 9.4          D. 10.1

43.

The percentage of the above tank that is filled with water is MOST NEARLY

A. 33          B. 35          C. 37          D. 39

44.

44.____

The top and front view of an object are shown above. The right side view will MOST likely look like

A.

B.

C.

D.

45.

45.____

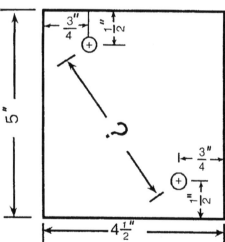

The distance between centers of the holes in the above diagram is MOST NEARLY

A.  $4\frac{1}{2}$"

B.  4 3/4"

C.  5"

D.  $5\frac{1}{4}$"

Questions 46-48.

DIRECTIONS:   Questions 46 through 48, inclusive, are to be answered in accordance with the paragraph below.

*A steam heating system with steam having a pressure of less than 10 pounds is called a low-pressure system. The majority of steam-heating systems are of this type. The steam may be provided by low-pressure boilers installed* <u>expressly</u> *for the purpose, or it may be gener-*

*ated in boilers at a higher pressure and reduced in pressure before admitted to the heating mains. In other instances, it may be possible to use exhaust steam which has been made to run engines and other machines and which still contains enough heat to be utilized in the heating system. The first case represents the system of heating used in the ordinary residence or other small building; the other two represent the systems of heating employed in industrial buildings where a power plant is installed for general power purposes.*

46.  According to the above paragraph, whether or not a steam heating system is considered    46.____
     a low pressure system is determined by the pressure

     A.  generated by the boiler
     B.  in the heating main
     C.  at the inlet side of the reducing valve
     D.  of the exhaust

47.  According to the above paragraph, steam used for heating is sometimes obtained from    47.____
     steam

     A.  generated principally to operate machinery
     B.  exhausted from larger boilers
     C.  generated at low pressure and brought up to high pressure before being used
     D.  generated by engines other than boilers

48.  As used in the above paragraph, the word *expressly* means    48.____

     A.  rapidly                              B.  specifically
     C.  usually                              D.  mainly

49.  Of the following words, the one that is CORRECTLY spelled is    49.____

     A.  suficient                            B.  sufficiant
     C.  sufficient                           D.  suficiant

50.  Of the following words, the one that is CORRECTLY spelled is    50.____

     A.  fairly          B.  fairley          C.  farely          D.  fairlie

---

# KEY (CORRECT ANSWERS)

| | | | | | | | | | |
|---|---|---|---|---|---|---|---|---|---|
| 1. | B | 11. | B | 21. | C | 31. | B | 41. | D |
| 2. | A | 12. | D | 22. | C | 32. | A | 42. | B |
| 3. | A | 13. | D | 23. | B | 33. | D | 43. | D |
| 4. | C | 14. | B | 24. | A | 34. | B | 44. | A |
| 5. | C | 15. | C | 25. | C | 35. | D | 45. | C |
| 6. | C | 16. | C | 26. | C | 36. | A | 46. | B |
| 7. | B | 17. | B | 27. | B | 37. | B | 47. | A |
| 8. | A | 18. | D | 28. | B | 38. | B | 48. | B |
| 9. | C | 19. | B | 29. | A | 39. | C | 49. | C |
| 10. | B | 20. | A | 30. | B | 40. | D | 50. | A |

---

# TOOLS

## EXAMINATION SECTION
## TEST 1

DIRECTIONS: Each question or incomplete statement is followed by several suggested answers or completions. Select the one that BEST answers the question or completes the statement. *PRINT THE LETTER OF THE CORRECT ANSWER IN THE SPACE AT THE RIGHT.*

1. It is NOT good practice to cut thin-walled copper tubing with an ordinary three-wheel pipe cutter because

    A. the cutters will be dulled
    B. too much time is required
    C. the tubing end must be reamed after cutting
    D. the tubing is likely to collapse

1.____

2. Wedges are used under vertical shoring timbers to

    A. utilize scrap wood
    B. permit the use of very short timbers
    C. obtain rigid shoring
    D. absorb construction noise

2.____

3. The LONGEST nail of the following is a _____-penny nail.

    A. 12        B. 10        C. 6        D. 4

3.____

4. A commonly used priming coat for structural steel is

    A. enamel        B. varnish        C. red lead        D. lacquer

4.____

5. A nail set is a tool used for

    A. straightening bent nails
    B. cutting nails to specified size
    C. sinking a nail head in wood
    D. measuring nail size

5.____

6. The sketch at the right shows a gauge used to
    A. measure the depth of a hole
    B. determine if a board has been smoothly planed
    C. check the width of a brick
    D. scribe a line on a board parallel to its edge

GAUGE

6.____

7. The gauge box shown at the right is used for measuring the dry volume of a concrete mix. If the gauge box is to have a volume of 1 cubic yard, dimension H must be APPROXIMATELY _____ feet.

   A. 2.39
   B. 1.69
   C. 1.45
   D. .63

Questions 8-27.

DIRECTIONS:   Questions 8 through 27 refer to the use of tools shown below. Refer to these tools when answering these questions.

8. Tool number 38 is properly called a(n) _____ wrench.     8.____

   A. box       B. open-end       C. socket       D. tool

9. Two tools which are used for cutting large circular holes in thin sheets are numbers _____ and _____.     9.____

   A. 12; 31       B. 28; 33       C. 12; 28       D. 31; 33

10. If there is a possible danger of electric shock when you are taking measurements, it would be BEST to use number     10.____

   A. 1       B. 4       C. 18       D. 32

11. A 1/2-inch steel pipe is preferably cut with number     11.____

   A. 14       B. 23       C. 27       D. 29

12. A nut for a #8 machine screw should be tightened using number     12.____

   A. 9       B. 15       C. 17       D. 38

13. The hexagon nut for a 1/2-inch diameter machine bolt should be tightened using number     13.____

   A. 5       B. 10       C. 22       D. 26

14. If a small piece must be chipped off a brick in order to clear an obstruction when a brick wall is being built, the MOST suitable tool to use is number     14.____

   A. 16       B. 19       C. 20       D. 33

15. A large number of wood screws can be screwed into a board MOST quickly by using number     15.____

   A. 7       B. 8       C. 11       D. 17

16. A number of different diameter holes can be MOST easily bored through a heavy wood plank by using number     16.____

   A. 3       B. 13       C. 21       D. 31

17. The tool to use in order to form threads in a hole in a steel block is number     17.____

   A. 2       B. 3       C. 27       D. 31

18. Curved designs in thin wood are preferably cut with number     18.____

   A. 12       B. 23       C. 29       D. 37

19. The driving of Phillips-head screws requires the use of number     19.____

   A. 7       B. 8       C. 11       D. 34

20. In order to properly flare one end of a piece of copper tubing, the tool to use is number     20.____

   A. 13       B. 25       C. 33       D. 35

21. Tool number 16 is used for     21.____

   A. counterboring       B. cutting concrete
   C. countersinking       D. reaming

22. A tool that can be used to drill a hole in a concrete wall to install a lead anchor is number    22._____

    A.  3            B.  16            C.  21            D.  25

23. After cutting a piece of steel pipe, the burrs are BEST removed from the inside edge with    23._____
    number

    A.  6            B.  13            C.  16            D.  33

24. The MOST convenient tool for measuring the depth of a 1/2-inch diameter hole is num-    24._____
    ber

    A.  24           B.  31            C.  32            D.  36

25. A 1" x 1" x 1/8" angle iron would usually be cut using number    25._____

    A.  12           B.  26            C.  29            D.  37

26. Wood screws located in positions NOT accessible to an ordinary screwdriver would be    26._____
    removed using number

    A.  2            B.  8             C.  13            D.  30

27. A small hole can be quickly bored through an 1/8-inch thick plywood board with number    27._____

    A.  3            B.  7             C.  21            D.  31

28. The hammer shown to the right would be used by a    28._____
    A.  carpenter
    B.  bricklayer
    C.  tinsmith
    D.  plumber

29. Which of the following pairs of tools would be used to tighten a nut on a screw?    29._____

    A.  Two open-end wrenches
    B.  One open-end wrench and one adjustable wrench
    C.  A screwdriver and a wrench
    D.  A vise wrench and an adjustable screwdriver

30. In order to determine if a surface is truly horizontal, it should be checked with a    30._____

    A.  carpenter's square            B.  plumb bob
    C.  steel rule                    D.  spirit level

# KEY (CORRECT ANSWERS)

| | | | | |
|---|---|---|---|---|
| 1. | D | | 16. | D |
| 2. | C | | 17. | B |
| 3. | A | | 18. | B |
| 4. | C | | 19. | D |
| 5. | C | | 20. | D |
| | | | | |
| 6. | D | | 21. | C |
| 7. | B | | 22. | D |
| 8. | C | | 23. | D |
| 9. | A | | 24. | A |
| 10. | A | | 25. | D |
| | | | | |
| 11. | A | | 26. | B |
| 12. | C | | 27. | C |
| 13. | B | | 28. | B |
| 14. | B | | 29. | C |
| 15. | A | | 30. | D |

———

# TEST 2

DIRECTIONS: Each question or incomplete statement is followed by several suggested answers or completions. Select the one that BEST answers the question or completes the statement. *PRINT THE LETTER OF THE CORRECT ANSWER IN THE SPACE AT THE RIGHT.*

1. After a wedge-shaped hole has been cut into the large stone, the three-legged lifting device is inserted to lift the stone. The CORRECT order for inserting the three legs is

    A.  1, 2, 3
    B.  3, 2, 1
    C.  2, 3, 1
    D.  1, 3, 2

1.____

2. Brushes which have been used to apply shellac are BEST cleaned with

    A.  alcohol              B.  water
    C.  carbon tetrachloride  D.  acetic acid

2.____

3. When timbers are bolted together, a flat washer is GENERALLY used under the head of the bolt to

    A.  prevent the bolt from turning
    B.  increase the strength of the bolt
    C.  reduce crushing of the wood when the bolt is tightened
    D.  make it easier to turn the bolt

3.____

4. A claw hammer is PROPERLY used for

    A.  driving a cold chisel
    B.  driving brads
    C.  setting rivets
    D.  flattening a 1/4" metal bar

4.____

5. Open-end wrenches are made with the sides of the jaws at about a 15° angle to the line of the handle. This angle

    A.  is useful when working the wrench in close quarters
    B.  increases the strength of the jaws
    C.  prevents extending the handle with a piece of pipe
    D.  serves only to improve the appearance of the wrench

5.____

6. It is BEST to cut a piece of sheet metal with a pair of snips by starting each cut with the metal sheet       6.\_\_\_\_

    A. out near the points of the snips
    B. as far back in the jaws as possible
    C. midway between the snip points and the pivot
    D. one-quarter the way between the snip points and the pivot

7. Cement-lined drain pipe should be cut with a       7.\_\_\_\_

    A. chisel                    B. file
    C. star drill            D. hacksaw

8. A riser is GENERALLY a pipe run which is       8.\_\_\_\_

    A. horizontal          B. curved
    C. vertical             D. at a 45 angle

Questions 9-18.

DIRECTIONS: Questions 9 through 18 refer to the use of the tools shown below. Read the item, and for the operation given, select the PROPER tool to be used from those shown.

9. Turning a screw tap when threading a hole in a steel block.

9.___

10. Boring a number of different diameter holes through a heavy wood plank.

10.___

11. Quickly screwing a number of wood screws into a board.

11.___

12. Setting a groove in a cement floor before hardening of the cement.

12.___

13. Plastering a wall.

13.___

14. Chipping a small piece out of a brick to clear a projecting steel rod when building a brick wall.

14.___

15. Tightening a large nut.

15.___

16. Quickly boring a small hole through a 1/8" board.

16.___

17. Unfastening wood screws located in a position inaccessible to an ordinary screwdriver.

17.___

18. Making a 1 1/2" hole in a steel plate.

18.___

19. A pneumatic bucker is used in

19.___

    A. riveting             B. brazing
    C. soldering         D. reinforcing concrete

20. To make certain two points separated by a vertical distance of 8 feet are in perfect vertical alignment, it would be BEST to use a

20.___

    A. surface gage        B. height gage
    C. protractor           D. plumb bob

21. When repair work is being done on the elevated structure, canvas spreads are suspended under the working area MAINLY to

21.___

    A. reduce noise         B. discourage crowds
    C. protect the structure     D. protect pedestrians

22. When grinding a weld smooth, it is MOST important to avoid.

22.___

    A. overheating the surrounding metal
    B. grinding too much of the weld away
    C. grinding too slowly
    D. grinding after the weld has cooled off

23. A gouge is a tool used for

23.___

    A. planing wood smooth      B. grinding metal
    C. drilling steel              D. chiseling wood

24. The tool that should be used to cut a 1" x 4" plank down to a 3" width is a

24.___

    A. hacksaw             B. crosscut saw
    C. rip saw               D. backsaw

25. Threads are cut on the ends of a length of steel pipe by the use of a          25.____

    A.  brace and bit               B.  counterbore
    C.  stock and die             D.  doweling jig

26. A bit brace can be locked so that the bit will turn in only one direction by means of a          26.____

    A.  feed screw               B.  rachet device
    C.  universal chuck          D.  ball-bearing device

27. A reamer is used to          27.____

    A.  enlarge drilled holes to an exact size
    B.  punch holes to desired size
    C.  line up adjacent holes
    D.  lay out holes before drilling

28. The tool shown at the right is a          28.____
    A.  countersink
    B.  counterbore
    C.  star drill
    D.  burring reamer

29. The saw shown at the right would be used to cut          29.____
    A.  curved designs in thin wood
    B.  strap iron
    C.  asphalt tiles to fit against walls
    D.  soft lead pipe

30. The tool shown at the right is a          30.____
    A.  float
    B.  finishing trowel
    C.  hawk
    D.  roofing seamer

# KEY (CORRECT ANSWERS)

| | | | | |
|---|---|---|---|---|
| 1. | D | | 16. | C |
| 2. | A | | 17. | D |
| 3. | C | | 18. | B |
| 4. | B | | 19. | B |
| 5. | A | | 20. | D |
| | | | | |
| 6. | B | | 21. | C |
| 7. | D | | 22. | B |
| 8. | C | | 23. | D |
| 9. | P | | 24. | C |
| 10. | A | | 25. | C |
| | | | | |
| 11. | E | | 26. | B |
| 12. | V | | 27. | A |
| 13. | T | | 28. | D |
| 14. | J | | 29. | A |
| 15. | M | | 30. | A |

# TEST 3

DIRECTIONS: Each question or incomplete statement is followed by several suggested answers or completions. Select the one that BEST answers the question or completes the Statement. *PRINT THE LETTER OF THE CORRECT ANSWER IN THE SPACE AT THE RIGHT.*

Questions 1-8.

DIRECTIONS: Questions 1 through 8 are to be answered on the basis of the following items. The sizes of the items shown are NOT their actual sizes. Each item is identified by a number, For each question, select the answer which gives the identifying number of the item that BEST answers the question.

1. Which one of the following items should be connected to a hydrant and used to put out a fire?

   A.  5          B.  7          C.  8          D.  17         1._____

2. Which one of the following pairs of items should be used after a fire to clean a floor covered with small pieces of burned material?

   A.  1 and 14      B.  4 and 6      C.  10 and 12      D.  11 and 13     2._____

3. Which one of the following pairs of items should be used for cutting a branch from a tree?

   A.  2 and 3      B.  8 and 9      C.  11 and 12      D.  14 and 15     3._____

4. Which one of the following items should be used to rescue a victim from a second floor window?

   A.  1          B.  10          C.  15          D.  20         4._____

5. Which one of the following pairs of items should be used to tighten a nut on a screw?

   A.  2 and 3      B.  8 and 19      C.  9 and 14      D.  16 and 18     5._____

6. Which one of the following items should be used to repair a leaky faucet?

   A.  4          B.  5          C.  12          D.  13         6._____

7. Which one of the following items should be used as a source of water at a fire?

   A.  2          B.  6          C.  9          D.  20         7._____

8. Which item should be used for cutting metal?

   A.  6          B.  13          C.  15          D.  18         8._____

Questions 9-18.

DIRECTIONS: Questions 9 through 18, inclusive, in Column I are articles or terms used in structure maintenance and repair work, each of which is associated primarily (though not exclusively) with one of the trade specialties listed in Column II. For each article or term in Column I, select the trade specialty from Column II in which it is in greatest use. Indicate in the space at the right, the letter preceding your selected trade specialty.

| COLUMN I (Articles or Terms) | COLUMN II (Trade Specialties) | |
|---|---|---|
| 9.  Drift pin | A.  Carpentry | 9._____ |
| 10.  Studding | | 10._____ |
| 11.  Elbow | B.  Masonry | 11._____ |
| 12.  Header course | | 12._____ |
| 13.  Dowel | C.  Ironwork | 13._____ |
| 14.  Screeding | | 14._____ |
| 15.  Cleanout | D.  Plumbing | 15._____ |
| 16.  Air jam | | 16._____ |
| 17.  Curing | | 17._____ |
| 18.  Mortise and tenon | | 18._____ |

19. Practically all valves used in plumbing work are made so that the handwheel is turned     19.___
    clockwise instead of counterclockwise to close the valve.
    The PROBABLE reason is that

    A.  it is easier to remember since screws and nuts move inward when turned clock-
        wise
    B.  the handwheel is less likely to loosen
    C.  greater force can be exerted
    D.  most people are righthanded

20. Sharpening a hand saw consists of     20.___

    A.  jointing, shaping, setting, and filing
    B.  adzing, clinching, forging, and machining
    C.  brazing, chiseling, grinding, and mitering
    D.  bushing, dressing, lapping, and machining

21. A hacksaw blade having 32 teeth to the inch is the BEST blade to use when cutting     21.___

    A.  cold rolled steel shafting
    B.  wrought iron pipe
    C.  stainless steel plate
    D.  copper tubing

22. Good practice dictates that an adjustable open-end wrench should be used PRIMARILY     22.___
    when the

    A.  nut to be turned is soft and must not be scored
    B.  extra leverage is needed
    C.  proper size of fixed wrench is not available
    D.  location is cramped permitting only a small turning angle

23. When a hacksaw blade is designated as an 18-32, the numbers 18 and 32 refer to,     23.___
    respectively, the blade's

    A.  stroke and thickness
    B.  thickness and length
    C.  length and teeth per inch
    D.  teeth per inch and stroke

24. When a machine screw is designated as a 10-32, the numbers 10 and 32 refer to,     24.___
    respectively, the screw's

    A.  length and head type
    B.  threads per inch and length
    C.  diameter and threads per inch
    D.  head type and diameter

25. An offset screwdriver is MOST useful for turning a wood screw when     25.___

    A.  a strong force needs to be applied
    B.  the screw head is marred
    C.  space is limited
    D.  speed is desired

26. Of the following orders for tools or materials used in the building trades, the one which is INCOMPLETE is

    A. 1 paintbrush, flat, 2 in. wide
    B. 1 drill, twist, straight shank, high speed, 3/8 in.
    C. 1 snake, steel, 3/4 in. wide by 1/8 in. thick
    D. 1 keg of nails, 10 penny, common wire, galvanized

26.____

27. The tool that is GENERALLY used to slightly elongate a round hole in strap-iron is a

    A. rat-tail file
    C. drill
    B. reamer
    D. rasp

27.____

28. The BEST way to locate a point on the floor directly below a given point on the ceiling is by using a

    A. plumber's snake
    C. flashlight
    B. plumb bob
    D. chalk line

28.____

29. The wrench that would prove LEAST useful in uncoupling several pieces of pipe is a _____ wrench.

    A. socket    B. chain    C. strap    D. stillson

29.____

30. Of the following, the tool that is LEAST easily broken is a

    A. file
    C. folding rule
    B. pry bar
    D. hacksaw blade

30.____

# KEY (CORRECT ANSWERS)

| | | | | |
|---|---|---|---|---|
| 1. | B | | 16. | C |
| 2. | B | | 17. | B |
| 3. | C | | 18. | A |
| 4. | A | | 19. | A |
| 5. | D | | 20. | A |
| | | | | |
| 6. | D | | 21. | D |
| 7. | D | | 22. | C |
| 8. | C | | 23. | C |
| 9. | C | | 24. | C |
| 10. | A | | 25. | C |
| | | | | |
| 11. | B | | 26. | C |
| 12. | D | | 27. | A |
| 13. | A | | 28. | B |
| 14. | B | | 29. | A |
| 15. | D | | 30. | B |

# EXAMINATION SECTION
## TEST 1

DIRECTIONS: Each question or incomplete statement is followed by several suggested answers or completions. Select the one that *BEST* answers the question or completes the statement. *PRINT THE LETTER OF THE CORRECT ANSWER IN THE SPACE AT THE RIGHT.*

1. Asbestos was used as a wire covering mainly for protection against          1.____
   A. humidity          B. vibration          C. corrosion          D. heat

2. A wattmeter is used for making a direct measurement of          2.____
   A. current          B. voltage          C. power          D. resistance

3. The number of connection points to a two-pole, double-throw knife switch is          3.____
   A. 2          B. 4          C. 6          D. 8

4. Wires are pulled through conduit with the aid of          4.____
   A. a hickey                    B. an extension bit
   C. a snake                     D. a nipple

5. To smooth out the ripples present in rectified a.c., the device commonly used is a          5.____
   A. filter          B. relay          C. spark gap          D. booster

6. A tachometer is used for measuring          6.____
   A. r.p.m.                      B. torque
   C. power factor               D. specific gravity

7. Rubber insulation deteriorates most rapidly when in contact with          7.____
   A. water          B. oil          C. lead          D. aluminum

8. The microfarad is a unit of measurement used for condenser          8.____
   A. ohmic resistance           B. power loss
   C. leakage current            D. capacity

9. A "megger" is an electrical instrument used to measure          9.____
   A. current                    B. resistance
   C. voltage                    D. wattage

10. When a run of conduit would require many right angle bends, it is necessary to install pull          10.____
    boxes because

    A. conduit cannot be bent
    B. otherwise injury to the wires may result during installation
    C. conduit comes in fixed lengths
    D. the conduit requires support

11. The metal frames of some electrical units are grounded mainly to     11.____

    A. eliminate short-circuits
    B. save insulating material
    C. protect against shock
    D. prevent overloading

12. A motor which can be operated only from an a.c. power source is     12.____

    A. a shunt motor          B. a series motor
    C. a compound motor     D. an induction motor

13. Of the following, the poorest conductor of electricity is     13.____

    A. mercury           B. sulphuric acid
    C. distilled water       D. salt water

14. The insulation provided between commutator bars on a d.c. motor is generally     14.____

    A. mica      B. lucite      C. porcelain      D. transite

15. Nichrome wire should be most suitable for use in     15.____

    A. a transformer          B. a motor
    C. an incandescent lamp    D. a heating element

16. Electrical outlet boxes do not have to be drilled for the entrance of conduit into the boxes     16.____
if they are provided with

    A. bushings      B. knockouts      C. hickeys      D. couplings

17. The minimum number of field windings in a compound motor is     17.____

    A. 1      B. 2      C. 3      D. 4

18. The motor most likely to reach a dangerous speed if operated at normal voltage and no     18.____
load is a

    A. shunt motor          B. series motor
    C. compound motor      D. synchronous motor

19. If three 6-volt batteries are connected in parallel, the resultant voltage will be     19.____

    A. 18 volts      B. 9 volts      C. 6 volts      D. 2 volts

20. If an incandescent lamp is operated at a voltage below its rated voltage then it     20.____

    A. will operate more efficiently
    B. will have a longer life
    C. will take more power
    D. is more likely to fail by arcing

21. Four resistors, having respective current ratings of 1, 2, 3 and 4 amperes, are connected     21.____
in series. If the resistors are not to be overloaded, the maximum current permissable in
this circuit is

    A. 1 ampere          B. 2.5 amperes
    C. 4 amperes         D. 10 amperes

22. Conduit is reamed mainly to 22.____

    A. protect the wires against sharp edges
    B. make threading easier
    C. increase its electrical conductivity
    D. improve its appearance

23. Two 25-watt, 120-volt lamps are connected in parallel to a 120-volt source. The two 23.____
lamps will take a total of

    A. 12.5 watts                 B. 25 watts
    C. 50 watts                  D. 100 watts

24. An advantage of the mercury arc rectifiers when compared to rotary converters is that 24.____
the mercury arc rectifiers

    A. are relatively quiet
    B. eliminate the use of transformers
    C. operate at lower voltage
    D. operate for shorter periods

25. A bushing is usually provided on the end of a conduit running into a panel box. An impor- 25.____
tant function of the bushing is to

    A. insulate the conduit from the panel box
    B. support the panel box
    C. separate one conduit from another
    D. prevent injury to the wires

26. An alternator is 26.____

    A. an a.c. generator
    B. a ground detector device
    C. a choke coil
    D. a frequency meter

27. The best immediate first-aid treatment for a scraped knee is to 27.____

    A. apply plain vaseline
    B. use a knee splint
    C. apply heat
    D. wash it with soap and water

Questions 28 - 34.

Questions 28 through 34 are based on the Signal System Emergency Power Supply Information given below. Read this information carefully before answering these questions.

### SIGNAL SYSTEM EMERGENCY POWER SUPPLY INFORMATION

The signal mains operate on 115 volts a.c. and are fed from either a normal power supply or an emergency power supply. When the normal power supply goes below 90 volts, a transfer switch automatically switches the signal mains to the emergency power. With normal feed, the transfer switch is held in the normal or energized position. When the normal power supply falls, the transfer switch changes to the emergency supply by means of gravity and a control spring. The operation of the transfer switch is controlled by means of a potential relay which opens on less than 90 volts. Once the transfer switch has changed to the emergency side, it can only be reset to the normal side by first closing the potential relay by hand. If the normal supply is satisfactory, this relay will remain closed. Then by pushing a reset button, the transfer switch will swing to the normal side and remain-closed through its retaining circuit. A special push button is provided for checking the transfer switch for proper operation.

28. The transfer switch will automatically connect the signal mains to emergency power when the normal power supply voltage is  28.____

    A.  120 volts     B.  115 volts     C.  95 volts     D.  85 volts

29. The *FIRST* step in resetting the transfer switch to the normal side is to  29.____

    A.  open the potential relay        B.  push the reset button
    C.  operate the special button     D.  close the potential relay

30. The special push button is provided for  30.____

    A.  checking the operation of the transfer switch
    B.  disconnecting the emergency supply
    C.  automatically closing the potential relay
    D.  resetting the control spring

31. The reset button is used to  31.____

    A.  swing the transfer switch to the normal side
    B.  swing the transfer switch to the emergency side
    C.  energize the potential relay
    D.  de-energize the potential relay

32. The signal mains receive their power through the  32.____

    A.  potential relay        B.  transfer switch
    C.  reset button          D.  special push button

33. When the emergency power is feeding the signal mains, then the  33.____

    A.  transfer switch is automatically energized
    B.  potential relay automatically goes to the closed position
    C.  transfer switch is in the de-energized position
    D.  special push button must be pressed to restore the normal power supply

34. The transfer switch is held in the emergency supply position by  34.____

    A.  a retaining circuit
    B.  a special push button
    C.  gravity and a control spring
    D.  a reset button

35. To reduce the pitting of relay contacts which make and break frequently, the unit generally connected across them is a  35.____

    A.  transistor        B.  spark gap
    C.  condenser       D.  switch

36. As compared to a solid conductor, a stranded conductor of the same diameter      36.____

    A. has greater flexibility
    B. requires less insulation
    C. has greater resistance to corrosion
    D. does not require soldered connections

37. The electrolyte in a lead storage battery is      37.____

    A. sodium bicarbonate      B. sulphuric acid
    C. muriatic acid      D. ammonia

38. Twisted pair wire is desirable for telephone circuits mainly because it      38.____

    A. is less likely to pick up electrical interference
    B. can be run in long stretches without any support
    C. can carry heavy currents
    D. can withstand high voltage

39. In the subway, heavy copper bonds are connected across the joints of the track rails.      39.____
With the bonds installed, a voltage drop measurement is taken across the track rail joint.
This test would be used mainly to determine the bond

    A. temperature      B. electrical resistance
    C. breakdown voltage      D. leakage current

40. In a polarized electric cord plug, the contact blades of the plug are      40.____

    A. magnetized
    B. of different color
    C. parallel to each other
    D. perpendicular to each other

41. A capacity rating expressed in ampere-hours is commonly used for      41.____

    A. insulators      B. storage batteries
    C. switches      D. inductances

42. The number of ordinary flashlight cells which must be connected together to obtain 6      42.____
volts is

    A. 1      B. 2      C. 3      D. 4

43. A bank of five 120-volt lamps connected in series is used for test purposes in the subway.      43.____
This test bank would be best utilized in checking a circuit having

    A. 120 volts d.c.      B. 120 volts a.c.
    C. 24 volts      D. 600 volts

44. A step-up transformer is used to step up      44.____

    A. voltage      B. current      C. power      D. frequency

45. A photoelectric cell is a device for changing

    A. light into electricity
    B. electricity into light
    C. electricity into heat
    D. sound into electricity

45.\_\_\_\_

46. Decreasing the length of a wire conductor will

    A. increase the current carrying capacity
    B. decrease the current carrying capacity
    C. decrease the resistance
    D. increase the resistance

46.\_\_\_\_

47. The proper tool to use in making a hole through a transite panel is

    A. a star drill                B. a countersink
    C. a twist drill               D. an auger

47.\_\_\_\_

48. Copper is a preferred metal in the construction of large knife switches because it is

    A. soft                    B. flexible
    C. a good conductor      D. light in weight

48.\_\_\_\_

49. The process of removing the insulation from a wire is called

    A. sweating              B. skinning
    C. tinning                D. braiding

49.\_\_\_\_

50. The electric lamp which is used for providing heat is

    A. a sodium vapor lamp     B. a mercury vapor lamp
    C. a neon lamp            D. an infra-red lamp

50.\_\_\_\_

---

# KEY (CORRECT ANSWERS)

| | | | | | | | | | |
|---|---|---|---|---|---|---|---|---|---|
| 1. | D | 11. | C | 21. | A | 31. | A | 41. | B |
| 2. | C | 12. | D | 22. | A | 32. | B | 42. | D |
| 3. | C | 13. | C | 23. | C | 33. | C | 43. | D |
| 4. | C | 14. | A | 24. | A | 34. | C | 44. | A |
| 5. | A | 15. | D | 25. | D | 35. | C | 45. | A |
| 6. | A | 16. | B | 26. | A | 36. | A | 46. | C |
| 7. | B | 17. | B | 27. | D | 37. | B | 47. | C |
| 8. | D | 18. | B | 28. | D | 38. | A | 48. | C |
| 9. | B | 19. | C | 29. | D | 39. | B | 49. | B |
| 10. | B | 20. | B | 30. | A | 40. | D | 50. | D |

---

# TEST 2

DIRECTIONS: Each question or incomplete statement is followed by several suggested answers or completions. Select the one that *BEST* answers the question or completes the statement. *PRINT THE LETTER OF THE CORRECT ANSWER IN THE SPACE AT THE RIGHT.*

Questions 1-7

Questions 1 through 7 are based on the above wiring diagram. Refer to this diagram when answering these questions.

1. Starting with all switches open, then to light the lamp it is necessary to close switch          1._____

    A. No. 1        B. No. 2        C. No. 3        D. No . 4

2. Closing one of the four switches will prevent the lamp from being lighted. This switch is          2._____

    A. No. 1        B. No. 2        C. No. 3        D. No. 4

3. The two switches which must be in the closed position to obtain a reading on the voltme-          3._____
ter are

    A. No. 1 and No. 4                B. No. 2 and No. 3
    C. No. 3 and No. 4                D. No.1 and No. 2

4. To obtain a reading on the ammeter it is necessary to have          4._____

    A. switch No. 2 open
    B. switch No. 4 closed
    C. switch No. 3 closed and switch No. 1 open
    D. switch No. 3 open and switch No. 1 closed

5. When current is flowing through the 10-ohm resistors, the voltmeter reading will be    5._____

    A.  100 volts        B.  60 volts        C.  40 volts        D.  24 volts

6. In this circuit the ammeter should have a scale range of at least zero to    6._____

    A.  1 ampere        B.  2 amperes       C.  3 amperes       D.  4 amperes

7. With the switches set for this circuit to take maximum current from the line, then the current through the fuse will be approximately    7._____

    A.  1 ampere        B.  2 amperes       C.  4 amperes       D.  10 amperes

8. The abbreviations I.D. and O.D. used in describing conduit directly refer to its    8._____

    A.  diameter        B.  length        C.  conductivity       D.  weight

9. To cut off a piece of #0000 insulated copper cable it is best to use    9._____

    A.  a hacksaw                  B.  side-cutting pliers
    C.  an electrician's knife       D.  light nippers

10. Conduit is galvanized in order to    10._____

    A.  improve electrical conductivity       B.  protect it from corrosion
    C.  obtain a smooth surface            D.  insulate it

11. The best material for an electrical contact finger subjected to constant bending is    11._____

    A.  brass                  B.  aluminum
    C.  tin                    D.  phosphor bronze

12. One disadvantage of porcelain as an insulator is that it is    12._____

    A.  only good for low voltage
    B.  not satisfactory on a-c circuits
    C.  a brittle material
    D.  easily compressed

13. To vary the speed of a d-c motor-generator set, it would be necessary to    13._____

    A.  use a rheostat in the generator field
    B.  use a voltage regulator on the generator output
    C.  use a rheostat in the motor field
    D.  shift the brushes on the generator

14. The ordinary telephone transmitter contains granules of    14._____

    A.  sulphur        B.  carbon        C.  borax        D.  lucite

15. A stubby screwdriver is especially designed for turning screws    15._____

    A.  having a damaged screw slot
    B.  which are jammed tight
    C.  with stripped threads
    D.  inaccessible to a longer screwdriver

16. It is important to make certain a ladle does not contain water before using it to scoop up molten solder since the water may    16.____

    A. cause serious personal injury
    B. prevent the solder from sticking
    C. cool the solder
    D. dilute the solder

17. Steel helmets give workers the most protection from    17.____

    A. eye injuries                        B. falling objects
    C. fire                               D. electric shock

18. A slight coating of rust on small tools is best removed by    18.____

    A. applying a heavy coat of vaseline
    B. rubbing with kerosene and fine steel wool
    C. scraping with a sharp knife
    D. rubbing with a dry cloth

19. In the case of an auto-transformer, it is *INCORRECT* to say that    19.____

    A. the primary is insulated from the secondary
    B. a magnetic core is used
    C. a.c. is required
    D. it can be used for power purposes

20. The number 6-32 for a machine screw specifies the diameter and the    20.____

    A. length
    B. the number of threads per inch
    C. type of head
    D. hardness

21. It is undesirable to allow a soldering iron to overheat since this would cause    21.____

    A. softening of the copper tip
    B. hardening of the copper tip
    C. the soldering fumes to become poisonous
    D. damage to the tinned surface of the tip

22. To measure the small gap between relay contacts, it would be best to use a    22.____

    A. vernier caliper               B. depth gage
    C. feeler gage                   D. micrometer

23. Acid is not a desirable flux to use in soldering small connections mainly because it    23.____

    A. is corrosive
    B. is expensive
    C. requires skill in handling
    D. requires a very hot iron

24. It is good practice to use standard electrician's pliers to         24.____

    A. tighten nuts
    B. remove insulation from a wire
    C. cut BX sheath
    D. shorten a wood screw

25. Three resistors having respective resistances of 12 ohms, 5 ohms, and 1 ohm are con-    25.____
nected in parallel. The combined resistance will be

    A. 18 ohms                 B. 6 ohms
    C. 4 ohms                  D. less than 1 ohm

26. The star drill is a multiple-pointed chisel used for drilling         26.____

    A. brass                     B. stone and concrete
    C. wood                     D. aluminum

27. A screwdriver in good condition should have a blade whose bottom edge is    27.____

    A. rounded                 B. knife-sharp
    C. chisel-shaped           D. flat

28. From the standpoint of management, the most desirable characteristic in a newly    28.____
appointed helper would be

    A. the lack of outside personal interests
    B. the ability to keep to himself and away from the other employees
    C. the ability to satisfactorily perform his assigned duties
    D. eagerness to ask questions about all phases of the work

29. To provide transit employees with quick assistance in the case of minor injuries it would    29.____
be most logical to

    A. instruct the employees in first-aid techniques
    B. provide each employee with a first-aid kit
    C. have one centrally located medical office for the transit system
    D. equip all employees with walkie-talkie devices

30. One result of corrosion of an electrical connection is that        30.____

    A. its resistance increases
    B. its resistance decreases
    C. its temperature drops
    D. the current in the circuit increases

31. Subway cars are equipped with storage batteries. These batteries are *LEAST* likely to be    31.____
used to supply power to the car

    A. traction motors
    B. emergency lights
    C. public address system
    D. motorman-conductor communication system

32. The size of a screwdriver is defined by the     32.____

    A. length of the handle         B. thickness of the blade
    C. length of the blade          D. diameter of the handle

33. A newly appointed helper would be expected to do his work in the manner prescribed by   33.____
his foreman because

    A. it insures discipline
    B. good results are more certain with less supervision
    C. no other method would work
    D. it permits speed-up

34. When a soldered splice is covered with both rubber and friction tape, the main function of   34.____
the friction tape is to

    A. provide extra electrical insulation
    B. protect the rubber tape
    C. make the splice water-tight
    D. increase the mechanical strength of the splice

35. Powdered graphite is a good     35.____

    A. lubricant     B. abrasive     C. adhesive     D. insulator

36. A zero adjusting screw will be found on most     36.____

    A. overload relays         B. lightning arrestors
    C. voltmeters            D. switches

37. Lock nuts are frequently used in making electrical connections on terminal boards. The   37.____
purpose of the lock-nuts is to

    A. keep the connections from loosening through vibration
    B. prevent unauthorized personnel from tampering with the connections
    C. eliminate the use of flat washers
    D. increase the contact area at the connection point

38. The abbreviation D.P.D.T. used in electrical work describes a type of     38.____

    A. switch     B. motor     C. fuse     D. generator

39. A wire has a resistance of 2 ohms per 1000 feet. A piece of this wire 1500 feet long will   39.____
have a resistance of

    A. 1 ohm     B. 1.5 ohms     C. 2.5 ohms     D. 3 ohms

40. The dielectric strength of the oil used in an oil filled transformer is a direct measure of the   40.____
oil's

    A. viscosity          B. weight
    C. breakdown voltage     D. current carrying capacity

41. The power fed to a mercury arc rectifier would probably come from　　41.____

    A. a rotary converter　　　　　　B. a d.c.generator
    C. an a.c.source　　　　　　　　D. a battery

42. The ordinary plug fuse has　　42.____

    A. knife blade contacts　　　　B. screw base contacts
    C. ferrule contacts　　　　　　D. jack contacts

43. When using a hacksaw, it is good practice to　　43.____

    A. tighten the blade in the frame by using pliers on the wing nut
    B. use heavy pressure on both the forward and return strokes
    C. slow the speed of cutting when the piece is almost cut through
    D. use very short, very rapid strokes

44. A new helper is told by an experienced helper that he is not doing a particular job prop-　　44.____
erly. The best reason for the new helper to give this advice due consideration is that the
other helper

    A. has the authority to enforce his advice
    B. has more experience on the job
    C. will be resentful if his advice is not taken
    D. will not help the new man again if his advice is not taken

45. The main purpose of the oil in an oil circuit breaker is to　　45.____

    A. quench the arc　　　　　　B. lubricate the moving parts
    C. prevent corrosion　　　　　D. absorb moisture

46. A piece of electrical equipment which does *NOT* require a magnetic field for its operation　　46.____
is

    A. a motor　　　　　　　　　　B. a generator
    C. a transformer　　　　　　　D. an electrostatic voltmeter

47. The rating term "20-watts, 500-ohm" would generally be applied to a　　47.____

    A. resistor　　　　　　　　　　B. condenser
    C. switch　　　　　　　　　　　D. circuit breaker

48. The core of an electro-magnet is usually made of　　48.____

    A. lead　　　　B. iron　　　　C. brass　　　　D. bakelite

49. The A.W.G. size is used in specifying　　49.____

    A. wires　　　B. condensers　　　C. switches　　　D. fuses

50. The metal which is preferred for use in relay contacts is　　50.____

    A. brass　　　B. tin　　　C. silver　　　D. aluminum

# KEY (CORRECT ANSWERS)

| | | | | | | | | | |
|---|---|---|---|---|---|---|---|---|---|
| 1. | A | 11. | D | 21. | D | 31. | A | 41. | C |
| 2. | D | 12. | C | 22. | C | 32. | C | 42. | B |
| 3. | D | 13. | C | 23. | A | 33. | B | 43. | C |
| 4. | B | 14. | B | 24. | B | 34. | B | 44. | B |
| 5. | D | 15. | D | 25. | D | 35. | A | 45. | A |
| 6. | D | 16. | A | 26. | B | 36. | C | 46. | D |
| 7. | D | 17. | B | 27. | D | 37. | A | 47. | A |
| 8. | A | 18. | B | 28. | C | 38. | A | 48. | B |
| 9. | A | 19. | A | 29. | A | 39. | D | 49. | A |
| 10. | B | 20. | B | 30. | A | 40. | C | 50. | C |

# EXAMINATION SECTION
## TEST 1

DIRECTIONS: Each question or incomplete statement is followed by several suggested answers or completions. Select the one that BEST answers the question or completes the statement. *PRINT THE LETTER OF THE CORRECT ANSWER IN THE SPACE AT THE RIGHT.*

1. Three resistors, each of 12 ohms, connected in parallel with each other, are connected in series to a resistor of 6 ohms and to a 60 volt source.
   The current, in amperes, through the 6 ohms resistor will be

   A. 5      B. 6      C. 10      D. 15

   1.____

2. Two electrical condensers have capacitances of 9 and 18 microfarads, respectively, are connected in series.
   The capacitance, in microfarads, of the two connected together will be

   A. 6      B. 9      C. 13.5      D. 27

   2.____

3. The current in a coil having an inductance of 32 millihenries increases in magnitude from 2 to 6 amperes in 0.05 second.
   The voltage of self-induction will equal

   A. 1.28      B. 1.60      C. 1.92      D. 2.56

   3.____

4. A variable electrical condenser of the type used in radio sets is completely immersed in oil whose dielectric strength is 3.5.
   As compared to its former state, its

   A. ability to withstand high voltages has been reduced
   B. capacitance has been increased
   C. capacitance has been decreased
   D. capacitance remains unaffected

   4.____

5. A shunt motor having an armature whose resistance is 0.5 ohm is attached to a 120 volt supply. The armature current at full speed is 10 amperes.
   The back EMF, in volts, will be

   A. 5      B. 10      C. 115      D. 125

   5.____

6. An electron stream sent horizontally through a magnetic field whose lines of force are horizontal and at right angles to the electron stream will

   A. curve in a horizontal plane
   B. curve in a vertical plane
   C. curve in a plane neither horizontal nor vertical
   D. pass through without curving

   6.____

7. In a series wound DC electrical generator, the current in the line is

   A. the same as the field current
   B. half the current through either brush
   C. twice the current through either brush
   D. independent of the field current

   7.____

8. The MOST economical 0.1 mfd condenser to be used, without danger of shorting, on a 250-volt AC line is one whose DC working voltage is rated at

    A. 250        B. 300        C. 400        D. 600

8.____

9. As the frequency of an alternating EMF in a given circuit increases, the current in the circuit at first increases, then decreases.
The circuit contains

    A. only capacitative reactance
    B. only inductive reactance
    C. both capacitative and inductive reactance
    D. a constant impedance

9.____

10. A storage cell is connected in series with a resistance of 0.3 ohms.
If the resistance of the cell is 0.2 ohms and its EMF is 2.5 volts, the current, expressed in amperes, in the circuit is

    A. 1/5        B. 5        C. 7.5        D. 12.5

10.____

11. A battery has an open circuit voltage of 20 volts and an internal resistance of 0.25 ohm. When it delivers a current of 10 amperes, the terminal voltage will be

    A. 15        B. 17.5        C. 18        D. 20

11.____

12. The core of an electromagnet is made of soft iron because soft iron

    A. is an electrical conductor
    B. is easily magnetized and demagnetized
    C. is easy to shape
    D. retains its magnetism

12.____

13. The wire in the primary of a step-up transformer is usually thicker than the wire in the secondary because the primary has the

    A. higher current        B. higher resistance
    C. higher voltage        D. lower current

13.____

14. Direct current is necessary in order to

    A. charge storage batteries
    B. operate lights
    C. produce heat
    D. run electric motors

14.____

15. Very small electric currents are measured by a(n)

    A. galvanometer        B. micrometer
    C. ohmmeter        D. wattmeter

15.____

16. Of the following, the STRONGEST electromagnet is one having _____ amperes and _____ turns.

    A. 5; 10        B. 10; 5        C. 5; 5        D. 10; 10

16.____

17. In describing an alternating current, the term *60 cycles per second* refers to the

    A. amplitude        B. frequency        C. voltage        D. wavelength

17.____

18. In a parallel circuit, the device with the LOWEST resistance has the     18.\_\_\_\_

    A. least heating effect            B. highest wattage
    C. lowest current                 D. lowest voltage drop

19. When a current is made to flow in a circuit consisting of two unlike metals, heat is     19.\_\_\_\_
absorbed at one of the junctions and given off at the other junction.
This phenomenon is known as the _____ effect

    A. Tyndall          B. Stark          C. Purkinje          D. Peltier

20. Assume that a length of wire having a resistance of 20 ohms is cut into four equal     20.\_\_\_\_
lengths. The four resistors then are connected in parallel with each other and their resistance measured.
The resistance, in ohms, will be

    A. 1.25          B. 2.50          C. 5          D. 10

21. Two adjacent turns in a helical coil through which a constant current is passing will     21.\_\_\_\_

    A. repel each other
    B. attract each other
    C. have no effect on each other
    D. have a voltage induced in them

22. When several capacitors are connected in series and to a source of direct current, each     22.\_\_\_\_
capacitor must have the same

    A. voltage                   B. dielectric strength
    C. charge                    D. capacitance

23. The current in an alternating current circuit is equal to the voltage multiplied by the     23.\_\_\_\_

    A. impedance              B. admittance
    C. capacitance            D. inductance

24. The penetrating power of the x-rays produced by a Coolidge x-ray tube can be increased     24.\_\_\_\_
by increasing the

    A. number of electrons emitted from the filament
    B. distance between cathode and anode
    C. mass of the anode
    D. voltage between cathode and anode

25. The combined resistance, in ohms, of four 100-ohm resistors connected in series is     25.\_\_\_\_

    A. 100          B. 200          C. 25          D. 400

26. Four resistors of sixty ohms each are connected in parallel.     26.\_\_\_\_
Their combined resistance, in ohms, is

    A. 15          B. 30          C. 60          D. 240

27. Resistors of 5, 10, 15, and 30 ohms are connected in series to a battery.     27.\_\_\_\_
The GREATEST voltage drop will be across the resistor of _____ ohms.

    A. 5          B. 10          C. 15          D. 30

28. Eight Christmas tree lamps are connected in series on a 120-volt circuit. The voltage across each lamp is     28.____

     A. 15         B. 112         C. 120         D. 960

29. A flow of electricity in a copper wire consists of a movement of     29.____

     A. ions         B. electrons         C. positrons         D. protons

30. A wire 50 feet long has a resistance of 10 ohms. The resistance of 25 feet of this wire is _____ ohms.     30.____

     A. 2.5         B. 5         C. 20         D. 40

31. All of the following devices can be operated from a steady direct current EXCEPT a     31.____

     A. flatiron         B. rheostat
     C. toaster         D. transformer

32. The alloy used for lead-in wires of electric lamps is chosen PRINCIPALLY because it     32.____

     A. does not expand on heating
     B. expands at the same rate as glass
     C. has a high specific heat
     D. has a low melting point

33. A voltmeter is a galvanometer that has its movable coil connected with a _____ resistance in _____.     33.____

     A. high; parallel         B. high; series
     C. low; parallel         D. low; series

34. A commutator on a direct-current motor     34.____

     A. reverses the direction of the current in the field magnet
     B. reverses the direction of the current in the armature coils
     C. changes low voltage DC to higher voltage DC
     D. changes low voltage AC to higher voltage AC

35. One great advantage of AC over DC is that AC     35.____

     A. can be stored
     B. can be transmitted more economically
     C. operates heating devices better
     D. requires less insulation

36. Steady direct current cannot be used to operate a(n)     36.____

     A. doorbell         B. electric heater
     C. lamp         D. transformer

37. Only direct-current electricity may be used to     37.____

     A. operate a transformer
     B. charge a storage battery
     C. heat a radio-tube filament
     D. operate a doorbell

38. In speaking of 60-cycle alternating current, the term *60 cycle* refers to          38.____

    A. amplitude                     B. frequency
    C. velocity                       D. wavelength

39. Of the following, the device that should NOT be connected to a DC source is a          39.____

    A. flatiron                      B. heating coil
    C. lamp                        D. transformer

40. The armature in an electric doorbell moves away from the magnet because it is          40.____

    A. moved back by the electromagnet
    B. moved back by the spring
    C. repelled by the gong
    D. repelled by the interrupter

41. A condenser is used to          41.____

    A. change AC to DC             B. charge batteries
    C. generate electricity         D. store electricity

42. The potential difference in a circuit is measured in          42.____

    A. amperes     B. ohms         C. volts         D. watts

43. The current in a fuse is _____ the current in the circuit it protects.          43.____

    A. much less than          B. the same as
    C. slightly greater than      D. much greater than

44. A condenser is connected in series with a 25-watt lamp to a 120-volt DC source.          44.____
The lamp will

    A. operate normally         B. burn out
    C. glow dimly            D. not operate

45. A galvanometer has a resistance of 50 ohms and requires 0.05 amperes for full-scale          45.____
The voltage required for half-scale deflection is

    A. 0.0001     B. 0.05       C. 1.25       D. 2.5

46. If the capacitance in an oscillator circuit of frequency F is increased fourfold, the frequency of the oscillator becomes          46.____

    A. F/4     B. F/2       C. 2F       D. 4F

47. In circuit A, one ampere of AC flows for 1 hour and generates X calories. In circuit B, one          47.____
ampere of DC flows for 1 hour.
The heat generated in circuit B is

    A. 0.707X                     B. the same as in A

    C. $\dfrac{X}{0.707}$               D. 0.24 IRT

48. Two 50-watt, 120-volt heaters are connected in parallel to a 120-volt DC line. The power consumption is now X times as great as it would be if they were connected in series. Assuming no change in resistance, X will be

   A.  2         B.  1/2        C.  1/4        D.  4

48.\_\_\_\_

49. In an AC circuit in which the current and voltage are out of phase by 90°, an ammeter reads 2 and a voltmeter reads 120.
The power expended by this circuit, in watts, equals

   A.  zero       B.  60        C.  120        D.  240

49.\_\_\_\_

50. A voltmeter showed a reading, when connected to a circuit carrying a sinusoidal alternating current, of 100 volts (RMS value).
The MAXIMUM instantaneous voltage was

   A.  100       B.  141       C.  173       D.  200

50.\_\_\_\_

———

# KEY (CORRECT ANSWERS)

| | | | | | | | | | |
|---|---|---|---|---|---|---|---|---|---|
| 1. | B | 11. | B | 21. | B | 31. | D | 41. | D |
| 2. | A | 12. | B | 22. | C | 32. | B | 42. | C |
| 3. | D | 13. | A | 23. | B | 33. | B | 43. | B |
| 4. | B | 14. | A | 24. | D | 34. | B | 44. | D |
| 5. | C | 15. | A | 25. | D | 35. | B | 45. | C |
| 6. | B | 16. | D | 26. | A | 36. | D | 46. | B |
| 7. | A | 17. | B | 27. | D | 37. | B | 47. | B |
| 8. | C | 18. | B | 28. | A | 38. | B | 48. | D |
| 9. | C | 19. | D | 29. | B | 39. | D | 49. | A |
| 10. | B | 20. | A | 30. | B | 40. | B | 50. | B |

———

# TEST 2

DIRECTIONS: Each question or incomplete statement is followed by several suggested answers or completions. Select the one that BEST answers the question or completes the statement. *PRINT THE LETTER OF THE CORRECT ANSWER IN THE SPACE AT THE RIGHT.*

1. A three-element vacuum tube in an electric circuit

   A. generates signals of increased voltage
   B. amplifies the grid bias
   C. controls the electron flow in the circuit
   D. rectifies the B-battery output
   E. increases the signal frequency

   1.____

2. A simple series circuit consists of a cell, an ammeter, and a rheostat of resistance R. The ammeter reads 5 amps. When the resistance of the rheostat is increased by 2 ohms, the ammeter reading drops to 4 amps.
   The original resistance, in ohms, of the rheostat R is

   A. 2.5        B. 4.0        C. 8.0        D. 10.0        E. 12.0

   2.____

3. Two lamps need 50V and 2 amp each in order to operate at a desired brilliancy.
   If they are to be connected in series across a 120V line, the resistance, in ohms, of the rheostat that must be placed in series with the lamps needs to be

   A. 4        B. 10        C. 20        D. 100        E. 200

   3.____

4. As the photon is a quantum in electromagnetic field theory, which one of the following is considered to be the quantum in the nuclear field?

   A. Neutrino        B. Electron        C. Meson
   D. Neutron         E. None of the above

   4.____

5. Which symbol represents an electrical ground connection?

   A        B        C        D        E

   5.____

6. Which of the following circuits could you wire from the diagram at the right?
   A. Code oscillator
   B. Doorbell system
   C. Electric chime
   D. Radio receiving set
   E. Electric train signal

   6.____

7. The rate of electron flow in an electric circuit is measured with a(n)

   A. ammeter        B. voltmeter        C. ohmmeter
   D. wattmeter      E. none of the above

   7.____

8. Which one of the following is characteristic of a parallel electrical circuit?   8._____

    A. The current is the same in all parts of the circuit.
    B. The voltage across all the branches is the same.
    C. A break through any part of the circuit will stop the flow of current throughout the circuit.
    D. The total resistance is equal to the sum of the resistances of the component parts.

9. When sphere A, with a large negative charge, is touched by sphere B, with a smaller negative charge, which one of the following will occur?   9._____

    A. Electrons flow from A to B
    B. Electrons flow from B to A
    C. Protons flow from A to B
    D. Protons flow from B to A

10. Rectifiers are LEAST often made from which one of the following elements?   10._____

    A. Si        B. Ge        C. Se        D. Cu

11. Which of the following is GENERALLY used to convert a galvanometer to an ammeter?   11._____

    A. Capacitor        B. Inductor
    C. Oscillator        D. Resistor

12. The tuned circuits of a radio receiver consist BASICALLY of which one of the pairs of components below?   12._____

    A. Rectifier and antenna
    B. Tube or transistor and coil
    C. Potentiometer and oscillator
    D. Capacitor and coil

13. Often a 2-ohm and a 4-ohm resistor are connected to a 12-volt battery in series. The number of amperes flowing through the 2-ohm resistor is   13._____

    A. 0.5        B. 1        C. 2        D. 6

14. A radio wave 6 meters long will have a frequency CLOSEST to which one of the following?   14._____

    A. 6 cycles        B. 6 kilocycles
    C. 6 megacycles        D. 50 megacycles

15. Which one of the instruments below sometimes uses an internal battery?   15._____

    A. Ammeter        B. Voltmeter
    C. Wattmeter        D. Ohmmeter

16. Which one of the following kinds of rays is bent MOST by a magnetic field?   16._____

    A. Alpha        B. Beta        C. Gamma        D. Cosmic

17. A battery having an emf of 6.0 volts and an internal resistance of 0.20 ohms is being The charging current is 10 amperes.
The potential difference at the terminals of the battery is, in volts, which one of the following?   17._____

A.  4.0          B.  5.8          C.  6.0          D.  8.0

18.  Whenever magnetic lines of force are cut by a conductor,                    18.____

    A.  an induced current results
    B.  a magnetic field is induced
    C.  an emf is induced
    D.  the motion will be opposed by an induced magnetic field

19.  The oil drop experiment performed by Robert Millikan was used to measure          19.____

    A.  energy of emitted photoelectrons
    B.  charge of an electron
    C.  thin film interference
    D.  surface tension of oil

20.  Of the following, a dielectric is MOST similar to a(n)                    20.____

    A.  conductor                    B.  capacitor
    C.  inductor                     D.  insulator

21.  To measure the electric power consumed by a direct current circuit, the MINIMUM appa-    21.____
    ratus required is a(n)

    A.  ammeter                       B.  voltmeter
    C.  ammeter and a voltmeter       D.  ohmmeter

22.  An AC circuit has a capacitive reactance of 100 ohms, an inductive reactance of 100     22.____
    ohms, and a resistance of 100 ohms.
    The impedance, in ohms, of the circuit is

    A.  33.3          B.  100          C.  150          D.  300

23.  A series electric circuit consists of a 20 ohm resistor, a 10 volt battery, and a switch.    23.____
    If the switch is closed for 6 seconds, the energy consumed by the circuit, in joules, is

    A.  10          B.  20          C.  30          D.  40

24.  A 10 ohm resistor and a 50 ohm resistor are connected in parallel.                24.____
    If the current in the 10 ohm resistor is 5 amperes, the current, in amperes, in the 50
    ohm resistor will be

    A.  1          B.  5          C.  25          D.  50

25.  Assuming a core of adequate size, of the following, the MOST powerful electromagnet     25.____
    would have _____ turns and draw _____ amperes.

    A.  100; 6          B.  50; 13          C.  200; 2          D.  150; 5

26.  Resistors of 2 ohms, 4 ohms, and 6 ohms are connected in series to a 24 volt battery.    26.____
    The current, in amps, through the 4 ohm resistor is

    A.  2          B.  4          C.  6          D.  22

27.  An electric circuit consisting of a 10V battery and two resistors connected in series has 5    27.____
    amperes of current. If a 5 microfarad capacitor is placed in series with the resistors, the
    current after a few minutes will be

A.  5 amperes
B.  more than 5 amperes
C.  between 1 and 5 amperes
D.  zero

28. Resistance CANNOT be measured if the only instruments available are a voltmeter and a(n)    28.____

   A.  ammeter
   B.  Wheatstone Bridge
   C.  galvanometer
   D.  ohmmeter

29. In the absence of external magnetic fields, ground state electronic energy levels depend ALMOST ENTIRELY on the quantum numbers    29.____

   A.  $n$ and $m_1$    B.  $n$ and $1$    C.  $m_1$ and $m_s$    D.  $1$ and $m_s$

30. A small object having a charge of -2 microcoulombs is placed in a uniform electric field of 10 volts/meter.    30.____
   The force, in micronewtons, on the object due to the electric field is

   A.  0.2    B.  5.0    C.  8.0    D.  20.0

31. A 50 microfarad capacitor is fully charged by a 100 volt power supply.    31.____
   The electric energy, in joules, stored in the capacitor is

   A.  0.25    B.  0.50    C.  1.50    D.  5.00

32. A thin-walled, hollow metal sphere has a diameter of 2.0 meters and is given a charge of +9 microcoulombs.    32.____
   The electric potential 8.0 meters above the top of the sphere, in volts, is

   A.  80    B.  1000    C.  1200    D.  9000

33. Assume that a length of wire having a resistance of 20 ohms is cut into four equal lengths. The four resistors then are connected in parallel with each other and their resistance measured.    33.____
   The resistance, in ohms, will be

   A.  1.25    B.  2.50    C.  5    D.  10

34. Two adjacent turns in a helical coil through which a constant current is passing will    34.____

   A.  repel each other
   B.  attract each other
   C.  have no effect on each other
   D.  have a voltage induced in them

35. When several capacitors are connected in series and to a source of direct current, each capacitor must have the same    35.____

   A.  voltage
   B.  dielectric strength
   C.  charge
   D.  capacitance

36. The current in an alternating current circuit is equal to the voltage multiplied by the    36.____

   A.  impedance
   B.  admittance
   C.  capacitance
   D.  inductance

37. The penetrating power of the x-rays produced by a Coolidge x-ray tube can be increased   37.____
by increasing the

  A.  number of electrons emitted from the filament
  B.  distance between cathode and anode
  C.  mass of the anode
  D.  voltage between cathode and anode

38. A shunt motor having an armature whose resistance is 0.5 ohm is attached to a 120 volt   38.____
supply. The armature current at full speed is 10 amperes.
The back EMF, in volts, will be

  A.  5          B.  10          C.  115          D.  125

39. An electron stream sent horizontally through a magnetic field whose lines of force are   39.____
horizontal and at right angles to the electron stream will

  A.  curve in a horizontal plane
  B.  curve in a vertical plane
  C.  curve in a plane neither horizontal nor vertical
  D.  pass through without curving

40. In a series wound DC electrical generator, the current in the line is   40.____

  A.  the same as the field current
  B.  half the current through either brush
  C.  twice the current through either brush
  D.  independent of the field current

41. The MOST economical 0,1 mfd condenser to be used, without danger of shorting, on a   41.____
250 volt AC line is one whose DC working voltage is rated at

  A.  250          B.  300          C.  400          D.  600

42. As the frequency of an alternating EMF in a given circuit increases, the current in the cir-   42.____
cuit at first increases, then decreases.
The circuit contains

  A.  only capacitative reactance
  B.  only inductive reactance
  C.  both capacitative and inductive reactance
  D.  a constant impedance

43. A storage cell is connected in series with a resistance of 0.3 ohms.   43.____
If the resistance of the cell is 0.2 ohms and its EMF is 2.5 volts, the current, expressed
in amperes, in the circuit is

  A.  1/5          B.  5          C.  7.5          D.  12.5

44. A condenser of capacitance C is charged to a potential V by a quantity of charge Q.   44.____
The energy stored in the condenser is

  A.  1/2CV          B.  1/2CV$^2$          C.  CV          D.  1/2CQ$^2$

45. Two 50-watt, 120-volt heaters are connected in parallel to a 120-volt DC line. The power consumption is now X times as great as it would be if they were connected in series. Assuming no change in resistance, X will be

   A.  2         B.  1/2         C.  1/4         D.  4

45._____

46. The wire in the primary of a step-up transformer is usually of larger diameter than the wire in the secondary because the primary has the higher

   A.  voltage                       B.  resistance
   C.  current                     D.  number of turns

46._____

47. A spark coil operated in the classroom can produce a spark about 2 inches long. This represents a voltage of about

   A.  400         B.  4000         C.  40,000         D.  400,000

47._____

48. A substance with a magnetic permeability less than one is called

   A.  ferromagnetic              B.  diamagnetic
   C.  paramagnetic             D.  isomagnetic

48._____

49. The constant current in a simple series circuit is 5 amperes and the resistance of the circuit is 10 ohms. The circuit is closed for exactly 4 minutes.
During this time, the net quantity of electricity transferred past any cross-section of the circuit is, in coulombs,

   A.  20         B.  120         C.  200         D.  1200

49._____

50. The Curie point is the

   A.  temperature at which a magnetic substance loses its magnetism
   B.  temperature above which a gas cannot be liquefied by pressure
   C.  pressure needed to inhibit radioactivity
   D.  temperature at which the addition of heat causes contraction

50._____

---

# KEY (CORRECT ANSWERS)

| | | | | |
|---|---|---|---|---|
| 1. C | 11. D | 21. C | 31. B | 41. C |
| 2. C | 12. D | 22. B | 32. C | 42. C |
| 3. B | 13. C | 23. C | 33. A | 43. B |
| 4. C | 14. D | 24. A | 34. B | 44. B |
| 5. C | 15. D | 25. D | 35. C | 45. D |
| 6. D | 16. B | 26. A | 36. B | 46. C |
| 7. A | 17. D | 27. D | 37. D | 47. C |
| 8. B | 18. C | 28. C | 38. C | 48. B |
| 9. A | 19. B | 29. A | 39. B | 49. D |
| 10. D | 20. D | 30. D | 40. A | 50. A |

---

# EXAMINATION SECTION
# TEST 1

DIRECTIONS:    Each question or incomplete statement is followed by several suggested
answers or completions. Select the one that BEST answers the question or
completes the statement. *PRINT THE LETTER OF THE CORRECT ANSWER
IN THE SPACE AT THE RIGHT.*

Questions 1-8.

DIRECTIONS:    Questions 1 through 8 involve tests on the fuse box arrangement shown
below. All tests are to be performed with a neon tester or a lamp test bank consisting of two 6-watt, 120-volt lamps connected in series. Do not make any
assumptions about the conditions of the circuits. Draw your conclusions only
from the information obtained with the neon tester or the two-lamp test bank,
applied to the circuits as called for.

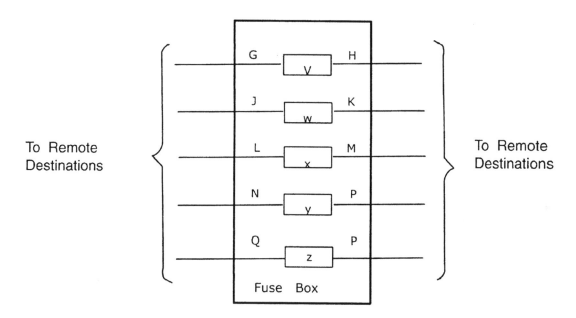

1.  The two lamp test bank is placed from point G to joint J, and both lamps light.          1._____
One of the lamps is momentarily removed from its socket; during that instant, the other
lamp in the series-connected test bank should

    A.  go dark
    B.  get dimmer
    C.  remain at same brightness
    D.  get brighter

2.  The test bank with two 60-watt, 120-volt lamps in series should be used on circuits with      2._____

    A.  wattages only from 60 to 120 watts
    B.  wattages only from 0 to 120 watts
    C.  voltages only from 120 to 240 volts
    D.  voltages only from 0 to 240 volts

3. The neon tester is placed from point G to point J and only one-half of the neon tester lights.
   It should be concluded that

   3.____

   A. half of the tester has gone bad
   B. a wire has become disconnected in the circuit
   C. the voltage is AC
   D. the voltage is DC

4. If both lamps in the test bank light when placed directly across one of the above fuses, it should be concluded that

   4.____

   A. the fuse is good
   B. the fuse is blown
   C. the fuse is overrated
   D. further tests have to be made to determine the condition of the fuse

5. If the lamp test bank does not light when placed directly across one of the above fuses, it should be concluded that

   5.____

   A. the fuse is good
   B. the fuse is blown
   C. the fuse is overrated
   D. further tests have to be made to determine the condition of the fuse

6. The lamp test bank lights when placed from point G to point J but does not light when placed from point H to point J.
   It should be concluded that

   6.____

   A. the wire to point H has become disconnected
   B. the wire to point J has become disconnected
   C. fuse v is bad
   D. fuse w is bad

7. The lamp test bank lights when placed from point L to point N but does not light when placed from point M to point P.
   It should be concluded that

   7.____

   A. both fuses x and y are bad
   B. either fuse x or fuse y is bad or both are bad
   C. both fuses x and y are good
   D. these tests do not indicate the condition of any fuse

8. The lamp test bank is placed from point L to point N, then from N to point Q, and finally from point L to point Q. In each case, both lamps light to full brightness.
   It should be concluded that points L, N, and Q have

   8.____

   A. three-phase, 120 volts, AC, line-to-line
   B. plus and minus 120 volts, DC
   C. three-phase, 208 volts, AC
   D. plus and minus 240 volts, DC

9. The resistance of a copper wire to the flow of electricity _____ as the _____ of the wire _____.    9.____

    A. increases; diameter; increases
    B. decreases; diameter; decreases
    C. decreases; length; increases
    D. increases; length; increases

10. Where galvanized steel conduit is used, the PRIMARY purpose of the galvanizing is to    10.____

    A. increase mechanical strength
    B. retard rusting
    C. provide a good surface for painting
    D. provide good electrical contact for grounding

11. The lamps used for station and tunnel lighting in subways are generally operated at slightly less than their rated voltage.
The LOGICAL reason for this is to    11.____

    A. prevent overloading of circuits
    B. increase the life of the lamps
    C. decrease glare
    D. obtain a more even distribution of light

12. The CORRECT method of measuring the power taken by an AC electric motor is to use a    12.____

    A. wattmeter           B. voltmeter and an ammeter
    C. power factor meter     D. tachometer

13. Wood ladders should NOT be painted because the paint may    13.____

    A. deteriorate the wood     B. make ladders slippery
    C. be inflammable         D. cover cracks or defects

14. Goggles would be LEAST necessary when    14.____

    A. recharging soda-acid fire extinguishers
    B. chipping stone
    C. putting electrolyte into an Edison battery
    D. scraping rubber insulation from a wire

15. The number and type of precautions to be taken on a job generally depend LEAST on the    15.____

    A. nature of the job
    B. length of time the job is expected to last
    C. kind of tools and materials being used
    D. location of the work

16. When training workers in the use of tools and equipment, safety precautions related to their use should be FIRST mentioned    16.____

    A. in the introductory training session before the workers begin to use the equipment or tools
    B. during training sessions when workers practice operating the tools or equipment

C. after the workers are qualified to use the equipment in their daily tasks
D. when an agency safety bulletin related to the tools and equipment is received

17. Artificial respiration should be started immediately on a man who has suffered an electric shock if he is   17.____

   A. *unconscious* and breathing
   B. *unconscious* and not breathing
   C. *conscious* and in a daze
   D. *conscious* and badly burned

18. The fuse of a certain circuit has blown and is replaced with a fuse of the same rating which also blows when the switch is closed.
In this case,   18.____

   A. a fuse of higher current rating should be used
   B. a fuse of higher voltage rating should be used
   C. the fuse should be temporarily replaced by a heavy piece of wire
   D. the circuit should be checked

19. Operating an incandescent electric light bulb at less than its rated voltage will result in   19.____

   A. shorter life and brighter light
   B. longer life and dimmer light
   C. brighter light and longer life
   D. dimmer light and shorter life

20. In order to control a lamp from two different positions, it is necessary to use   20.____

   A. two single pole switches
   B. one single pole switch and one four-way switch
   C. two three-way switches
   D. one single pole switch and one four-way switch

21. One method of testing fuses is to connect a pair of test lamps in the circuit in such a manner that the test lamp will light up if the fuse is good and will remain dark if the fuse is bad. In the illustration at the right, 1 and 2 are fuses.
In order to test if fuse 1 is bad, test lamps should be connected between   21.____

   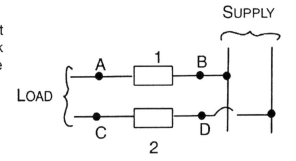

   A. A and B
   B. B and D
   C. A and D
   D. C and B

22. The PRINCIPAL reason for the grounding of electrical equipment and circuits is to   22.____

   A. prevent short circuits      B. insure safety from shock
   C. save power                  D. increase voltage

23. An interlock is generally installed on electronic equipment to

    A. prevent loss of power
    B. maintain VHF frequencies
    C. keep the vacuum tubes lit
    D. prevent electric shock during maintenance operations

23.____

24. A flame should not be used to inspect the electrolyte level in a lead-acid battery because the battery cells give off highly flammable

24.____

    A. hydrogen              B. lead oxide
    C. lithium               D. xenon

25. The purpose of the third prong in a three-prong male electric plug used in a 120 volt circuit is to

25.____

    A. make a firm connection          B. strengthen the plug
    C. ground to prevent shock         D. act as a transducer

---

# KEY (CORRECT ANSWERS)

| | | | |
|---|---|---|---|
| 1. | A | 11. | B |
| 2. | D | 12. | A |
| 3. | D | 13. | D |
| 4. | B | 14. | D |
| 5. | D | 15. | B |
| 6. | C | 16. | A |
| 7. | B | 17. | B |
| 8. | C | 18. | D |
| 9. | D | 19. | B |
| 10. | B | 20. | C |

| | |
|---|---|
| 21. | C |
| 22. | B |
| 23. | D |
| 24. | A |
| 25. | C |

---

# TEST 2

DIRECTIONS:    Each question or incomplete statement is followed by several suggested answers or completions. Select the one that BEST answers the question or completes the statement. *PRINT THE LETTER OF THE CORRECT ANSWER IN THE SPACE AT THE RIGHT.*

1.    The BEST procedure to follow when replacing a blown fuse is to          1._____

    A.    immediately replace it with the same size fuse
    B.    immediately replace it with a larger size fuse
    C.    immediately replace it with a smaller size fuse
    D.    correct the cause of the fuse failure and replace it with the correct size

2.    The amperage rating of the fuse to be used in an electrical circuit is determined by the          2._____

    A.    size of the connected load
    B.    size of the wire in the circuit
    C.    voltage of the circuit
    D.    ambient temperature

3.    In a 208 volt, three-phase, 4 wire circuit, the voltage, in volts, from any line to the grounded neutral is APPROXIMATELY          3._____

    A.    208          B.    150          C.    120          D.    zero

4.    The device commonly used to change an AC voltage to a DC voltage is called a          4._____

    A.    transformer          B.    rectifier
    C.    relay          D.    capacitor or condenser

5.    Where conduit enters a knock-out in an outlet box, it should be provided with a          5._____

    A.    bushing on the inside and locknut on the outside
    B.    locknut on the inside and bushing on the outside
    C.    union on the outside and a nipple on the inside
    D.    nipple on the outside and a union on the inside

6.    The electric circuit to a ten kilowatt electric hot water heater which is automatically controlled by an aquastat will also require a          6._____

    A.    transistor          B.    choke coil
    C.    magnetic contactor          D.    limit switch

7.    An electric power consumption meter USUALLY indicates the power used in          7._____

    A.    watts          B.    volt-hours
    C.    amperes          D.    kilowatt-hours

8.    Of the following sizes of copper wire, the one which can SAFELY carry the greatest amount of amperes is          8._____

    A.    14 ga. stranded          B.    12 ga. stranded
    C.    12 ga. solid          D.    10 ga. solid

9. If a 110 volt lamp were used on a 220 volt circuit, the     9.____

    A. fuse would burn out        B. lamp would burn out
    C. line would overheat        D. lamp would flicker

10. The material which is LEAST likely to be found in use as the outer covering of rubber insulated wires or cables is     10.____

    A. cotton        B. varnished cambric
    C. lead        D. neoprene

11. In measuring to determine the size of a stranded insulated conductor, the PROPER place to use the wire gauge is on     11.____

    A. the insulation
    B. the outer covering
    C. the stranded conductor
    D. one strand of the conductor

12. Rubber insulation on an electrical conductor would MOST quickly be damaged by continuous contact with     12.____

    A. acid        B. water        C. oil        D. alkali

13. If a fuse clip becomes hot under normal circuit load, the MOST probable cause is that the     13.____

    A. clip makes poor contact with the fuse ferrule
    B. circuit wires are too small
    C. current rating of the fuse is too high
    D. voltage rating of the fuse is too low

14. If the input to a 10 to 1 step-down transformer is 15 amperes at 2400 volts, the secondary output would be NEAREST to _____ amperes at _____ volts.     14.____

    A. 1.5; 24,000        B. 150; 240
    C. 1.5; 240        D. 150; 24,000

15. In a two-wire electrical system, the color of the wire which is grounded is USUALLY     15.____

    A. white        B. red        C. black        D. green

16. It is generally recommended that wooden ladders be kept coated with a suitable protective coating.
The one of the following which is NOT a suitable protective coating is     16.____

    A. clear lacquer        B. clear varnish
    C. linseed oil        D. paint

17. The tool you should use to mend metal by soldering is     17.____

A.

B.

C.

D.

18. The one of the following that is NOT part of an electric motor is a          18.____

    A. brush        B. rheostat        C. pole        D. commutator

19. An electrical transformer would be used to          19.____

    A. change current from AC to DC
    B. raise or lower the power
    C. raise or lower the voltage
    D. change the frequency

20. The piece of equipment that would be rated in ampere hours is a          20.____

    A. storage battery        B. bus bar
    C. rectifier           D. capacitor

21. A ballast is a necessity in a(n)          21.____

    A. motor generator set
    B. fluorescent lighting system
    C. oil circuit breaker
    D. synchronous converter

22. The power factor in an AC circuit is on when    22.____

    A.   no current is flowing
    B.   the voltage at the source is a minimum
    C.   the voltage and current are in phase
    D.   there is no load

23. Neglecting the internal resistance in the battery, the current flowing through the battery shown at the right is _____ amp.    23.____

    A.   3
    B.   6
    C.   9
    D.   12

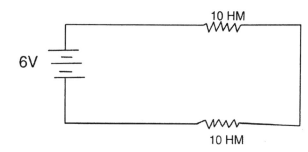

24. Using a fuse with a LARGER rated capacity than that of the circuit is    24.____

    A.   *advisable;* such use prevents the fuse from blowing
    B.   *advisable;* larger capacity fuses last longer than smaller capacity fuses
    C.   *inadvisable;* larger capacity fuses are more expensive than smaller capacity fuses
    D.   *inadvisable;* such use may cause a fire

25. You can MOST easily tell when a screw-in type fuse has blown because the center of the strip of metal in the fuse is    25.____

    A.   broken                B.   visible
    C.   nicked               D.   cool to the touch

———

# KEY (CORRECT ANSWERS)

| 1. | D | | 11. | D |
|----|---|---|-----|---|
| 2. | B | | 12. | C |
| 3. | C | | 13. | A |
| 4. | B | | 14. | B |
| 5. | A | | 15. | A |
| 6. | C | | 16. | D |
| 7. | D | | 17. | B |
| 8. | D | | 18. | B |
| 9. | B | | 19. | C |
| 10. | B | | 20. | A |

| 21. | B |
|-----|---|
| 22. | C |
| 23. | A |
| 24. | D |
| 25. | A |

———

# TEST 3

DIRECTIONS:   Each question or incomplete statement is followed by several suggested answers or completions. Select the one that BEST answers the question or completes the statement. *PRINT THE LETTER OF THE CORRECT ANSWER IN THE SPACE AT THE RIGHT.*

1.  The ordinary single-pole flush wall type switch must be connected          1.____

    A.   across the line
    B.   in the hot conductor
    C.   in the grounded conductor
    D.   in the white conductor

2.  A DC shunt motor runs in the wrong direction.          2.____
    This fault can be CORRECTED by

    A.   reversing the connections of both the field and the armature
    B.   interchanging the connections of either main or auxiliary windings
    C.   interchanging the connections to either the field or the armature windings
    D.   interchanging the connections to the line of the power leads

3.  The MOST common type of motor that can be used with both AC and DC sources is the          3.____
    _____ motor.

    A.   compound      B.   repulsion      C.   series      D.   shunt

4.  A fluorescent fixture in a new building has been in use for several months without trouble.          4.____
    Recently, the ends of the fluorescent lamp have remained lighted when the light was switched off.
    The BEST way to clear up this trouble is to replace the

    A.   lamp      B.   ballast      C.   starter      D.   sockets

5.  A ballast is a part of a(n)          5.____

    A.   fluorescent light fixture
    B.   electric motor
    C.   doorbell circuit
    D.   incandescent light fixture

6.  Most of the lighting circuits in buildings operate on _____ volts.          6.____
    A.   6      B.   12      C.   120      D.   208

7.  An ordinary wall switch called a *silent switch* contains a liquid called          7.____

    A.   water      B.   mercury      C.   oil      D.   naptha

8.  The rating of the circuit breaker in a lighting circuit is determined by the          8.____

    A.   load connected to the circuit
    B.   current carrying capacity of the wire
    C.   ambient temperature
    D.   length of the wire

9. One ADVANTAGE of rubber insulation is that it         9.____

    A. does not deteriorate with age
    B. is able to withstand high temperatures
    C. does not absorb much moisture
    D. is not damaged by oil

10. The SIMPLEST device for interrupting an overloaded electrical circuit is a     10.____

    A. fuse                     B. relay
    C. capacitor              D. choke coil

11. Electric service meters are read in             11.____

    A. kilowatt hours         B. electrons
    C. amperes               D. volts

12. The device used to reduce the voltage of an electric circuit is the      12.____

    A. voltmeter             B. fuse
    C. circuit breaker        D. transformer

13. Ordinary light bulbs are USUALLY rated in          13.____

    A. watts        B. ohms        C. amperes        D. filaments

14. The electric plug on a scrubbing machine should be plugged into a      14.____

    A. light socket          B. wall outlet
    C. fuse receptacle        D. dimmer switch

15. The device which should be used to connect the output shaft of an electric motor to the    15.____
input shaft of a centrifugal pump is the

    A. flexible coupling       B. petcock
    C. alemite fitting         D. clutch

16. When comparing a 60 watt yellow bulb with a 60 watt clear bulb, it can be said that they   16.____
BOTH

    A. give the same amount of light
    B. use the same amount of power
    C. will burn for at least 60 hours
    D. will burn for at least 60 days

17. The output capacity of an electric motor is USUALLY rated in      17.____

    A. kilowatts            B. horsepower
    C. percent              D. cubic feet

18. A fuse will burn out whenever it is subjected to excessive      18.____

    A. resistance           B. voltage
    C. current             D. capacitance

19. The one of the following that is BEST to use to smooth a commutator is     19.____

    A. Number 1/0 emery cloth     B. Number 00 sandpaper
    C. Number 2 steel wool       D. a safe edge file

20. The electric service that is provided to MOST schools in the city is NOMINALLY _____     20.____
    volt- _____ phase - _____ wire - _____ volts to ground.

    A.  208; 3; 4; 120                          B.  208; 3; 3; 208
    C.  220; 2; 3; 110                          D.  440; 3; 4; 240

21. All the fuses in an electrical panel are good but the clips on the fuse in circuit No. 1 are     21.____
    much hotter than the clips of the other fuses.
    Of the following, the MOST likely cause of this condition is that

    A.  circuit No. 1 is greatly overloaded
    B.  circuit No. 1 is carrying much less than rated load
    C.  the room temperature is abnormally high
    D.  the fuse in circuit No. 1 is very loose in its clips

22. Before putting two DC engine generators on the line in parallel, it is USUALLY necessary     22.____
    to

    A.  adjust the speeds so that both are running at exactly the same speed
    B.  adjust the loads so that each machine will take its proportionate share
    C.  adjust the field of the incoming unit
    D.  lower the line voltage

23. Of the following, the BEST type of AC motor to use for direct connection to a timing     23.____
    device which must be very accurate is a _____ motor.

    A.  synchronous                             B.  squirrel cage
    C.  wound rotor                             D.  single phase capacitor

24. In running temporary electric wiring for a display requiring the use of 30 incandescent 50-     24.____
    watt lamps at the usual lighting voltage, the two main 120V loads supplying this load
    would carry MOST NEARLY _____ amps.

    A.  23.9            B.  12.5            C.  17.8            D.  9.5

25. The BEST of the following tools to use for cutting off a piece of single conductor #6 rub-     25.____
    ber insulated lead covered cable is a

    A.  pair of electrician's pliers
    B.  hacksaw
    C.  hammer and cold chisel
    D.  lead knife

# KEY (CORRECT ANSWERS)

| | | | | |
|---|---|---|---|---|
| 1. | B | | 11. | A |
| 2. | C | | 12. | D |
| 3. | C | | 13. | A |
| 4. | C | | 14. | B |
| 5. | A | | 15. | A |
| 6. | C | | 16. | B |
| 7. | B | | 17. | B |
| 8. | B | | 18. | C |
| 9. | C | | 19. | B |
| 10. | A | | 20. | A |

| | |
|---|---|
| 21. | D |
| 22. | C |
| 23. | A |
| 24. | B |
| 25. | B |

———

# TEST 4

DIRECTIONS: Each question or incomplete statement is followed by several suggested answers or completions. Select the one that BEST answers the question or completes the statement. *PRINT THE LETTER OF THE CORRECT ANSWER IN THE SPACE AT THE RIGHT.*

1. An indication that a fluorescent lamp in a fixture should be replaced is          1.____

   A. humming in the fixture
   B. the ends of the lamp remain black when the lamp is lit
   C. poor or slow starting
   D. the lamp does not shut off each time the OFF button is pressed

2. Asbestos is used as a covering on electrical wires to provide protection from          2.____

   A. high voltage                    B. high temperatures
   C. water damage                    D. electrolysis

3. Many electric power tools, such as drills, have a third conductor in the line cord which          3.____
   should be connected to a grounded part of the power receptacle.
   The reason for this is to

   A. have a spare wire in case one power wire should break
   B. strengthen the power lead so that it cannot be easily damaged
   C. protect the user of the tool from electrical shocks
   D. allow use of the tool for extended periods of time without overheating

4. A riser diagram is an electrical drawing which would give information about the          4.____

   A. voltage drop in feeders
   B. size of feeders and panel loads
   C. external connections to equipment
   D. sequence of operation of devices and equipment

5. An electric motor driven air compressor is automatically started and stopped by a          5.____

   A. thermostat                      B. line air valve
   C. pressure switch                 D. float trap

6. The term *kilowatt hours* describes the consumption of          6.____

   A. energy                          B. radiation
   C. cooling capacity                D. conductance

7. AC voltage may be converted to DC voltage by means of a          7.____

   A. magnet                          B. rectifier
   C. voltage regulator               D. transducer

8. The metal which has the GREATEST resistance to the flow of electricity is          8.____

   A. steel          B. copper          C. silver          D. gold

9. Tinning a soldering iron means

   A. applying flux to the tip
   B. cleaning the tip to make it bright
   C. applying a coat of solder to the tip
   D. heating the iron to the proper temperature

9.____

10. Electricians working around *live wires* should wear gloves made of

    A. asbestos              B. metal mesh
    C. leather               D. rubber

10.____

11.

11.____

### METER READING AT BEGENNING OF PERIOD

### METER READING AT END OF PERIOD

The above are the readings on the electric meter at the beginning and end of a period.
The TOTAL kilowatt hour consumption is

A. 264          B. 570          C. 61          D. 175

12. The modern multiple-circuit program instrument which automatically controls bell signals
    in a school USUALLY includes

    A. automatic resetting of electric clocks throughout the school
    B. automatic ringing of room bells when the fire bell switch is closed
    C. prevention of manual control of schedules by eliminating manual control switches
    D. provision for automatic cutout of the schedule for any 24-hour day desired

12.____

13. Of the following, the device which uses the GREATEST amount of electric power is the

    A. electric typewriter

    B. $\frac{1}{4}$ inch electric drill
    C. floor scrubbing machine
    D. oil burner ignition transformer

13.____

14. Meters which indicate the electric power consumed in a public building are read in

    A. kilowatt-hours         B. volts
    C. cubic feet             D. degree days

14.____

15. The MAIN reason for grounding the outer shell of an electric fixture is to      15.____

    A. provide additional support for the fixture
    B. reduce the cost of installation of the fixture
    C. provide a terminal to which the wires can be attached
    D. reduce the chance of electric shock

16. The BEST way to determine whether the locknuts on terminals in an electrical terminal      16.____
box have become loose is to

    A. use an electric tester
    B. try to tighten the nuts with an appropriate wrench
    C. tap the nuts with an insulated handle
    D. try to loosen the nuts with a pair of pliers

17. The PROPER flux to use for soldering electric wire connections is      17.____

    A. rosin             B. killed acid
    C. borax           D. zinc chloride

18. A fusestat differs from an ordinary plug fuse in that a fusestat has      18.____

    A. less current carrying capacity
    B. different size threads
    C. an aluminum shell instead of a copper shell
    D. no threads

19. A grounding type 120-volt receptacle differs from an ordinary electric receptacle MAINLY      19.____
in that a grounding receptacle

    A. is larger than the ordinary receptacle
    B. has openings for a three prong plug
    C. can be used for larger machinery
    D. has a built-in circuit breaker

20. In a 110-220 volt three-wire circuit, the neutral wire is USUALLY      20.____

    A. black          B. red          C. white          D. green

21. Brushes on fractional horsepower universal motors are MOST often made of      21.____

    A. flexible copper strands          B. rigid carbon blocks
    C. thin wire strips               D. collector rings

22. A ground wire that is too small is dangerous because it will      22.____

    A. generate heat             B. blow a fuse
    C. increase the voltage         D. increase the current

23. A 115-volt hot water heater has a resistance of 5.75 ohms. The current it will take at      23.____
rated voltage is

    A. 15           B. 20          C. 13          D. 23

24. If a 30 ampere fuse is placed in a fuse box for a circuit requiring a 15 ampere fuse,      24._____

    A. serious damage to the circuit may result from an overload
    B. better protection will be provided for the circuit
    C. the larger fuse will tend to blow more often since it carries more current
    D. it will eliminate maintenance problems

25. Metal tubing through which electric wires of buildings are run is called      25._____

    A. insulation          B. conduit
    C. duct               D. sleeve

_____

# KEY (CORRECT ANSWERS)

| | | | | |
|---|---|---|---|---|
| 1. | B | | 11. | D |
| 2. | B | | 12. | A |
| 3. | C | | 13. | C |
| 4. | B | | 14. | A |
| 5. | C | | 15. | D |
| 6. | A | | 16. | B |
| 7. | B | | 17. | A |
| 8. | A | | 18. | B |
| 9. | C | | 19. | B |
| 10. | D | | 20. | C |

| | |
|---|---|
| 21. | B |
| 22. | A |
| 23. | B |
| 24. | A |
| 25. | B |

_____

# TEST 5

DIRECTIONS: Each question or incomplete statement is followed by several suggested answers or completions. Select the one that BEST answers the question or completes the statement. *PRINT THE LETTER OF THE CORRECT ANSWER IN THE SPACE AT THE RIGHT.*

1. *Found reading* and *left reading* are terms associated with                                    1.____

   A.  petrometers                          B.  electric meters
   C.  gas meters                           D.  water meters

2. When lamps are wired in parallel, the failure of one lamp will                                    2.____

   A.  break the electric circuit to the other lamps
   B.  have no effect on the power supply to the other lamps
   C.  increase noticeably the light production of the other lamps
   D.  cause excessive current to flow through the other lamps

3. The MAIN objection to using a copper penny in place of a blown fuse is that                       3.____

   A.  the penny will conduct electric current
   B.  the penny will reduce the current flowing in the line
   C.  melting of the penny will probably occur
   D.  the line will not be protected against excessive current

4. The term *mogul base* is GENERALLY associated with                                               4.____

   A.  boiler compound                      B.  stock cleaning solution
   C.  insecticide                          D.  lamps

5. When connecting lamp sockets to a lighting circuit, the shell should ALWAYS be con-              5.____
   nected to the white wire of the circuit to

   A.  balance the load on the system
   B.  reduce the possibility of accidental shock
   C.  eliminate blowing the fuse in case the socket becomes grounded
   D.  protect the circuit against reverse current

6. The MAIN purpose of periodic inspections and tests of electrical equipment is to                 6.____

   A.  encourage the workers to take better care of the equipment
   B.  familiarize the workers with the equipment
   C.  keep the workers busy during otherwise slack periods
   D.  discover minor faults before they develop into major faults

7. The current rating of the fuse to use in a lighting circuit is determined by the                 7.____

   A.  connected load                       B.  line voltage
   C.  capacity of the wiring               D.  rating of the switch

8. Artificial respiration after a severe electric shock is ALWAYS necessary when the shock          8.____
   results in

   A.  unconsciousness                      B.  stoppage of breathing
   C.  bleeding                             D.  a burn

9. If you find a co-worker lying unconscious across an electric wire, the FIRST thing you should do is

    A.  get him off the wire
    B.  call the foreman
    C.  get a doctor
    D.  shut off the power

9.____

10. A solenoid valve is actuated by

    A.  air pressure
    B.  electric current
    C.  temperature change
    D.  light rays

10.____

11.

11.____

The electrician's bit is indicated by the number

    A.  1        B.  2        C.  3        D.  4

12. BX is a designation for a type of

    A.  flexible armored electric cable
    B.  flexible gas line
    C.  rigid conduit
    D.  electrical insulation

12.____

13. *WYE-WYE* and *DELTA-WYE* are two

    A.  types of DC motor windings
    B.  arrangements of 3-phase transformer connections
    C.  types of electrical splices
    D.  shapes of commutator bars

13.____

14. When joining electric wires together in a fixture box, the BEST thing to use are wire

    A.  connectors
    B.  couplings
    C.  clamps
    D.  bolts

14.____

15. If the name plate of a motor indicates that it is a split phase motor, it is LIKELY that this motor 15.____

    A. is a universal motor
    B. operates on DC only
    C. operates on AC only
    D. operates either on DC at full power or on AC at reduced power

16. Rigid steel conduit used for the protection of electrical wiring is GENERALLY either galvanized or enameled both inside and out in order to 16.____

    A. prevent damage to the wire insulation
    B. make threading of the conduit easier
    C. prevent corrosion of the conduit
    D. make the conduit easier to handle

17. If a test lamp does not light when placed in series with a fuse and an appropriate battery, it is a GOOD indication that the fuse 17.____

    A. is open-circuited
    B. is short-circuited
    C. is in operating condition
    D. has zero resistance

18. The process of removing the insulation from a wire is called 18.____

    A. braiding    B. skinning    C. sweating    D. tinning

19. A 10-to-1 step-down transformer has an input of 1 ampere at 120 volts AC. If the losses are negligible, the output of the transformer is _____ volts. 19.____

    A. 1 ampere at 12    B. .1 ampere at 1200
    C. 10 amperes at 12    D. 10 amperes at 120

20. In city schools, wiring for motors or lighting is _____ volt, _____. 20.____

    A. 208-220; 4 wire, 60 cycle
    B. 240-110; 3 wire, 4 phase
    C. 120-208; 3 phase, 4 wire
    D. 160-210; 4 phase, 3 wire

21. When using a voltmeter in testing an electric circuit, the voltmeter should be connected 21.____

    A. across the circuit
    B. in series with the circuit
    C. in parallel or series with the circuit
    D. in series with the active element

22. A kilowatt is _____ watts. 22.____

    A. 500    B. 2,000    C. 1,500    D. 1,000

23. Of the following classifications, the one which pertains to fires in electrical equipment is Class 23.____

    A. A    B. B    C. C    D. D

24. The lighting systems in public buildings usually operate MOST NEARLY on _____ volts.  24.____
    A. 6              B. 24              C. 115              D. 220

25. A type of portable tool used to bend electrical conduit is called a                25.____
    A. helve          B. newel           C. spandrel        D. hickey

─────────

# KEY (CORRECT ANSWERS)

| | | | | |
|---|---|---|---|---|
| 1. | B | | 11. | C |
| 2. | B | | 12. | A |
| 3. | D | | 13. | B |
| 4. | D | | 14. | A |
| 5. | B | | 15. | C |
| 6. | D | | 16. | C |
| 7. | C | | 17. | A |
| 8. | B | | 18. | B |
| 9. | D | | 19. | C |
| 10. | B | | 20. | B |

21. A
22. D
23. C
24. C
25. D

─────────

# TEST 6

DIRECTIONS:  Each question or incomplete statement is followed by several suggested answers or completions. Select the one that BEST answers the question or completes the statement. *PRINT THE LETTER OF THE CORRECT ANSWER IN THE SPACE AT THE RIGHT.*

1.  In a 4-wire, 3-phase electrical supply system, the voltage between one phase and ground used for the lighting load is MOST NEARLY

    A.  440        B.  230        C.  208        D.  115

1._____

2.  Of the following, the one that takes the place of a fuse in an electrical circuit is a

    A.  transformer              B.  circuit breaker
    C.  condenser               D.  knife switch

2._____

3.  Escutcheons are USUALLY located

    A.  on switch plates
    B.  on electrical outlets
    C.  around pipes, to cover pipe sleeve openings
    D.  around armored electric cable going into a gem box

3._____

4.  It is ADVISABLE to remove broken bulbs from light sockets with

    A.  a wooden or hard rubber wedge
    B.  pliers
    C.  a hammer and chisel
    D.  a fuse puller

4._____

5.  A 3-ohm resistor placed across a 12-volt battery will dissipate _____ watts.

    A.  3        B.  4        C.  12        D.  48

5._____

6.  Instead of using fuses, modern electric wiring uses

    A.  quick switches          B.  circuit breakers
    C.  fusible links            D.  lag blocks

6._____

7.  In order to reverse the direction of rotation of a series motor, the

    A.  connections to the armature should be reversed
    B.  connections to both the armature and the series field should be reversed
    C.  connections of the motor to the power lines should be reversed
    D.  series field should be placed in shunt with the armature

7._____

8.  The BEST flux to use when soldering copper wires in an electric circuit is

    A.  sal ammoniac          B.  zinc chloride
    C.  rosin                D.  borax

8._____

9.  A megger is an instrument used to measure

    A.  capacitance           B.  insulation resistance
    C.  power              D.  illumination levels

9._____

10. An electrical drawing is drawn to a scale of 1/4" = 1'.    10.____
    If a length of conduit on the drawing measures 7 3/8", the actual length of the conduit,
    in feet, is MOST NEARLY

    A. 7.5'          B. 15.5'          C. 22.5'          D. 29.5'

11. Standard 120-volt plug-type fuses are GENERALLY rated in    11.____

    A. farads        B. ohms           C. watts          D. amperes

12. Standard 120-volt electric light bulbs are GENERALLY rated in    12.____

    A. farads        B. ohms           C. watts          D. amperes

13. Of the following colors of electrical conductor coverings, the one which indicates a con-    13.____
    ductor used SOLELY for grounding portable or fixed electrical equipment is

    A. blue          B. green          C. red            D. black

14. A device that operates to vary the resistance of an electrical circuit is USUALLY part of a    14.____
    _____ pressuretrol.

    A. high-limit                       B. low-limit
    C. manual-reset                     D. modulating

15. The type of screwdriver SPECIALLY made to be used in tight spots is the    15.____

    A. Phillips                         B. offset
    C. square shank                     D. truss

16. On a plan, the symbol shown at the right USUALLY represents a(n)    16.____
    A. duplex receptacle
    B. electric switch
    C. ceiling outlet
    D. pull box

17. Electric power is measured in    17.____

    A. volts         B. amperes        C. watts          D. ohms

18. Of the following sizes of copper conductors, the one which has the LEAST current-carry-    18.____
    ing capacity is _____ AWG.

    A. 000           B. 0              C. 8              D. 12

19. When excess current flows, a circuit breaker is opened directly by the action of a    19.____

    A. condenser                        B. transistor
    C. relay                            D. solenoid

20. Conduit is used in electrical wiring in order to the wires.    20.____

    A. waterproof                       B. color code
    C. protect                          D. insulate

# KEY (CORRECT ANSWERS)

| | | | | |
|---|---|---|---|---|
| 1. | D | – | 11. | D |
| 2. | B | | 12. | C |
| 3. | D | | 13. | B |
| 4. | A | | 14. | D |
| 5. | B | | 15. | B |
| 6. | B | | 16. | C |
| 7. | A | | 17. | C |
| 8. | C | | 18. | D |
| 9. | B | | 19. | D |
| 10. | D | | 20. | C |

# EXAMINATION SECTION
## TEST 1

DIRECTIONS: Each question or incomplete statement is followed by several suggested answers or completions. Select the one that BEST answers the question or completes the statement. *PRINT THE LETTER OF THE CORRECT ANSWER IN THE SPACE AT THE RIGHT.*

1. If a nichrome wire 2 meters long has a resistance of 10 ohms, the resistance of another nichrome wire 1 meter long and with a cross-sectional area half that of the longer wire is, in ohms,

    A.  5        B.  10        C.  20        D.  40

1.____

2. Two nichrome wires of exactly the same composition have the same weight, but one is 5 times as long as the other. If the resistance of the shorter wire is R, the resistance of the other is

    A.  R        B.  5R        C.  25R        D.  50R

2.____

3. A magnet pole has a strength of 400 units.
The magnetic field intensity in air due to this pole and at a distance 4 cm from this pole is _____ oersteds.

    A.  25        B.  50        C.  100        D.  $25\pi$

3.____

4. The number of revolutions per minute that a 6-pole alternator must make to produce a frequency of 60 cycles/sec is

    A.  1080        B.  1200        C.  2160        D.  21,600

4.____

5. A voltmeter having a full scale deflection of 10 volts has an internal resistance of 1000 ohms.
To convert this instrument to a voltmeter having a full scale deflection of 300 volts requires, in ohms, a multiplier of

    A.  3000        B.  6000        C.  9000        D.  12,000

5.____

6. Which one of the following scientists is NOT directly connected with the invention and development of the transistor?

    A.  John Bardeen        B.  William B. Shockley
    C.  Polykarp Kusch        D.  Walter H. Brattain

6.____

7. If there is a current of 0.1 ampere through a lamp for 100 seconds, the number of coulombs passing through in that time is

    A.  0.1        B.  1        C.  10        D.  100

7.____

8. If the core of an electromagnet is made of 2 pieces of iron, each running the full length of the electromagnet, when a direct current is sent through the coil, the 2 core pieces will

    A.  attract each other
    B.  repel each other
    C.  attract and repel alternately
    D.  have no effect on each other

8.____

9. If a 25-watt, 120-volt lamp and a 100-watt, 12-volt lamp are connected in a series to a 120-volt source,

    A. both lamps light normally
    B. neither lamp lights
    C. the 100-watt lamp is brighter
    D. the 25-watt lamp is brighter

9._____

10. A 30-watt, 120-volt resistor is connected to a 120-volt, 60-cycle source. The maximum current flow in the lamp, in amperes, is APPROXIMATELY

    A. 0.18    B. 0.25    C. 0.35    D. 0.4

10._____

11. A 0-20 milliampere meter has a resistance of 20 ohms. To convert this meter to a voltmeter with a range of 0-10 volts, one should connect a resistance of APPROXIMATELY _____ ohms in _____.

    A. 200; series    B. 200; parallel
    C. 500; series    D. 500; parallel

11._____

12. The current flow through a galvanometer is $10^{-5}$ milliamperes and produces a deflection of 1 scale division. If the resistance of the moving coil is 200 ohms, the voltage across the coil, in volts, is

    A. $2 \times 10^{-3}$    B. $5 \times 10^{-10}$    C. $5 \times 10^{-5}$    D. $2 \times 10^{-6}$

12._____

13. A capacitor using a dielectric whose coefficient is 5 has a capacitance of A. An identical capacitor using a dielectric whose coefficient is 20 will have a capacitance equal to

    A. 2A    B. 4A    C. 10A    D. 100A

13._____

14. When resonance occurs in a circuit supplied with an alternating voltage, the

    A. impedance equals zero
    B. inductance equals the reciprocal of the capacitance
    C. capacitance equals the inductance
    D. inductive reactance equals the capacitive reactance

14._____

15. An electric heating coil of 6 ohms resistance is connected across a 120-volt line for 10 minutes. The energy liberated, in joules, in this period of time equals

    A. $7.2 \times 10^3$    B. $14.4 \times 10^5$
    C. $25.8 \times 10^4$    D. $43.2 \times 10^4$

15._____

16. If a triode has its plate current increased 20 milliamperes when the plate voltage is increased from 50 to 90 volts and the plate current is also increased 20 milliamperes when the grid potential changes 4 volts, the amplification factor of the tube is

    A. 1.8    B. 5.0    C. 10.0    D. 40.0

16._____

17. A charge of 30 coulombs passes through a wire in 3 seconds. The current flow in this wire, in amperes, equals

    A. 3.3    B. 10    C. 30    D. 90

17._____

18. The heat developed by 5 amperes flowing through a resistance of 4 ohms is     18._____

    A.   20 calories                 B.   24 calories per second

    C.   100 calories               D.   4.8 calories per degree

19. 1 e.s.u. of potential difference equals     19._____

    A.   1 volt                      B.   300 joules/coulomb

    C.   $10^8$ e.m.u. of potential     D.   4.187 volts

20. Two electrical condensers having capacitances of 6 and 12 microfarads, respectively, are     20._____
connected in series. The TOTAL capacitance, in microfarads, of this combination is

    A.   2            B.   4            C.   9            D.   18

21. The voltage induced in a coil with an inductance of 0.25 henries when the current     21._____
decreased uniformly from 2 amperes to zero amperes in 1/16 second is

    A.   4            B.   8            C.   16          D.   24

22. A transformer placed on DC is LIKELY to burn out because of the absence of     22._____

    A.   a fuse                   B.   voltage regulation

    C.   hysteresis              D.   inductive reactance

23. If the effective AC voltage of a given circuit is 100, the maximum voltage is CLOSEST to     23._____
which one of the following?

    A.   0            B.   71          C.   141        D.   173

24. One milliampere produces full scale deflection in a galvanometer whose internal resis-     24._____
tance is 50 ohms.
To convert this instrument into an ammeter whose full scale deflection is 1 amp, it
should be shunted with a resistance, in ohms, CLOSEST to which one of the following?

    A.   0.005         B.   0.05        C.   0.5         D.   5.0

25. The results of the Millikan oil drop experiment lead to the conclusion that     25._____

    A.   electric charges are negative

    B.   electric charges are due to a transfer of electrons

    C.   there is a fundamental unit of charge

    D.   there are no isolated magnetic poles

26. A 60-watt, 120-volt incandescent lamp has a resistance, in ohms, of     26._____

    A.   0.5         B.   2.0         C.   60         D.   240

27. A 0-5 amp ammeter reads full scale when its 2-ohm movable coil has a voltage of 0.01     27._____
applied across it.
The shunt has a resistance, in ohms, CLOSEST to which one of the following?

    A.   0.001        B.   0.002       C.   250        D.   500

28. The heat in kilocalories (1 kilocalorie = 4200 joules) developed by a 60 watt lamp in one     28._____
hour is APPROXIMATELY

    A.   36         B.   50         C.   60         D.   95

29. Assume that a circuit consisting of a coil and a capacitor is adjusted to give resonance. If some turns are removed from the coil, then resonance can be restored by    29._____

    A. increasing the frequency
    B. decreasing the capacitance
    C. decreasing the frequency
    D. decreasing the inductance

30. A series AC circuit contains a resistance of 40 ohms, an inductive reactance of 100 ohms, and a capacitive reactance of 70 ohms.    30._____
    The impedance of this circuit is, in ohms,

    A. 50          B. 110          C. 150          D. 210

31. A series AC circuit contains a 20-ohm resistance, a 40-ohm resistance, a 60-ohm inductive reactance, and an 80-ohm capacitive reactance.    31._____
    The GREATEST amount of heat per second produced by any of these will be produced by the

    A. 20-ohm resistance          B. 40-ohm resistance
    C. 60-ohm reactance           D. 80-ohm reactance

32. If a sheet of glass is slipped between the plates of an air capacitor, the capacitance of the combination    32._____

    A. drops to zero
    B. is reduced to approximately one-half of the original value
    C. increases
    D. has a value which depends on the charge of the capacitor

33. The resistance of a piece of wire is 16 ohms.    33._____
    The resistance, in ohms, of a piece of the same wire twice as long and twice the diameter is

    A. 8          B. 16          C. 32          D. 64

34. A circuit containing resistance, capacitance, and inductance is in resonance when supplied with an alternating current of a given frequency.    34._____
    An increase in the frequency of this current will

    A. decrease the inductive reactance
    B. increase the capacitive reactance
    C. increase the total current in the circuit
    D. decrease the impedance

35. The heat developed by a 5 ampere current flowing through a resistance of 4 ohms is    35._____

    A. 20 calories          B. 24 calories/sec
    C. 100 calories         D. 4.8 calories per degree

36. A capacitor stores 50 joules of energy when charged by a 5000 volt source.    36._____
    The capacitance of the capacitor, in microfarads, is

    A. .02          B. .04          C. 2.0          D. 4.0

37. The amplification factor of a triode is represented BEST by which one of the following expressions?
    The

    A. change in grid voltage divided by the change in filament voltage
    B. plate current
    C. change in plate voltage divided by the change in grid voltage needed to produce that change in plate current
    D. change in plate voltage divided by the change in plate current needed to produce that change in grid voltage

    37._____

38. Kirchhoff's Laws with regard to the current in an electrical circuit states that

    A. current is directly proportional to voltage
    B. the algebraic sum of the currents at a junction equals zero
    C. current is inversely proportional to electrical resistance
    D. the total current in a parallel circuit equals the sum of the currents in the individual parallel branches

    38._____

39. A Fleming valve or diode performs which one of the following functions?

    A. Converts rectified DC to AC
    B. Converts AC to half-wave rectified DC
    C. Converts AC to smooth DC
    D. Steps up low voltage AC to high voltage AC

    39._____

40. A capacitor discharges at a certain frequency through a circuit containing an inductance. If the capacitance is multiplied by four, the oscillation frequency is multiplied by

    A. $\dfrac{1}{4}$      B. $\dfrac{1}{2}$      C. 2      D. 4

    40._____

41. A coil of 100 turns is wound on an iron core. The coil is connected to an AC source. Suitable connections are made to display applied voltage and circuit current on an oscilloscope.
    It is found that the current _____ the voltage by _____.

    A. leads; 90°                 B. lags behind; 90°
    C. leads; an acute angle      D. lags behind; an acute angle

    41._____

42. The mixing of an audio frequency electric current with a radio frequency carrier in a broadcasting station is known as

    A. oscillation                B. modulation
    C. amplification            D. rectification

    42._____

43. An electron is accelerated through a potential difference of 20,000 volts.
    Its gain in kinetic energy is 20,000

    A. volts                    B. joules
    C. electron volts          D. ergs

    43._____

44. The radius of the circular path of a charged particle moving at right angles to a uniform magnetic field is DIRECTLY proportional to the

    A. momentum of the particle
    B. flux density
    C. charge on the particle
    D. wavelength of its radiation

44._____

45. The direction of an induced current is always such that the magnetic field belonging to it tends to oppose the change in the strength of the magnetic field belonging to the primary current.
This law was FIRST enunciated by

    A. Ampere        B. Faraday        C. Henry        D. Lenz

45._____

46. A split ring commutator will be found on a

    A. synchronous motor
    B. AC generator
    C. DC motor
    D. induction-repulsion type of motor

46._____

47. A ballistic galvanometer is used MAINLY to measure which one of the following?

    A. Electric charge        B. Electric current
    C. EMF                D. Resistance

47._____

48. If a calibrated oscilloscope shows a sinusoidal current having a peak to peak value of 2.0 amperes, the effective value of the current as measured by an ammeter and expressed in amperes would be

    A. 0.50        B. 0.71        C. 1.0        D. 2.0

48._____

49. Of the following, the pair of functions of a vacuum tube that are MOST closely allied are

    A. rectification and amplification
    B. oscillation and rectification
    C. amplification and detection
    D. detection and rectification

49._____

50. If a thin sheet of metal is placed halfway between the two plates of a parallel-plate, air-dielectric capacitor, the capacitance is

    A. quadrupled
    B. doubled
    C. decreased to 1/2 of the original value
    D. decreased to 1/4

50._____

# KEY (CORRECT ANSWERS)

| | | | | | | | | | |
|---|---|---|---|---|---|---|---|---|---|
| 1. | B | 11. | C | 21. | B | 31. | B | 41. | D |
| 2. | C | 12. | D | 22. | D | 32. | C | 42. | B |
| 3. | A | 13. | B | 23. | C | 33. | A | 43. | C |
| 4. | B | 14. | D | 24. | B | 34. | B | 44. | A |
| 5. | C | 15. | B | 25. | C | 35. | B | 45. | D |
| 6. | C | 16. | C | 26. | D | 36. | D | 46. | C |
| 7. | C | 17. | B | 27. | B | 37. | C | 47. | A |
| 8. | B | 18. | B | 28. | B | 38. | B | 48. | B |
| 9. | D | 19. | B | 29. | A | 39. | B | 49. | D |
| 10. | C | 20. | B | 30. | A | 40. | B | 50. | C |

# TEST 2

DIRECTIONS: Each question or incomplete statement is followed by several suggested answers or completions. Select the one that BEST answers the question or completes the statement. *PRINT THE LETTER OF THE CORRECT ANSWER IN THE SPACE AT THE RIGHT.*

1. If a 1 mfd capacitor and a 2 mfd capacitor are connected in series across a 120-volt source, the potential difference across the 1 mfd capacitor is _____ volts.      1.____

    A.  30           B.  40           C.  60           D.  80

2. If a battery having an EMF of 6 volts and internal resistance of 0.6 ohms is supplying a current of 0.5 amperes, the terminal voltage is _____ volts.      2.____

    A.  5.4           B.  5.5           C.  5.6           D.  5.7

3. A capacitor C and inductor L are connected in series across an AC source. As the value of C is increased, the current in the circuit      3.____

    A.  increases                      B.  decreases
    C.  remains constant        D.  may increase or decrease

4. As the frequency of a generator is decreased, the impedance of a circuit      4.____

    A.  increases
    B.  decreases
    C.  may increase or decrease
    D.  does not change

5. It is desired to determine the direction of electron flow in a vertical conductor carrying direct current.      5.____
This may be done with the aid of a compass placed

    A.  to the right of the wire
    B.  to the left of the wire
    C.  behind the wire
    D.  in any of the above listed positions

6. If the current flow in a circular coil consisting of a single turn of wire of 1 cm radius is 2 abamperes, it will produce a magnetic field intensity at the center of the coil equal, in oersteds, to      6.____

    A.  $\pi$           B.  $2\pi$           C.  $4\pi$           D.  $8\pi$

7. Ampere's Law is concerned with      7.____

    A.  the force on a wire carrying a current in a magnetic field
    B.  electrochemical equivalents
    C.  rms values
    D.  unit magnetic poles

8. A 60-watt, 120-volt and a 40-watt, 120-volt lamp are joined in series and connected to a 120-volt line.      8.____
The current flow in the circuit, in amperes, is

    A.  more than 0.5          B.  between 0.5 and 0.3
    C.  0.2                    D.  less than 0.2

9. The function of the grid in a three element vacuum tube is to                                    9.____

    A.  aid electron flow at reduced cathode temperatures
    B.  reduce the loss of heat from the cathode
    C.  prevent secondary emission of electrons from the plate
    D.  control the electron flow to the plate

10. Three capacitors of 4 mfd, 10 mfd, and 20 mfd are connected in parallel.            10.____
The equivalent capacitance of this group equals, in mfd,

    A.  2.5         B.  17         C.  34         D.  800

11. Two 60-watt, 120-volt heaters are connected in series on a 120-volt DC line. The power     11.____
consumption is now X times as great as it would be if they were connected in parallel.
Assuming no change in resistance, X would be

    A.  1/4         B.  1/2         C.  2         D.  4

12. The current in an alternating current circuit is equal to the voltage divided by the          12.____

    A.  impedance                B.  capacitance
    C.  reluctance               D.  inductance

13. The core of a transformer is laminated largely for the purpose of                          13.____

    A.  reducing eddy currents
    B.  aiding in heat dissipation
    C.  increasing self-inductance
    D.  increasing impedance

14. Kirchhoff's First Law is really a restatement of                                          14.____

    A.  Lenz' Law
    B.  Ohm's Law
    C.  Faraday's Law of Electrolysis
    D.  Law of Conservation of Energy

15. A condenser designed for use across a 220-volt AC line should have a peak inverse volt-    15.____
age rating of AT LEAST _____ volts.

    A.  110         B.  220         C.  250         D.  325

16. The voltage between the cathode and target of an x-ray tube is V volts.                    16.____
If e is the charge on the electron in e.s.u., then Ve has the dimensions of

    A.  work         B.  current         C.  force         D.  momentum

17. A transformer with 50 turns on the primary and 100 turns on the secondary is connected    17.____
to a 6-volt battery.
The voltage on the secondary will be

    A.  zero
    B.  equal to that on the primary
    C.  twice the voltage on the primary
    D.  half the voltage on the primary

18. When a 60 cycle source of e.m.f. is connected between the plate and the cathode of a diode, the current between the cathode and plate will

18.____

    A. reverse 60 times per second
    B. reverse 120 times per second
    C. flow continuously
    D. flow intermittently in the same direction

19. Inside a dry cell that is delivering current,

19.____

    A. electrons flow from + to -
    B. there is no resistance
    C. there is no current
    D. electrons flow from - to +

20. In a circuit containing an alternating source and a coil, increasing both the frequency of the source and the inductance of the coil (without changing the e.m.f.) will result in

20.____

    A. increased current
    B. decreased current
    C. same current
    D. increased or decreased current, depending on which factor is increased more

21. If the plate current of a triode electronic tube increases 10 milliamperes when the plate voltage is increased from 60 to 80 volts or when the grid potential changes 2 volts, the amplification factor of the tube is

21.____

    A. 5        B. 10        C. 20        D. 40

22. A series circuit with a capacitive reactance of 20 ohms, an inductive reactance of 50 ohms, and a resistance of 40 ohms has an overall impedance, in ohms, of

22.____

    A. 10        B. 50        C. 70        D. 110

23. Waves of 3 cm in length radiated by an electronic oscillator would have a frequency, in cycles/sec, of

23.____

    A. $10^6$        B. $10^8$        C. $10^{10}$        D. $10^{12}$

24. If a student, in finding the resistance of a lamp on a 120-volt line, places the voltmeter in series with the lamp and the ammeter in parallel with the lamp, the

24.____

    A. ammeter will burn out        B. voltmeter will burn out
    C. lamp will burn out        D. lamp may not light

25. If a 120-volt, 60-cycle source is connected to a circuit containing resistance, inductive reactance, and capacitive reactance, each of 16 ohms, the current in the circuit is _____ amperes.

25.____

    A. 5        B. 7.5        C. 15        D. 30

26. If a nail is attracted to an electromagnet carrying direct current, and the current is quickly reversed, the nail will

    A. fall to the ground
    B. be repelled by the electromagnet
    C. heat up
    D. still be attracted

26.____

27. The volt is NOT a unit of

    A. charge per unit time    B. e.m.f.
    C. work per unit charge    D. potential difference

27.____

28. The energy used to carry unit charge around an electrical circuit is measured by the

    A. current    B. potential difference
    C. power    D. resistance of the circuit

28.____

29. Two 1 mfd capacitors are connected in parallel and the combination is then charged. If the capacitance, charge, and potential of each capacitor are C, Q, and V, respectively, the corresponding three values for the combination is which one of the following?

    A. C/2, 2Q, V    B. 2C, 2Q, V
    C. 2C, Q, V    D. 2C, 2Q, V/2

29.____

30. The resonant frequency f of an alternating e.m.f. in a circuit containing in series an inductance L, a capacitance C, and a resistance R, is given by the formula f =

    A.  $2\pi\sqrt{LC}$    B.  $\frac{1}{2}\pi\sqrt{LC}$    C.  $\frac{1}{2\pi\sqrt{LC}}$    D.  $\frac{R}{2\pi\sqrt{LC}}$

30.____

31. In a series resonant circuit, the circuit impedance is ALWAYS

    A. equal to the inductive reactance
    B. greater than the capacitive reactance
    C. equal to the capacitive reactance
    D. equal to the resistance

31.____

32. Two resistances of 30 ohms and 20 ohms, respectively, are joined in parallel in an electric circuit.
The equivalent resistance, in ohms, of this parallel pair is

    A. 12    B. 25    C. 50    D. 600

32.____

33. A solenoid has an inductance of 0.32 henry.
Its reactance, in ohms, to an alternating current having a frequency of 1000 cycles/sec is

    A. 2010    B. 3125    C. 3200    D. 3310

33.____

34. If, with an impressed voltage of 240 volts and a current of 13 amp, a shunt-wound DC motor delivers 4 horsepower, its efficiency, in percent, is

    A. 80    B. 86    C. 90    D. 96

34.____

35. If the maximum value of an alternating voltage is 110, its value, in volts, at the 30° phase    35.____
is

    A.  55           B.  78           C.  155           D.  220

36. A coil of 2.5 henries inductance would resonate with a 1 microfarad capacitance at a fre-    36.____
quency, in cycles/sec, of

    A.  100         B.  1,000       C.  10,000      D.  100,000

37. When an alternating emf is supplied to a circuit consisting, in addition to the source, of    37.____
wiring a 40 watt lamp and an 80 mf capacitor, the voltage in the circuit

    A.   leads to current
    B.   lags behind the current
    C.   is in phase with the current
    D.   becomes and remains zero after a few minutes

38. Of the following, the one which is incorporated in a DC generator but NOT in an AC gen-    38.____
erator is the

    A.   slip rings                  B.   commutator
    C.   series field               D.   permanent magnets

39. When a capacitor C, an inductance L, and a resistance R are joined in series and an    39.____
alternating emf is supplied to the circuit, the resonant frequency of this circuit can be
decreased by doing which one of the following?

    A.   Increasing L             B.   Decreasing R
    C.   Decreasing C           D.   Decreasing L

40. Three 6 mfd capacitors are connected in parallel across a 120-volt AC line.    40.____
The equivalent capacitance, in mfd, of this circuit is

    A.  2            B.  6            C.  18           D.  20

41. Assume that two capacitors, one of 3 microfarad capacitance and the other of 6 micro-    41.____
farad capacitance, are connected in series and charged to a difference of potential of
120 volts.
The potential difference, in volts, across the 3 microfarad capacitor is

    A.  40          B.  80          C.  180          D.  360

42. Three resistors are connected to form the sides of a triangle ABC. The resistance of side    42.____
AB is 40 ohms, of side BC 60 ohms, and of side CA 100 ohms.
The effective resistance between points A and B, in ohms, is

    A.  32          B.  50          C.  64          D.  200

43. When a current of 2 amperes flows through a conductor of 2 ohms resistance for 3 sec-    43.____
onds, the heat produced, in joules, is

    A.  12          B.  24          C.  36          D.  72

44. A length of wire, diameter 2 mils, has a resistance of 6 ohms.                    44._____
The same length of wire of the same material having a diameter of 4 mils has a resistance, in ohms, of

    A.  1.5        B.  3        C.  12        D.  24

45. The generalization that the algebraic sum of the currents at a junction in a circuit equals    45._____
zero was postulated by

    A.  Ohm        B.  Kirchhoff        C.  Onnes        D.  Seebeck

46. It is desired to charge an electroscope negatively by induction.                    46._____
One of the steps that must be performed is to

    A.  use a negatively charged rod
    B.  remove positive charges
    C.  remove electrons
    D.  ground the electroscope

47. A series AC circuit contains an inductance L, a capacitance C, and a resistor R.    47._____
The impedance of this circuit equals

    A.  $R^2 + X_L + X_C$                 B.  $\sqrt{R^2 + (X_L - X_C)^2}$

    C.  $R^2 + \sqrt{X_L - X_C}$            D.  $R^2 - X_L - X^2_C$

48. In a selenium rectifier, current flow practically ceases when the                   48._____

    A.  selenium becomes negative
    B.  selenium becomes positive
    C.  accompanying alloy becomes negative
    D.  applied voltage exceeds the critical value

49. An alternating current generator having 4 poles rotates at 60 revolutions per second.  49._____
The frequency of the current produced, in cycles per second, is

    A.  60        B.  15        C.  120        D.  240

50. If an AC circuit contains resistance only, then current                             50._____

    A.  and voltage are in phase
    B.  lags by 45°
    C.  leads by 90°
    D.  lags by 45° and voltage leads by 45°

# KEY (CORRECT ANSWERS)

| | | | | |
|---|---|---|---|---|
| 1. D | 11. A | 21. B | 31. D | 41. B |
| 2. D | 12. A | 22. B | 32. A | 42. A |
| 3. D | 13. A | 23. C | 33. A | 43. B |
| 4. C | 14. D | 24. D | 34. D | 44. A |
| 5. D | 15. D | 25. B | 35. A | 45. B |
| 6. C | 16. A | 26. D | 36. A | 46. D |
| 7. A | 17. A | 27. A | 37. B | 47. B |
| 8. C | 18. D | 28. B | 38. B | 48. A |
| 9. D | 19. A | 29. B | 39. A | 49. C |
| 10. C | 20. B | 30. C | 40. C | 50. A |

# EXAMINATION SECTION
## TEST 1

DIRECTIONS: Each question or incomplete statement is followed by several suggested answers or completions. Select the one that BEST answers the question or completes the statement. *PRINT THE LETTER OF THE CORRECT ANSWER IN THE SPACE AT THE RIGHT.*

1. Which of the following capacitors could be damaged by a reversal in polarity? A(n) _____ capacitor.

    A. ceramic        B. paper        C. mica
    D. electrolytic     E. vacuum

1.____

2. If the current through a resistor is 6 amperes and the voltage drop across it is 100 volts, what is the approximate value of the resistor in ohm(s)?

    A. 1660    B. 166    C. 16.6    D. 1.66    E. 0.0166

2.____

3. What is the CORRECT use for an arbor press?

    A. Bending sheet metal        B. Driving self-tapping screws
    C. Removing screws           D. Removing "C" rings
    E. Removing bearings from shafts

3.____

4. Which one of the following is a tensioning device in bulk-belt-type conveyor systems?
    _____ take-up.

    A. Spring         B. Power        C. Hydraulic
    D. Fluid coupled    E. Flexible coupled

4.____

5. When $X_L = X_C$ in a series circuit, what condition exists?

    A. The circuit impedance is increasing
    B. The circuit is at resonant frequency
    C. The circuit current is minimum
    D. The circuit has no e.m.f. at this time
    E. None of the above

5.____

6. Which of the following pieces of information is NOT normally found on a schematic diagram?

    A. Functional stage name      B. Supply voltages
    C. Part symbols           D. Part values
    E. Physical location of parts

6.____

7. When a single-phase induction motor drawing 24 amps at 120 VAC is reconnected to 240 VAC, what will be the amperage at 240 VAC? _____amps.

    A. 6    B. 8    C. 12    D. 24    E. 36

7.____

8. Which one of the following meters measures the SMALLEST current?      8.____

    A. Kilometer            B. Milliammeter         C. Microvoltmeter
    D. Millivoltmeter        E. Kilovoltmeter

9. If the current through a 1000-ohm resistor is 3 milliamperes, the voltage drop      9.____
across the resistor is _____ volt(s).

    A. 1         B. 2.5        C. 3         D. 30        E. 300

10. The normally closed contacts of a relay are open when its solenoid is energized
with VDC. The voltage at which the contacts re-close will be

    A. dependent upon the current through the contacts
    B. dependent upon the voltage applied to the contacts
    C. 24 VDC through the coil
    D. more than 24 VDC through the contacts
    E. less than 24 VDC through the coil

11. Electrical energy is converted to mechanical rotation by what component in the
electric motor?

    A. Armature          B. Commutator        C. Field
    D. Start windings       E. Stator

12. Ohm's Law expresses the basic relationship of

    A. current, voltage, and resistance
    B. current, voltage, and power
    C. current, power, and resistance
    D. resistance, impedance, and voltage
    E. resistance, power, and impedance

13. In parallel circuits, the voltage is *always*

    A. variable           B. constant          C. alternating
    D. fluctuating        E. sporadic

14. Which one of the following is used as a voltage divider?

    A. Rotary converter      B. Potentiometer      C. Relay
    D. Circuit breaker         E. Voltmeter

Question 15.

Question 15 is based on the following diagram.

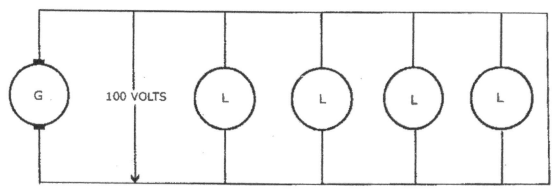

**CURRENT IN EACH LAMP 1/2 AMPERE**

15. What is the resistance of the entire circuit? _____ ohms.          15.____

    A. 15        B. 25        C. 35        D. 45        E. 50

16. Which one of the following tools is used to bring a bore to a specified          16.____
    tolerance?

    A. Tap              B. Reamer           C. Countersink
    D. Counterbore      E. Center drill

17. The primary function of a take-up pulley in a belt conveyor is to          17.____

    A. carry the belt on the return trip
    B. track the belt
    C. maintain the proper belt tension
    D. change the direction of the belt
    E. regulate the speed of the belt

Question 18.

Question 18 is based on the following diagram.

18. What is the name of the gears?          18.____

    A. Spur external        B. Spur internal        C. Helical
    D. Herringbone         D. Worm

Question 19.

Question 19 is based on the following diagram.

19.    The part labeled D is the                                                      19.____

     A.  sleeve           B.  thimble             C.  frame

     D.  anvil             E.  pindle

Question 20.

Question 20 is based on the following symbol.

20.    This symbol represents a _____ tube.                                        20.____

     A.  thyratron vacuum           B.  thyratron gas

     C.  variable-mu vacuum       D.  variable-mu gas

     E.  vacuum photo

21.    A diode can be substituted for which one of the following?                     21.____

     A.  Transformer         B.  Relay           C.  Rectifier

     D.  Condenser       E.  Rheostat

Question 22.

Question 22 is based on the following diagram.

22. The rate of amperes flowing in the circuit is:

    A. .03 1/3            B. .18            C. .24
    D. .30 1/3            E. .33 1/3

22._____

23. The firing point in a thyratron tube is *most usually* controlled by the

    A. cathode            B. grid            C. plate
    D. heater            E. envelope

23._____

Questions 24-25.

Questions 24 and 25 shall be answered in accordance with the diagram below.

24. With reference to the above diagram, the voltage difference between points c and f is, *most nearly,* in volts,

    A. 40        B. 20        C. 10        D. 5        E. 0

24._____

25. With reference to the above diagram, the current flowing through the resistance c d is, *most nearly,* in amperes,

    A. 10        B. 5        C. 4        D. 2        E. 1

25._____

# KEY (CORRECT ANSWERS)

| | | | | |
|---|---|---|---|---|
| 1. D | 6. E | 11. A | 16. B | 21. C |
| 2. C | 7. C | 12. A | 17. C | 22. E |
| 3. E | 8. B | 13. B | 18. A | 23. B |
| 4. A | 9. C | 14. B | 19. A | 24. E |
| 5. B | 10. E | 15. E | 20. B | 25. B |

———

# EXAMINATION SECTION
## TEST 1

DIRECTIONS: Each question or incomplete statement is followed by several suggested answers or completions. Select the one that BEST answers the question or completes the statement. *PRINT THE LETTER OF THE CORRECT ANSWER IN THE SPACE AT THE RIGHT.*

1. Two gears are meshed. The first gear has 20 teeth per inch and is rotating at 500 rpms. What is the speed of the second gear if it has 40 teeth per inch? _____ rpms.      1._____

    A. 500        B. 400        C. 250        D. 200

2. With two meshed gears, the first gear rotates at 100 rpms, the second gear rotates at 2000 rpms and has 10 teeth per inch.
The first gear has _____ number of teeth per inch.      2._____

    A. 200        B. 100        C. 50        D. 150

3. Two pulleys are connected. The first pulley has a diameter of 5 inches; the second pulley has a diameter of 15 inches and rotates at 25 rpms.
The speed of the first pulley is _____ rpms.      3._____

    A. 30        B. 75        C. 200        D. 400

4. Of two connected pulleys, the first has a radius of 10 inches and rotates at 50 rpms; the second rotates at 25 rpms.
The diameter of the second pulley is _____ inches.      4._____

    A. 40        B. 30        C. 20        D. 10

5. Two pulleys are connected. The first pulley rotates at 75 rpms; the second pulley rotates at 100 rpms and has a diameter of 9 inches.
The diameter of the first pulley is _____ inches.      5._____

    A. 10        B. 12        C. 15        D. 20

6. Of two connected pulleys, the first pulley has a radius of 12 inches and rotates at 60 rpms; the second pulley has a diameter of 16 inches.
The speed of the second pulley is _____ rpms.      6._____

    A. 1000        B. 1020        C. 1040        D. 1080

7. If $16_{10}$ were converted to base 2, 8, and 16, the results would be _____ base 2, _____ base 8, and _____ base 16, respectively.      7._____

    A. 10000; 20; 10        B. 1000; 2000; 20
    C. 20000; 200; 20        D. 2000; 100; 10

8. Converting $CAF_{16}$ to base 10 and base 8, the results would be _____ base 10 and _____ base 8, respectively.      8._____

    A. 2437; 2567        B. 3247; 6257
    C. 4327; 5267        D. 3427; 2657

9. Converting $101011001_2$ to base 8, 10, and 16, the results would be _____ base 8, _____ base 10, and _____ base 16, respectively.          9._____

    A.  135; 45; 59                                 B.  567; 435; 259
    C.  315; 245; 135                              D.  531; 345; 159

10. If $136_8$ were converted to base 2, 10, and 16, the results would be _____ base 2, _____ base 10, and _____ base 16, respectively.          10._____

    A.  001011110; 94, 5E                        B.  010100110; 92; 10E
    C.  00100000; 90; 15E                         D.  011001110; 96; 20E

11. It may be correctly stated that 1000 picofarads are equal to _____ microfarads.          11._____

    A.  .0001           B.  .001           C.  .01           D.  .1

12. If 5 megohms were converted to kohms, the result would be _____ kohms.          12._____

    A.  1000           B.  2000           C.  4000           D.  5000

13. 1 nanohenry would convert to _____ millihenries.          13._____

    A.  .001           B.  .0001           C.  .00001           D.  .0000001

14. If 7 milliamps were converted to microamps, the answer would be _____ microamps.          14._____

    A.  7000           B.  700           C.  70           D.  7

15. If two resistors are in parallel and are 100 ohms each, the total resistance is          15._____

    A.  100           B.  150           C.  50           D.  10

16. In reference to the circuit in Question 15, if the first resistor has 25 volts DC, (VDC) across it, the second resistor also has 25 VDC across it, and there are no other components in the circuit except for the power source, the total circuit voltage is _____ VDC.          16._____

    A.  25           B.  50           C.  250           D.  500

17. In reference to the circuit in Question 15, if the first resistor has 1 amp on it, and the second resistor also has 1 amp on it, the total circuit amperage is _____ amps.          17._____

    A.  1           B.  2           C.  3           D.  4

18. If two resistors are in series and are 100 ohms each, the total resistance is          18._____

    A.  50           B.  100           C.  150           D.  200

19. In reference to the circuit in Question 18, if the first resistor has 25 VDC across it and the second resistor also has 25 VDC across it, the total circuit voltage is          19._____

    A.  50           B.  100           C.  200           D.  500

20. In reference to the circuit in Question 18, if the first resistor has 1 amp across it and the second resistor also has 1 amp on it, the total circuit amperage is          20._____

    A.  1           B.  5           C.  10           D.  15

21. Where two resistors are in parallel, one is 100 ohms and the other is 300 ohms. The total resistance is _____ ohms.

    A. 25          B. 35          C. 55          D. 75

21._____

22. Three resistors in series are 25 ohms, 50 ohms, and 75 ohms, respectively. The total resistance is _____ ohms.

    A. 25          B. 50          C. 100          D. 150

22._____

23. Two inductors are in parallel; the first is 50 henries and the second is also 50 henries. The total inductance is _____ henries.

    A. 25          B. 50          C. 55          D. 60

23._____

24. Two inductors are in series and the first is 50 henries; the second is 50 henries. The total inductance is _____ henries.

    A. 25          B. 50          C. 75          D. 100

24._____

25. Where two inductors are in parallel, the first is 100 henries and the second is 200 henries. The total inductance is _____ henries.

    A. 50          B. 75          C. 65          D. 100

25._____

---

# KEY (CORRECT ANSWERS)

| | | | | |
|---|---|---|---|---|
| 1. C | 6. D | 11. B | 16. A | 21. D |
| 2. A | 7. A | 12. D | 17. B | 22. D |
| 3. B | 8. B | 13. D | 18. D | 23. A |
| 4. A | 9. D | 14. A | 19. A | 24. D |
| 5. B | 10. A | 15. C | 20. A | 25. B |

# TEST 2

DIRECTIONS: Each question or incomplete statement is followed by several suggested answers or completions. Select the one that BEST answers the question or completes the statement. *PRINT THE LETTER OF THE CORRECT ANSWER IN THE SPACE AT THE RIGHT.*

1. Two inductors are in series; the first inductor is 100 henries and the second is 200 henries.
   The total inductance is _____ henries.

   A. 200          B. 300          C. 400          D. 500

   1.____

2. Two capacitors are in parallel; each capacitor is 30 farads.
   The total capacitance is _____ farads.

   A. 60          B. 80          C. 100          D. 200

   2.____

3. Two capacitors are in series; each capacitor is 30 farads. The total capacitance is _____ farads.

   A. 10          B. 15          C. 20          D. 25

   3.____

4. Two capacitors are in parallel; the first is 50 farads and the second is 100 farads.
   The total capacitance is _____ farads.

   A. 50          B. 100          C. 125          D. 150

   4.____

5. Two capacitors are in series; the first is 50 farads and the second is 100 farads.
   The total capacitance is _____ farads.

   A. 33.333          B. 49.999          C. 13.333          D. 25.555

   5.____

6. A resistor's color codes are orange, blue, yellow, and gold, in that order.
   The value of the resistor is _____ kohms ± _____ %.

   A. 200; 2          B. 300; 4          C. 360; 5          D. 400; 7

   6.____

7. If a resistors color codes are red, black, and blue, the value of this resistor is _____ megohms ± _____ %.

   A. 20; 20          B. 40; 80          C. 30; 30          D. 50; 50

   7.____

8. If a resistor's color codes are gray, green, black, and silver, the resistor's value is _____ ohms ± _____ %.

   A. 55; 5          B. 75; 15          C. 85; 10          D. 100; 25

   8.____

9. One complete cycle of a sinewave takes 1000 microseconds. Its frequency is _____ hertz.

   A. 500          B. 1000          C. 2000          D. 5000

   9.____

10. If one complete cycle of a squarewave takes 5 microseconds, its frequency is _____ khertz.

    A. 200          B. 500          C. 700          D. 1000

    10.____

11. What is the PRT (pulse repetition time) of a 50 hertz (hz) sinewave?     11.____
    _____ milliseconds.

    A.  10          B.  20          C.  40          D.  60

12. The PRT of a 20 khz sawtooth signal is _____ megahertz.                12.____

    A.  50          B.  100         C.  200         D.  500

13. If a resistor measures 10 volts and 2 amps across it, the resistance is _____ ohms.   13.____

    A.  0           B.  2           C.  5           D.  10

14. If a 30 ohm resistor measures 10 volts, the power consumed by the resistor is _____   14.____
    watts.

    A.  3000        B.  5000        C.  6500        D.  7000

15. If a 50 ohm resistor measures 4 amps across, the power consumed by it is _____ watts.  15.____

    A.  200         B.  400         C.  600         D.  800

16. If a 100 ohm resistor measures 25 volts across, the current on it is _____ amps.       16.____

    A.  .15         B.  .25         C.  .55         D.  .65


Questions 17-23.

DIRECTIONS:    Questions 17 through 23 are to be answered on the basis of the following dia-
               gram.

SERIES CIRCUIT

$V_{supply} = V_A + V_B + V_C$
$I_{total} = I_A = I_B = I_C$

PARALLEL CIRCUIT

$V_{supply} = V_A = V_B = V_C$
$I_{total} = I_A + I_B + I_C$

17. In the series circuit above, if Vsupply = 100 VDC, resistor A is 10 ohms, resistor B is 50   17.____
    ohms, and resistor C is 5 ohms, the total circuit current is
    _____ amps.

    A.  1.538       B.  1.267       C.  1.358       D.  1.823

18. In the series circuit shown above, the current across each individual resistor is _____   18.____
    amps.

    A.  .5          B.  1.5         C.  2.5         D.  3.5

19. In the series circuit shown above, the total power drawn by the circuit is _____ watts.  19._____

  A. 140.25  B. 150.75  C. 153.38  D. 173.38

20. In the series circuit shown above, the power drawn from each individual resistor is  20._____
  _____ , _____ , and _____ watts, respectively.

  A. 23.65; 118.27; 11.827  B. 17.567; 123.27; 11.27
  C. 18.627; 145.27; 12.27  D. 21.735; 116.87; 11.83

21. In the parallel circuit shown above, if Vsupply = 100 VDC, resistor A is 10 ohms, resistor  21._____
  B is 50 ohms, and resistor C is 5 ohms, the total circuit current is _____ amps.

  A. 21  B. 27  C. 32  D. 45

22. In the parallel circuit shown above, the total power drawn by the circuit is _____ watts.  22._____

  A. 1200  B. 2300  C. 2700  D. 3200

23. In the parallel circuit above, the power drawn by each individual resistor is _____ watts,  23._____
  respectively.

  A. 100; 200; 2000  B. 200; 400; 5000
  C. 300; 500; 750  D. 450; 600; 1500

24. On an 0-scope display, one cycle of a signal takes up 4 1/2 divisions and the peak-to-  24._____
  peak amplitude of the signal takes up 3 3/4 divisions.
  With the volts/division knob set on 5 volts and the time/division knob set to 5 microseconds, the peak-to-peak amplitude and the frequency of the signal are _____ volts and
  _____ khz, respectively.

  A. 15.75; 100  B. 22.5; 200
  C. 37.5; 350  D. 45.75; 570

25. If a signal that has a peak-to-peak amplitude of 15 volts and a frequency of 5 megaherz  25._____
  is to be observed on an 0-scope with one complete cycle shown, the time/division knob
  and volts/division knob should be set on _____ microseconds and _____ volts per
  division, respectively.

  A. .02; 2  B. .05; 4  C. .07; 3.5  D. 10; 7.5

# KEY (CORRECT ANSWERS)

| | | | | | |
|---|---|---|---|---|---|
| 1. B | 6. C | 11. B | 16. B | 21. C |
| 2. A | 7. A | 12. A | 17. A | 22. D |
| 3. B | 8. C | 13. C | 18. B | 23. A |
| 4. D | 9. B | 14. A | 19. C | 24. B |
| 5. A | 10. A | 15. D | 20. A | 25. A |

———

# EXAMINATION SECTION
## TEST 1

DIRECTIONS: Each question or incomplete statement is followed by several suggested answers or completions. Select the one that BEST answers the question or completes the statement. *PRINT THE LETTER OF THE CORRECT ANSWER IN THE SPACE AT THE RIGHT.*

1. The gray code minimizes the possibility of ambiguity when changing state by:　　1.＿＿＿
   A. Changing state on leading or trailing pulse edges.
   B. Using a common clock to synchronize inputs.
   C. Changing only one bit at a time.
   D. Requiring coincidence between two or more samples.

2. Convert the decimal number 164 to hex.　　2.＿＿＿
   A. 104.　　　　　　B. A4.　　　　　　C. 10110100.　　　　D. 5B.

3. A computer memory location is designated FO9Fh. The decimal equivalent is:　　3.＿＿＿

   A. 4367.　　　　　B. 1010101.　　　　C. 10110100.　　　D. 61599.

4. Which of the following items is not an ASCII item?　　4.＿＿＿
   A. 8.　　　　　　B. BS.　　　　　　C. END.　　　　　D. A.

5. If the input lead to an operating TTL inverter became grounded, what would the output　　5.＿＿＿
   lead measure?
   A. +0 to +0.7 VDC.
   B. Ground.
   C. More than +5 VDC.
   D. Between +2.5 VDC and + 5VDC depending on load.

6. What is the range of supply voltage (VDD) to a CMOS logic IC?　　6.＿＿＿
   A. +4.5 to +5.5 VDC.　　　　　　C. +5 to +25 VDC.
   B. -3 VDC to +10 VDC.　　　　　D. + 3 VDC to +15 VDC.

7. Using positive logic, a TTL IC will recognize the following voltages levels as valid　　7.＿＿＿
   "1" and "0" levels in an operational logic circuit:
   A. Binary 0 = +0.4 VDC, Binary 1 = +3.6 VDC.
   B. Binary 0 = 0.0 VDC, Binary 1 = +5.0 VDC.
   C. Binary 0 = +0.3 VDC, Binary 1 = +4.7 VDC.
   D. All of these.

8. If the output of a TTL gate measures 2.0VDC:　　8.＿＿＿
   A. There is a problem either in the gate or the loading.
   B. This is a normal high.
   C. This is a normal low.
   D. None of these.

9. A digital logic chip has a supply voltage of -5.2V. This chip belongs to which family?　　9.＿＿＿
   A. ECL　　　　　B. TTL　　　　　C. CMOS　　　　D. RTL

10. Which of the following integrated circuit or semiconductors devices normally require　　10.＿＿＿
    special handling to avoid damage by static electricity?
    A. TTL　　　　　B. ECL　　　　　C. MOV　　　　　D. CMOS

**Figure 9C-1**

11. On Figure 9C-1, the function D is described as:
    A. AB (-C).      B. C + (-A) B.      C. C + AB.      D. A + BC.

11._____

12. ECL achieves high speed due to:
    A. The use of gallium arsenide conductors.
    B. Construction in small geometries.
    C. The operating transistors being unsaturated.
    D. Operation in low noise negative supply region.

12._____

13. By DeMorgan's Theorem, $(X + Y)$ =
    A. $-X + -Y$      B. $(X + Y)$      C. $-(X + Y)$      D. $X\,Y$

13._____

14. The logic family which typically has the largest fanout is:
    A. CMOS.      B. ECL.      C. TTL.      D. RTL.

14._____

15. In order of highest to lowest speed, the logic families are ranked:
    A. ECL, CMOS, Schottky TTL, Standard TTL.
    B. Schottky, Standard TTL, ECL, CMOS.
    C. CMOS, Standard TTL, Schottky TTL, ECL.
    D. ECL, Schottky TTL, Standard TTL, CMOS.

15._____

16. In a three bit binary ripple counter, the state following 111 will be:
    A. 110.      B. 000.      C. 001.      D. 111.

16._____

17. In a 4 bit BCD ripple counter the state following 1001 will be:
    A. 1111.      B. 1011.      C. 0000.      D. 1000.

17._____

18. Synchronous counters are distinguished from ripple in that:
    A. Logic inputs are applied in parallel.
    B. Counter feedback is synchronous.
    C. The clock is applied to all flip flops simultaneously.
    D. There is no ripple on synchronous counters.

18._____

**Figure 9C-2**

19. The circuit shown on Figure 9C-2:                                        19._____
    A. Is a wired exclusive or.
    B. Is a wired or.
    C. Is used for high speed operation.
    D. Uses open collector gates.

20. What is the result of adding binary 110111 and 1001:                     20._____
    A. 1000000.        B. 11111.        C. 100000.        D. 111111.

21. What is the binary result of multiplying hexadecimal 1C by 7?            21._____
    A. 11101100.       B. 11000100.     C. 11001100.      D. 11100100.

22. The value 123456 is based upon a number system which has a minimum radix of:   22._____
    A. 10.             B. 6.            C. 7.             D. 2.

23. A twos complement number is formed by the following method:             23._____
    A. Complement individual bits; then add 1.
    B. Add the number to all ones; then add 1.
    C. Subtract the number from all ones; then add 1.
    D. Add individual bits; then add 1.

24. Choose the correct solution to the following: 0101 + 0010 =19.          24._____
    A. 10111.          B. 1000.         C. 0111.          D. 01000.

**Figure 9C-3**

25. Refer to the waveforms shown on Figure 9C-3:20.                          25._____
With x and y as inputs to an "AND" gate, what is the output waveform?
    A. Waveform A                    C. Waveform C
    B. Waveform B                    D. Waveform D

26. Refer to the waveforms shown on Figure 9C-3:                            26._____
With x and y as inputs to an "OR" gate, what is the output waveform?
    A. Waveform D                    C. Waveform B
    B. Waveform C                    D. Waveform A

27. Refer to the waveforms shown on Diagram EL9C3C: With x and y as inputs to a   27._____
    "Exclusive OR" gate, what is the output waveform?
    A. Waveform A                    C. Waveform C
    B. Waveform B                    D. Waveform D

28. The standard serial output of a PC conforms to the following specification.          28._____
    A. 20 mA loop.               C. NMEA0180.
    B. RS232.@ @           D. Centronics

29. Which of the following logic levels are in a normal ran for TxD and Rxd signals on an          29._____
    RS232 interface line?
    A. 2.5 V and +2.5 V.          C. -10 V and +10 V.
    B. +0.20 V and + 4.5 V.     D. 10 V and 0 V.

30. What happens in a microprocessor system if electrical power input is interrupted?          30._____
    A.    Data stored in ROM is lost forever.
    B.    Data stored in ROM is lost, but can be restored by rebooting.
    C.    Data stored in RAM is lost.
    D.    Data stored in RAM is retained.

# KEY (CORRECT ANSWERS)

| | | |
|---|---|---|
| 1. C | 11. B | 21. B |
| 2. B | 12. C | 22. C |
| 3. D | 13. D | 23. A |
| 4. C | 14. A | 24. B |
| 5. B | 15. D | 25. B |
| 6. D | 16. A | 26. D |
| 7. D | 17. C | 27. C |
| 8. A | 18. C | 28. B |
| 9. A | 19. D | 29. C |
| 10. D | 20. A | 30. C |

# TEST 2

DIRECTIONS: Each question or incomplete statement is followed by several suggested answers or completions. Select the one that BEST answers the question or completes the statement. *PRINT THE LETTER OF THE CORRECT ANSWER IN THE SPACE AT THE RIGHT.*

1. Complete the following sentence. A bit string manipulated by a computer in one operation is usually called:
   A. A bit.
   B. A word.
   C. A byte.
   D. A nibble.

1._____

2. In a microcomputer, the program counter contains:
   A. The address of the next instruction to be executed.
   B. Data.
   C. A sequential instruction set.
   D. An instruction set.

2._____

3. Choose the most correct statement.
   A. A RISC processor requires two or more clock cycles to execute a command.
   B. A RISC processor has fewer instructions available than an equivalent non-RISC processor.
   C. A RISC processor is inherently limited to a 32 bit architecture.
   D. RISC processors cannot implement a stack.

3._____

4. A one dimensional data structure in which values are entered and removed one item at a time at one end is called what?
   A. A ring counter.
   B. A FIFO.
   C. A stack pointer.
   D. A pushdown stack.

4._____

5. The output of an assembler is:
   A. Used only for solving floating point problems.
   B. A higher level language.
   C. Equivalent machine language instructions called object code.
   D. Not in executable machine language form.

5_____

6. What is the DOS command used to copy files from one drive to another?
   A. RD.
   B. COPY.
   C. DEL.
   D. FC.

6._____

7. What is the command used to determine the version of DOS that the computer is currently using?
   A. MEM.
   B. VER.
   C. VERIFY.
   D. CHKDSK.

7._____

8. All DOS file names may contain a maximum of how many characters?
   A. 6.
   B. 11.@@
   C. 10.
   D. 7.

8._____

9. Compilers are used with which type of code?.    9._____
    A. High level languages.
    B. Assembly languages.
    C. Machine languages.
    D. High level languages and assembly languages.    10._____

10. Choose the correct answer:11._____
    A. A bit is one binary digit.        C. A byte is 8 bits.
    B. A nibble is 4 bits.               D. All answers are correct.

11. An interpreter is used with which type of code?    11._____
    A. Object codes.                     C. High level languages.
    B. Assembly languages.               D. Machine codes.

12. An internal short between the base and collector of a bipolar transistor might be    12._____
    indicated by which of the following?
    A. A weak signal at the collector, in phase with the input.
    B. No signal at the output.
    C. DC supply voltage on the collector.
    E. Little or no signal at the collector and a reversal of phase.

13. When attempting to test a bipolar silicon or germanium transistor, which of the    13._____
    following is likely to be correct if the test is conducted after the device has been
    removed from its circuit?
    A. If an ohmmeter is used without an external limiting resistor, excessive base
       current will destroy the device.
    B. If A PNP transistor is being tested, forward junction resistance will be greater
       than reverse resistance.
    C. Forward junction resistance should be less than reverse junction resistance.
    D. Circuit effects which cannot be accounted for, preclude the use of resistance
       measurements.

14. When replacing a diac which is used with a silicon controlled rectifier, which way    14._____
    must the diac be installed?
    A. The anode must be connected to the gate.
    B. Either way will work.
    C. The cathode must be connected to the gate.
    D. Either way, depending on the polarity of the SCR.

15. Which of the following statements about diac bidirectional trigger diodes is incorrect?    15._____
    A. A diac is a three layer device with two terminals.
    B. A diac switch functions in either direction.
    C. The breakover voltage is usually between 28 and 36 volts.
    D. Lamps and battery chargers are typical loads for a diac.

16. Which of the following statements correctly describes photo diode operation?    16._____
    A. Photodiodes generate light in response to incident photons.
    B. Reverse biased photodiodes are photoresistive.
    C. Efficiency is a measure of photons per electron.
    D. Dark current flows in response to black light.

17. Which of the following statements distinguish phototransistors from photodiodes.
    A. Phototransistors are faster than photodiodes.
    B. Photodiodes are more sensitive than phototransistors.
    C. Photodarlingtons are the fastest photoconductors
    D. None of these.

17._____

18. Photodiode reverse current is called:
    A. Dark current in the absence of light.
    B. Zener current if the diode is reverse biased.
    C. Photocurrent if the diode is forward biased.
    D. Dark current in very low illumination.

18._____

19. What is the life expectancy of a light emitting diode operated continuously under normal operating conditions?
    A. Up to 100 years.
    B. Light emitting diodes may last up to 20 years.
    C. Unlimited life expectancy.
    D. Approximately 87660 hours.

19._____

20. How may the polarity of the leads of an LED be identified prior to installation in a circuit?
    A. The cathode lead is usually longer than the anode lead.
    B. There may be a flat edge on the body near the anode.
    C. If the cathode can be seen, it is usually smaller.
    D. The ground lead is usually lighter in color.

20._____

21. In testing a GaAs light emitting diode within the manufacturer's operating parameters of voltage and current, it appears that no light is emitted. What explanation could be given:
    A. The LED is connected backwards.
    B. The LED may have run out of GaAs.
    C. The LED may be emitting invisible light.
    D. The LED is connected backwards and may be emitting invisible light.

21._____

22. What is the typical minimum bias voltage required for normal operation of a GaAsP light emitting diode?
    A. The LED will operate at 1.2 volts reverse bias.
    B. The LED will operate at 0.6 volts forward bias.
    C. The LED will operate at 2 volts reverse bias.
    D. The LED will operate at 1.2 volts forward bias.

22._____

23. Which of the following statements is not true of light emitting diodes?
    A. They can be manufactured to emit various wavelengths.
    B. They can operate at very high speed.
    C. They can be made to emit nearly pure white light.
    D. They are vulnerable to failure due to overcurrent.

23._____

24. What is the usual method of protecting a light emitting diode from damage that would result if the operating voltage became too high?
    A. A series current limiting resistor is used.
    B. A zener voltage regulator is used.
    C. A fast-blow fuse is used in series with the LED.
    D. The LED is attached to a heat sink.

24._____

25. Assuming that a light emitting diode has an internal resistance of 5 ohms, what value of series current limiting resistor should be used if the power supply voltage is 6 volts and the diode current is to be 0.05 Amperes at 1.6 Volts DC?
    A. 83 Ohms.
    C. 88 Ohms.
    B. b} 120 Ohms.
    D. 32 Ohms.

25._____

26. With regard to a 7-segment LED display, which statement is correct?
    A. Only one segment at a time can be illuminated.
    B. An external decoder/driver is usually used.
    C. They are often used as simple on-off indicators.
    D. Segments must be illuminated in sets of two.

26._____

27. Identify the statement below which is incorrect with respect to infrared light emitting diodes:
    A. Light from an IR LED is invisible.
    B. Photodiodes can be used with IR LEDs.
    C. Phototransistors can be used with IR LEDs.
    D. IR LEDs are often used in optical couplers but not in opto-isolators.

27._____

28. When a power MOSFET has OV from gate to source the following is true:
    A. It is in pinch off.
    C. It is in a conducting region.
    B. It is saturated.
    D. It is drawing gate current.

28._____

**Figure 9C-4**

29. The purpose of the diode in the circuit shown on Figure 9C-4 is to:
    A. Speed switching time.
    B. Protect the transistor.
    C. Increase current capacity.
    D. Compensate for thermal variations.

29._____

30. In the silicon transistor circuit below, you test the input and find that it is a 0.5V p-p sine wave centered about 4V. The output is a 1.5Vp-p sine wave centered about 7V. The most likely fact is that:
    A. The circuit is operating normally and is driving a high impedance.
    B. The circuit is operating normally and is heavily loaded.
    C. The transistor is bad.
    D. One of the circuit components is bad.

30._____

# KEY (CORRECT ANSWERS)

| | | |
|---|---|---|
| 1. B | 11. C | 21. C |
| 2. A | 12. C | 22. D |
| 3. B | 13. C | 23. C |
| 4. D | 14. B | 24. A |
| 5. C | 15. D | 25. A |
| 6. B | 16. B | 26. B |
| 7. B | 17. D | 27. D |
| 8. B | 18. A | 28. A |
| 9. D | 19. C | 29. B |
| 10. D | 20. A | 30. A |

# EXAMINATION SECTION
## TEST 1

DIRECTIONS: Each question or incomplete statement is followed by several suggested answers or completions. Select the one that BEST answers the question or completes the statement. *PRINT THE LETTER OF THE CORRECT ANSWER IN THE SPACE AT THE RIGHT.*

1. What is the voltage range considered to be valid logic low input in a TTL device operating at 5 volts?
   A. 2.0 to 5.5 volts.
   B. -2.0 to -5.5 volts.
   C. Zero to 0.8 volts.
   D. 5.2 to 34.8 volts.

   1._____

2. What is the voltage range considered to be a valid logic high input in a TTL device operating at 5.0 volts?
   A. 2.0 to 5.5 volts.
   B. 1.5 to 3.0 volts.
   C. to 1.5 volts.
   D. 5.2 to 34.8 volts.

   2._____

3. What is the common power supply voltage for TTL series integrated circuits?
   A. 12 volts.
   B. 13.6 volts.
   C. 1 volt.
   D. 5 volts.

   3._____

4. TTL inputs left open develop what logic state?
   A. A high-logic state.
   B. A low-logic state.
   C. Open inputs on a TTL device are ignored.
   D. Random high- and low-logic states.

   4._____

5. Which of the following instruments would be best for checking a TTL logic circuit?
   A. VOM.
   B. DMM.
   C. Continuity tester.
   D. Logic probe.

   5._____

6. What do the initials TTL stand for?
   A. Resistor-transistor logic.
   B. Transistor-transistor logic.
   C. Diode-transistor logic.
   D. Emitter-coupled logic.

   6._____

7. What is a characteristic of an AND gate?
   A. Produces a logic "0" at its output only if all inputs are logic "1".
   B. Produces a logic "1" at its output only if all inputs are logic "1".
   C. Produces a logic "1" at its output if only one input is a logic "1".
   D. Produces a logic "1" at its output if all inputs are logic "0".

   7._____

8. What is a characteristic of a NAND gate?                                    8._____
    A. Produces a logic "0" at its output only when all inputs are logic "0".
    B. Produces a logic "1" at its output only when all inputs are logic "1".
    C. Produces a logic "0" at its output if some but not all of its inputs are logic "1".
    D. Produces a logic "0" at its output only when all inputs are logic "1".

9. What is a characteristic of an OR gate?                                      9._____
    A. Produces a logic "1" at its output if any input is logic "1".
    B. Produces a logic "0" at its output if any input is logic "1".
    C. Produces a logic "0" at its output if all inputs are logic "1".
    D. Produces a logic "1" at its output if all inputs are logic "0".

10. What is a characteristic of a NOR gate?                                     10._____
    A. Produces a logic "0" at its output only if all inputs are logic "0".
    B. Produces a logic "1" at its output only if all inputs are logic "1".
    C. Produces a logic "0" at its output if any or all inputs are logic "1".
    D. Produces a logic "1" at its output if some but not all of its inputs are logic "V.

11. What is a characteristic of a NOT gate?                                     11._____
    A. Does not allow data transmission when its input is high.
    B. Produces logic "0" at its output when the input is logic "1" and vice versa.
    C. Allows data transmission only when its input is high.
    D. Produces a logic "1" at its output when the input is logic "1" and vice versa.

12. Which of the following logic gates will provide an active high out when both inputs    12._____
are active high?
    A. NAND.
    B. NOR.
    C. AND.
    D. XOR.

13. In a negative-logic circuit, what level is used to represent a logic 0?     13._____
    A. Low level.
    B. Positive-transition level.
    C. Negative-transition level
    D. High level

14. For the logic input levels shown in the following figure, what are the logic levels of test    14._____
points A, B and C in this circuit? (Assume positive logic.)
    A. A is high, B is low and C is low.
    B. A is low, B is high and C is high.
    C. A is high, B is high and C is low.
    D. A is low, B is high and C is low.

15. For the logic input levels given in the following figure, what are the logic levels of test points A, B and C in this circuit? (Assume positive logic.)
    A. A is low, B is low and C is high.
    B. A is low, B is high and C is low.
    C. A is high, B is high and C is high.
    D. A is high, B is low and C is low.

15._____

16. In a positive-logic circuit, what level is used to represent a logic 1?
    A. High level
    B. Low level
    C. Positive-transition level
    D. Negative-transition level

16._____

17. Given the input levels shown in the following figure, and assuming positive logic devices, what would the output be?
    A. A is low, B is high and C is high.
    B. A is high, B is high and C is low.
    C. A is low, B is low and C is high.
    D. None of the above are correct.

17._____

18. What is a truth table?
    A. A list of input combinations and their corresponding outputs that characterizes a digital device's function.
    B. A table of logic symbols that indicate the high logic states of an op-amp.
    C. A diagram showing logic states when the digital device's output is true.
    D. A table of logic symbols that indicates the low logic states of an op-amp.

18._____

19. It has been reported that a VHF transceiver is unusable, because the LCD display characters are "all black." Which of the following might get it working again?

    A. Warm the display up to 20 degrees C.
    B. Drain and replace the LCD liquid.
    C. Replace the display's current limiting resistor.
    D. Replace the crystal.

19._____

20. A flip-flop circuit is a binary logic element with how many stable states?

    A. 1
    B. 2
    C. 4
    D. 8

20._____

21. What is a flip-flop circuit? A binary sequential logic element with_____stable states.

    A. 1
    B. 4
    C. 2
    D. 8

21._____

22. How many flip-flops are required to divide a signal frequency by 4?

    A. 1
    B. 2
    C. 3
    D. 4

22._____

23. How many bits lof information can be stored in a single flip-flop circuit?.

    A. 1
    B. 2
    C. 3
    D. 4

23._____

24. How many R-S flip-flops would be required to construct an 8 bit storage register?

    A. 2
    B. 4
    C. 8
    D. 16

24._____

25. An R-S flip-flop is capable of doing all of the following except:

    A. Accept data input into R-S inputs with CLK initiated.
    B. Accept data input into PRE and CLR inputs without CLK being initiated.
    C. Refuse to accept synchronous data if asynchronous data is being input at same time.
    D. Operate in toggle mode with R-S inputs he ld constant and CLK initiated.

25._____

# KEY (CORRECT ANSWERS)

| | | | |
|---|---|---|---|
| 1. C | | 11. B | |
| 2. A | | 12. C | |
| 3. D | | 13. D | |
| 4. A | | 14. B | |
| 5. D | | 15. C | |
| 6. B | | 16. A | |
| 7. B | | 17. B | |
| 8. D | | 18. A | |
| 9. A | | 19. A | |
| 10. C | | 20. B | |

21. C
22. D
23. A
24. C
25. D

———

# TEST 2

DIRECTIONS: Each question or incomplete statement is followed by several suggested answers or completions. Select the one that BEST answers the question or completes the statement. *PRINT THE LETTER OF THE CORRECT ANSWER IN THE SPACE AT THE RIGHT.*

1. Which of the following procedures would be appropriate with metal oxide semiconductor integrated circuits while making equipment repairs:
   A. Use a non-conductive mat on the work surface.
   B. Wear a conductive wrist strap with a 1 million ohm resistor to ground.
   C. Touch each lead to equalize electrostatic potentials.
   D. Keep spare IC's neatly organized in styrofoam.

   1._____

2. The frequency of an AC signal can be divided electronically by what type of digital circuit?
   A. Free-running multivibrator.
   B. Bistable multivibrator.
   C. OR gate.
   D. Astable multivibrator.

   2._____

3. What is an astable multivibrator?
   A. A circuit that alternates between two stable states.
   B. A circuit that alternates between a stable state and an unstable state.
   C. A circuit set to block either a 0 pulse or a 1 pulse and pass the other.
   D. A circuit that alternates between two unstable states.

   3._____

4. What is a monostable multivibrator?
   A. A circuit that can be switched momentarily to the opposite binary state and then returns after a set time to its original state.
   B. A "clock" circuit that produces a continuous square wave oscillating between 1 and 0.
   C. A circuit designed to store one bit of data in either the 0 or the 1 configuration.
   D. A circuit that maintains a constant output voltage, regardless of variations in the input voltage.

   4._____

5. What is a bistable multivibrator circuit commonly named?
   A. AND gate.
   B. OR gate.
   C. Clock.
   D. Flip-flop.

   5._____

6. What is a bistable multivibrator circuit?
   A. Flip-flop.
   B. AND gate.
   C. OR gate.
   D. Clock.

   6._____

7. What wave form would appear on the voltage outputs at the collectors of an astable, multivibrator, common-emitter stage?
   A. Sine wave.
   B. Sawtooth wave.
   C. Square wave.
   D. Half-wave pulses.

   7._____

8. What is the name of the semiconductor memory IC whose digital data can be written or read, and whose memory word address can be accessed randomly?
    A. ROM — Read-Only Memory.
    B. PROM — Programmable Read-Only Memory.
    C. RAM — Random-Access Memory.
    D. EPROM — Electrically Programmable Read-Only Memory.

8._____

9. What is the name of the semiconductor IC that has a fixed pattern of digital data stored in its memory matrix?
    A. RAM — Random-Access Memory.
    B. ROM — Read-Only Memory.
    C. Register.
    D. Latch.

9._____

10. What does the term "IO" mean within a microprocessor system?
    A. Integrated oscillator.
    B. Integer operation.
    C. Input-output.
    D. D Internal operation.

10._____

11. What is the name for a microprocessor's sequence of commands and instructions?
    A. Program.
    B. Sequence.
    C. Data string.
    D. Data execution.

11._____

12. How many individual memory cells would be contained in a memory IC that has 4 data bus input/output pins and 4 address pins for connection to the address bus?
    A. 8
    B. 16
    C. 32
    D. 64

12._____

13. What is the name of the random-accessed semiconductor memory IC that must be refreshed periodically to maintain reliable data storage in its memory matrix?
    A. ROM — Read-Only Memory.
    B. DRAM — Dynamic Random-Access Memory.
    C. PROM — Programmable Read-Only Memory.
    D. PRAM — Programmable Random-Access Memory.

13._____

14. In a microprocessor-controlled two-way radio, a "watchdog" timer:
    A. Verifies that the microprocessor is executing the program.
    B. Assures that the transmission is exactly on frequency.
    C. Prevents the transmitter from exceeding allowed power out.
    D. Connects to the system RADAR presentation.

14._____

15. What does the term "DAC" refer to in a microprocessor circuit?
    A. Dynamic access controller.
    B. Digital to analog converter.
    C. Digital access counter.
    D. Dial analog control.

15._____

16. Which of the following is not part of a MCU processor?    16._____
    A. RAM
    B. ROM
    C. I/O
    D. Voltage Regulator

17. What portion of a microprocessor circuit is the pulse generator?    17._____
    A. Clock                C. ROM
    B. RAM                  D. PLL

18. In a microprocessor, what is the meaning of the term "ALU"?    18._____
    A. Automatic lock/unlock.
    B. Arithmetical logic unit.
    C. Auto latch undo.
    D. Answer local unit.

19. What circuit interconnects the microprocessor with the memory and input/output system?    19._____
    A. Control logic bus.
    B. PLL line.
    C. Data bus line.
    D. Directional coupler.

20. What is the purpose of a prescaler circuit?    20._____
    A. Converts the output of a JK flip-flop to that of an RS flip-flop.
    B. Multiplies an HF signal so a low-frequency counter can display the operating frequency.
    C. Prevents oscillation in a low frequency counter circuit.
    D. Divides an HF signal so that a low-frequency counter can display the operating frequency.

21. What does the term "BCD" mean?    21._____
    A. Binaural coded digit.
    B. Bit count decimal.
    C. Binary coded decimal.
    D. Broad course digit.

22. What is the function of a decade counter digital IC?    22._____
    A. Decode a decimal number for display on a seven-segment LED display.
    B. Produce one output pulse for every ten input pulses.
    C. Produce ten output pulses for every input pulse.
    D. Add two decimal numbers.

23. What integrated circuit device converts an analog signal to a digital signal?    23._____
    A. DAC          B. DCC          C. ADC          D. CDC

24. What integrated circuit device converts digital signals to analog signals?    24._____
    A. ADC          B. DCC          C. CDC          D. DAC

25. In binary numbers, how would you note the quantity TWO?    25._____
    A. 0010
    B. 0002
    C. 2000
    D. 0020

# KEY (CORRECT ANSWERS)

1. B
2. B
3. D
4. A
5. D
6. A
7. C
8. C
9. B
10. C

11. A
12. D
13. B
14. A
15. B
16. D
17. A
18. B
19. C
20. D

21. C
22. B
23. C
24. D
25. A

# EXAMINATION SECTION
## TEST 1

DIRECTIONS: Each question or incomplete statement is followed by several suggested answers or completions. Select the one that BEST answers the question or completes the statement. *PRINT THE LETTER OF THE CORRECT ANSWER IN THE SPACE AT THE RIGHT.*

1. The majority of simple electronics circuits are based upon a logic

    A. A and a logic B state
    B. *on* and a logic *off* state
    C. 0 and a logic 1 state
    D. *go* and *no-go* state

1.____

2. What voltage level exists in the 7400-series of 1C chips?

    A. -15 volts, ground, and +5 volts
    B. Ground, +5 volts, and +12 volts
    C. -12 volts, ground, and +5 volts
    D. +5 volts and ground

2.____

3. A clock pulse is a transition

    A. from a logic 0 to a logic 1
    B. from a logic 1 to a logic 0
    C. from a logic 0 to a logic 1 and back to logic 0
    D. both A and B are correct

3.____

4. The symbols shown to the right are those for a 2-input _____ gate and 2-input _____ gate.

    A. AND; NOR
    B. EXCLUSIVE-OR; NAND
    C. OR; NOR
    D. AND; NAND

4.____

5. For which type of gate is the following definition CORRECT?
A binary circuit with two or more inputs and single output, in which the output is a logic 1 only when all inputs are logic 1, and the output is logic 0 if any one of the inputs is logic 0.

    A. AND gate    B. NAND gate    C. OR gate    D. NOR gate

5.____

6. If the two inputs to a 2-input AND, NAND, OR, and NOR gate are both at logic 1, the outputs from the four gates are

    A. 1,1,0 and 0        B. 1,0,0 and 1
    C. 0,1,1 and 0        D. 1,0,1 and 0

6.____

7. The term *to enable* a gate is the opposite of which of the following terms?

    A. To close a gate        B. To disable a gate
    C. To block a gate        D. All of the above

7.____

8.  A gate and a switch differ in which of the following ways?                                8.___

    A.  A gate is essentially a one-way device, whereas a switch is a two-way device.
    B.  When a gate is closed, a signal can pass; when a switch is closed, a signal cannot pass,
    C.  When a gate is open, a signal can pass; when a switch is closed, a signal cannot pass.
    D.  A gate and a switch are identical in function.

9.  A gating input of logic 0 to a 2-input NOR gate will allow what type of digital information   9.___
    to appear at the output of the gate?

    A.  Logic 1 state                        B.  Logic 0 state
    C.  Unchanged input data                 D.  Inverted input data

10. A gating input of logic 0 to a 2-input NAND gate will allow what type of digital information  10.___
    to appear at the output of the gate?

    A.  Logic 1 state                        B.  Logic 0 state
    C.  Unchanged input data                 D.  Inverted input data

11. The 7400, 7402, 7408, and 7432 IC chips each contain                                      11.___

    A.  *only* a single gate                 B.  four gates
    C.  three gates                          D.  two gates

12. A common-anode 7 segment display has the following inputs to its segments: A, D, E=1       12.___
    and B, C, F, G = 0.
    What does the display read out?

    A.  Nine          B.  Four          C.  Six          D.  Three
    E.  None of these

13. A common cathode display has the following inputs to its segments: C,F.=0 and              13.___
    A,B,D,E,G=1.
    What does the display indicate?

    A.  Nine          B.  Four          C.  Two          D.  Five

14. What is the difference between a 7490 and a 7493 counter?                                  14.___

    A.  There is no difference.
    B.  The 7490 is a decade counter, whereas the 7493 is a binary counter.
    C.  The 7490 is a binary counter, whereas the 7493 is a decade counter.
    D.  They have different pin configurations

15. The truth table to the right applies for the _____ gate.                                 15.___
    A.  AND
    B.  OR
    C.  NAND
    D.  NOR
    E.  None of these

| IN | OUT |
|----|-----|
| AB | X |
| 00 | 1 |
| 01 | 1 |
| 10 | 1 |
| 11 | 1 |

16. In the truth tables for a 2-input AND, NAND, OR, and NOR gate, the unique output state is, respectively,     16.____

    A.  logic 1, logic 1, logic 0, logic 1
    B.  logic 1, logic 0, logic 0, logic 1
    C.  logic 0, logic 1, logic 1, logic 1
    D.  logic 1, logic 1, logic 1, logic 1

17. When one inverts the output from an AND gate, he converts it into a(n) _____ gate.     17.____

    A.  EXCLUSIVE-OR        B.  NAND
    C.  NOR                D.  AND-OR-INVERT

18. If the two inputs to a 2-input AND gate and a 2-input NOR gate are left unconnected, the outputs from these two gates are, respectively,     18.____

    A.  logic 1 and logic 0        B.  logic 0 and logic 1
    C.  logic 0 and logic 0        D.  logic 1 and logic 1

19. The 7400, 7420, and 7430 IC chips have gates that have, respectively, the following numbers of inputs:     19.____

    A.  two, three, five, and ten
    B.  one, two, three, four
    C.  two, three, four, eight
    D.  two, three, four, six

20. The 7400, 7420, 7430 IC chips are all _____ gates.     20.____

    A.  AND               B.  NAND
    C.  both AND and NAND    D.  NOR

21. A four decade counter can count from     21.____

    A.  0001 to 10000         B.  0001 to 9999
    C.  0000 to 9999          D.  0000 to 100000

22. In a positive clock pulse, the transition from logic 1 to logic 0 occurs on the _____ edge.     22.____

    A.  positive trailing         B.  positi.ve leading
    C.  negative trailing        D.  negative leading

23. The 74121-IC chip is a     23.____

    A.  counter             B.  flip-flop
    C.  monostable multivibrator    D.  programmable timer

24. When one debounces a SPDT switch, he     24.____

    A.  makes sure that the switching action occurs quickly
    B.  makes sure that the output from the switch can be controlled to produce a single clock pulse at a time
    C.  turns the SPDT into, basically, a monostable multivibrator
    D.  none of the above

25. When R=l megohm and C=l microfarad, the RC time constant has a value of     25.____

    A.  1 second             B.  .000001 seconds
    C.  .001 seconds          D.  .000001 hz

# KEY (CORRECT ANSWERS)

| | | | | |
|---|---|---|---|---|
| 1. | C | | 11. | B |
| 2. | D | | 12. | E |
| 3. | C | | 13. | C |
| 4. | A | | 14. | B |
| 5. | A | | 15. | E |
| | | | | |
| 6. | D | | 16. | B |
| 7. | D | | 17. | B |
| 8. | A | | 18. | A |
| 9. | D | | 19. | C |
| 10. | A | | 20. | B |

21. C
22. C
23. C
24. B
25. A

# TEST 2

DIRECTIONS: Each question or incomplete statement is followed by several suggested answers or completions. Select the one that BEST answers the question or completes the statement. *PRINT THE LETTER OF THE CORRECT ANSWER IN THE SPACE AT THE RIGHT.*

1. In HEXADECIMAL notation, the binary number DCBA = 1100 represents either _____ or the letter _____.

   A. eleven; B               B. eleven; A
   C. twelve; C               D. thirteen; D

   1.___

2. The binary number, 11111, represents which of the following decimal numbers?

   A. 32          B. 16          C. 15          D. 3

   2.___

3. A twelve-bit binary number can encode _____ decimal numbers.

   A. two thousand and forty-eight     B. four thousand and ninety-six
   C. five hundred and twelve          D. two hundred and fifty-six

   3.___

4. The binary number, 1111, appears on the seven-segment LED display as a

   A. blank display           B. decimal 15
   C. the letter F            D. 0

   4.__

5. The LARGEST binary number that can exist in binary-coded decimal (BCD) is

   A. 1000        B. 1111        C. 1001        D. 1010

   5.___

6. The quantity, 0111 = DCBA, is in binary-coded decimal equal to decimal

   A. 7           B. 5           C. 9           D. 6

   6.___

7. In which of the following choices are all of the IC chips either decoders or decoder-drivers?

   A. 7447, 7451, and 74150     B. 7448, 7451, and 74160
   C. 7442, 7447, and 74154     D. 7442, 7448, and 74150

   7.___

8. Which of the following IC chips is a 4-line-to-10-line decoder?

   A. 7447        B. 7451        C. 74150       D. 7442

   8.___

9. In a decade sequencer, one requires a

   A. 74150 chip and a decade counter such as the 7490
   B. 74150 chip and a binary counter such as the 7493
   C. 7451 chip and a decoder such as the 7442
   D. 7442 chip and a 7490 chip

   9.___

10. A demultiplexer is similar to a

    A. shift register
    B. decoder
    C. device that can select one of a number of inputs and pass the logic level on to the output
    D. data selector

    10.___

11. When connected in the proper way, the 74150 and 74154 chips can serve as a        11._____

    A. sequencer
    B. simultaneous decoder/driver
    C. multiplexer/demultiplexer circuit
    D. programmable sequencer

12. The current that passes through a light-emitting diode (LED) should generally NOT     12._____
exceed

    A. one ampere                  B. one milliampere
    C. 30 to 50 milliamperes       D. 300 milliampere

13. When the anode of a LED is connected to +5 volts and the cathode is connected to      13._____
ground, the LED will

    A. remain unlit
    B. become lit, although only slightly
    C. light up immediately, but it may become unlit owing to the lack of a current-limiting
       resistor
    D. burn out

14. One can construct a simple logic probe from a                          14._____

    A. light-emitting diode, capacitor, and battery
    B. LED, transistor, and battery
    C. LED and resistor
    D. LED and capacitor

15. When a logic probe is constructed from a LED and other components, a transistor is *usu-*   15._____
*ally* employed to

    A. make the LED light a bit more brighter
    B. conserve power
    C. *decrease* the current required to light the lamp monitor circuit
    D. *decrease* the voltage across the LED

16. A typical J-K flip-flop can have the following inputs:                   16._____

    A. Strobe, enable, count, clear, and present
    B. Clock, preset, J, K, and clear
    C. Clock, count, J, K, and clear
    D. Clock, J, K, clear, preset, Q, and Q

17. A flip-flop is a                                                17._____

    A. three state device
    B. two state device
    C. one state device
    D. either a one state or a two state depending upon the logic state appearing at the
       strobe input

18. With the aid of a single gate, a 74126 gate with three-state output can be converted into     18.____
    a

    A.  monostable multivibrator
    B.  bi-stable memory element
    C.  tri-stable memory element
    D.  none of the above

19. When J = 0 and K = 1 in a J-K flip-flop,     19.____

    A.  Q can go to or stay at logic 1, but cannot go to logic 0
    B.  Q can go to or stay at logic 0, but cannot go to logic 1
    C.  the flip-flop toggles
    D.  Q remains at its logic state; the clock has no effect

20. When present at the inputs or outputs of logic devices, the small circle o represents     20.____

    A.  that a positive clock pulse may be required to enable the device
    B.  that a positive leading edge may be required to enable the device
    C.  inversion
    D.  a shorthand form for an AND gate

21. The preset and clear inputs to a flip-flop     21.____

    A.  do not take precedence to the J-K inputs, but do take precedence to the clock input
    B.  do not take precedence to the clock input, but do take precedence to the J-K inputs
    C.  take precedence over all other inputs
    D.  none of the above

22. A typical read-only memory (ROM) IC chip has     22.____

    A.  memory cell select inputs, memory enable input, read/write select input, data
        inputs, and data outputs
    B.  data inputs, data outputs, memory enable input, and memory cell select inputs
    C.  memory enable input, memory cell select inputs, and data outputs
    D.  data inputs, data outputs, read/write select inputs, memory cell select input, and
        clock input

23. A typical random access memory (RAM) IC chip has     23.____

    A.  memory cell select inputs, memory enable input, read/write select input, data
        inputs, and data outputs
    B.  data inputs, data outputs, and memory cell select inputs
    C.  data outputs, memory cell select inputs, and memory enable input
    D.  data inputs, data outputs, read/write select input, memory cell select input, and
        clock input

24. Shift registers can     24.____

    A.  convert serial data into parallel data
    B.  convert parallel data into serial data
    C.  store both serial and parallel data
    D.  do all of the above, depending, of course, upon the nature of the specific shift reg-
        ister used

25. The 74194 shift register can
       25.\_

    A.  parallel load            B.  shift right
    C.  shift left                D.  all of the above

---

# KEY (CORRECT ANSWERS)

| | | | | |
|---|---|---|---|---|
| 1. | C | | 11. | C |
| 2. | D | | 12. | C |
| 3. | B | | 13. | C |
| 4. | C | | 14. | C |
| 5. | B | | 15. | C |
| 6. | A | | 16. | B |
| 7. | C | | 17. | B |
| 8. | D | | 18. | D |
| 9. | D | | 19. | B |
| 10. | C | | 20. | C |

| | |
|---|---|
| 21. | C |
| 22. | C |
| 23. | D |
| 24. | D |
| 25. | D |

---

# EXAMINATION SECTION
## TEST 1

DIRECTIONS: Each question or incomplete statement is followed by several suggested answers or completions. Select the one that BEST answers the question or completes the statement. *PRINT THE LETTER OF THE CORRECT ANSWER IN THE SPACE AT THE RIGHT.*

1. Which of the following is the equivalent NAND-NAND network for $x = a+c$?　　　　1.____

A.

B.

C.

D.

2. 1101 divided by $10_2$ equals　　　　2.____

   A. $11_2$　　　　B. $110.1_2$　　　　C. $101_2$　　　　D. $10_2$

3. $1101_2$ multiplied by $110_2$ equals　　　　3.____

   A. decimal 78　　　　　　B. decimal 64
   C. decimal 8　　　　　　D. octal 14

4. $1101_2$ minus $110_2$ equals　　　　4.____

   A. $111_2$　　　　　　B. $100_2$
   C. decimal 8　　　　　　D. octal 14

5. The BCD equivalent of decimal 46 is　　　　5.____

   A. 10101110　　　　B. 111010　　　　C. 101110　　　　D. 1000110

6. In boolean algebra, a and b is equal to c is written　　　　6.____

   A. $a+b = c$　　　　B. $ab+c$　　　　C. $a=b=c$　　　　D. $a/b=c$

7. Inspect the truth table shown at the right. From which logic function was it derived?　　　　7.____

   | a | b | x |
   |---|---|---|
   | 0 | 0 | 0 |
   | 0 | 1 | 0 |
   | 1 | 0 | 0 |
   | 1 | 1 | 1 |

   A. And　　　　　　C. Nand
   B. Or　　　　　　D. Exclusive or

8. Propagation delay in TTL devices refers to

    A. the noise immunity of the TTL device
    B. time between input change and output change
    C. how many TTL devices can be connected to output of the device
    D. how long it takes to connect these devices together

8.\_\_\_\_

9. Choose the CORRECT output signal.

9.\_\_\_\_

    A.      B.      C.      D.

10. Analog electronic techniques vs. digital electronic techniques.
The digital techniques allow

    A. multiplexing many signals on a common carrier
    B. greater accuracy of signal measurement
    C. long distance signal transmission with less distortion and signal loss
    D. all of the above

10.\_\_\_\_

11. The binary number 1010 is equal to the decimal

    A. 4      B. 5      C. 10      D. 17

11.\_\_\_\_

12. The octal number 166 is equal to the decimal number

    A. 83      B. 120      C. 63      D. 118

12.\_\_\_\_

13. There are _____ different digits in the octal number system.

    A. 2      B. 8      C. 10      D. 7

13.\_\_\_\_

14. The advantage of using integrated circuits in logic design is

    A. small size      B. low price
    C. reliability      D. all of the above

14.\_\_\_\_

15. If a logic zero is placed on the *J* input of J-K flip flop,

    A. it can never be set by the clock
    B. it can never be reset by the clock
    C. the set output of the f/f will become a one
    D. the f/f will topple on every clock pulse

15.\_\_\_\_

16. The Nand gate is the backbone of the 7400 TTL Series because     16._____

    A. it is the least expensive gate in the line
    B. other logic elements can be constructed using only Nand gates
    C. it is readily available
    D. all of the above

17. Which type of multivibrator circuit can change a non-pulse type input into a perfect pulse     17._____
output?

    A. Stable                        B. *One-shot*
    C. Schmitt trigger            D. Bistable

18. Which type of multivibrator can be used to change the width of the input pulse?     18._____

    A. Stable                        B. *One-shot*
    C. Ujt oscillator              D. Bistable

19. Which type of multivibrator is used to construct flip flops?     19._____

    A. Stable                        B. Mono-stable
    C. Schmitt trigger            D. Bistable

20. A one khz clock pulse is applied to the *T* input of an RST flip flop. The flip flop is initially     20._____
reset.
What is the state of the flip flop after 5 clock pulses?

    A. No change (reset)          B. Set output = 0
    C. Set output = 1             D. Indeterminate

---

# KEY (CORRECT ANSWERS)

| | | | |
|---|---|---|---|
| 1. | B | 11. | C |
| 2. | B | 12. | D |
| 3. | A | 13. | B |
| 4. | A | 14. | D |
| 5. | C | 15. | B |
| 6. | A | 16. | A |
| 7. | A | 17. | C |
| 8. | B | 18. | B |
| 9. | A | 19. | D |
| 10. | A | 20. | C |

---

# TEST 2

DIRECTIONS: Each question or incomplete statement is followed by several suggested answers or completions. Select the one that BEST answers the question or completes the statement. *PRINT THE LETTER OF THE CORRECT ANSWER IN THE SPACE AT THE RIGHT.*

1. The following counter is initially cleared (reset). What is the count after 5 clock pulses?

    A. a=0, b=0, c=1             B. a=1, b=1, c=1
    C. a=1, b=0, c=1             D. a=1, b=1, c=0

1.____

2. Which flip flop type has only one input and will toggle on every input pulse?

    A. D-type         B. RS         C. J-K         D. T-type

2.____

3. Which flip flop type has two inputs, one of which is the clock?

    A. D-type         B. RS         C. J-K         D. T-type

3.____

4. The output of a certain TTL device has very low impedance. This means that the device will have

    A. very fast switching speed
    B. very slow switching speed
    C. a reduced fan-out
    D. less output sensitivity

4.____

5. What voltage level exists in the 7400-series of IC chips?

    A. -15 volts, ground, and +5 volts
    B. Ground, +5 volts, and +12 volts
    C. -12 volts, ground, and +5 volts
    D. +5 volts and ground

5.____

6. For which type of gate is the following definition CORRECT? A binary circuit with two or more inputs and single ouput, in which the output is a logic 1 only when all inputs are logic 1, and the output is logic 0 if any one of the inputs is logic 0.

    _____ gate.

    A. AND         B. NAND         C. OR         D. NOR

6.____

7. A gating input of logic 0 to a 2-input NOR gate will allow what type of digital information to appear at the output of the gate?

    A. A logic 1 state             B. A logic 0 state
    C. Unchanged input data      D. Inverted input data

7.____

8. A gating input of logic 0 to a 2-input NAND gate will allow what type of digital information to appear at the output of the gate?

    A. A logic 1 state             B. A logic 0 state
    C. Unchanged input data      D. Inverted input data

8.____

9. A common-anode 7 segment display has the following inputs to its segments: A, D, E=1 and B, C, F, G=0.
   What does the display read out?

   A. Nine      B. Four      C. Six      D. Three

   9.\_\_\_\_

10. A common cathode display has the following inputs to its segments: C, F=0 and A, B, D, E, G=1.
    What does the display indicate?

    A. Nine      B. Four      C. Two      D. Five

    10.\_\_\_\_

11. When one inverts the output from an AND gate, he converts it into a _____ gate.

    A. exclusive-OR      B. NAND
    C. NOR      D. AND-OR-invert

    11.\_\_\_\_

12. A four decade counter can count from _____ to _____.

    A. 0001; 10000      B. 0001; 9999
    C. 0000; 9999      D. 0000; 100000

    12.\_\_\_\_

13. When one debounces a SPDT switch, he

    A. makes sure that the switching action occurs quickly
    B. makes sure that the output from the switch can be controlled to produce a single clock pulse at a time
    C. turns the SPDT into, basically, a monostable multivibrator
    D. none of the above

    13.\_\_\_\_

14. The binary number, 11111, represents which of the following decimal numbers?

    A. 32      B. 16      C. 15      D. 31

    14.\_\_\_\_

15. The binary number, 1111, appears on the seven-segment LED display as a

    A. blank display      B. decimal 15
    C. the letter F      D. 0

    15.\_\_\_\_

16. The largest binary number that can exist in binary coded decimal (BCD) is

    A. 1000      B. 1111      C. 1001      D. 1010

    16.\_\_\_\_

17. A demultiplexer is similar to a

    A. shift register
    B. decoder
    C. a device that can select one of a number of inputs and pass the logic level on to the output
    D. data selector

    17.\_\_\_\_

18. When a logic probe is constructed from a LED and other components, a transistor is USUALLY employed to

    A. make the LED light a bit more brightly
    B. conserve power
    C. decrease the current required to light the lamp monitor circuit
    D. decrease the voltage across the LED

    18.\_\_\_\_

19. A typical J-K flip flop can have the following inputs:   19.____

    A. Strobe, enable, count, clear, and preset
    B. Clock, preset, J, K, and clear
    C. Clock, count, J, K, and clear
    D. Clock, J, K, clear, preset, Q and Q

20. A preset and clear inputs to a flip flop   20.____

    A. don't take precedence to the J-K inputs, but do take precedence to the clock input
    B. don't take precedence to the clock input, but do take precedence to the J-K inputs
    C. take precedence over all other inputs
    D. none of the above

---

# KEY (CORRECT ANSWERS)

| | | | |
|---|---|---|---|
| 1. | C | 11. | B |
| 2. | D | 12. | C |
| 3. | A | 13. | B |
| 4. | D | 14. | D |
| 5. | D | 15. | C |
| 6. | A | 16. | B |
| 7. | A | 17. | C |
| 8. | A | 18. | C |
| 9. | B | 19. | B |
| 10. | C | 20. | C |

---